Passenger Transport after 2000 AD

Technology in the Third Millennium

Passenger Transport after 2000 AD

Edited by
G.B.R. Feilden,
A.H. Wickens and
I.R. Yates

Published by E & FN Spon for The Royal Society

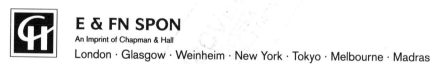

E & FN SPON
An Imprint of Chapman & Hall
London · Glasgow · Weinheim · New York · Tokyo · Melbourne · Madras

Published by E & FN Spon, an imprint of Chapman & Hall,
2–6 Boundary Row, London SE1 8HN, UK

Chapman & Hall, 2–6 Boundary Row, London SE1 8HN, UK

Blackie Academic & Professional, Wester Cleddens Road, Bishopbriggs, Glasgow G64 2NZ, UK

Chapman & Hall GmbH, Pappelallee 3, 69469 Weinheim, Germany

Chapman & Hall USA, One Penn Plaza, 41st Floor, New York NY 10119, USA

Chapman & Hall Japan, ITP-Japan, Kyowa Building, 3F, 2-2-1 Hirakawacho, Chiyoda-ku, Tokyo 102, Japan

Chapman & Hall Australia, Thomas Nelson Australia, 102 Dodds Street, South Melbourne, Victoria 3205, Australia

Chapman & Hall India, R. Seshadri, 32 Second Main Road, CIT East, Madras 600 035, India

First edition 1995

© 1992 The Royal Society and the authors of individual papers.

Typeset in 10/12 Times by Colset Typesetters Ltd, UK

Printed in Great Britain by
St Edmundsbury Press Ltd, Bury St Edmunds, Suffolk

ISBN 0 419 19470 3

Contents

Contributors

M.A. Ambrose
Director General
European Regional Airlines Association
The Baker Suite
Fairoaks Airport
Chobham, Woking
Surrey
GU24 8HX
UK

P.J. Braagaard
Department WD
Scandinavian Airline System
PO Box 150
DK 2770 Kastrup
Denmark

Professor W.P. Bradshaw
Chairman
Ulsterbus/Citybus Ltd
Milewater Road
Belfast
BT3 9BG
UK

Dr P. Davies
Castle Rock Consultants
Heathcoat Building
Highfields Science Park
University Boulevard
Nottingham
NG7 2QJ
UK

R.A. Davis
Vice President
Boeing Commercial Airplane Group
P.O. Box 3707, Mail Stop 75-06
Seattle, WA 98124-2207
USA

P. Essig
7, Avenue Fourcault de Pavaul
F-78000 Versailles
France

Dr G.B.R. Feilden, CBE, FEng, FRS
Feilden Associates
Verlands
Painswick
Gloucestershire
GL6 6XP
UK

W. Finkbohner
Passenger Traffic Manager
Swiss Federal Railways
SBB Regional Management III
Zürich
Switzerland

Sir F. Graham-Smith, FRS
Nuffield Radio Astronomy Labs
Jodrell Bank
Macclesfield
Cheshire
SK11 9DL
UK

C.E.W. Green
Managing Director
ScotRail
Caledonian Chambers
87 Union Street
Glasgow
G1 3TA

R. Kemp, BSc, CEng, FIEE, FIMechE
TMST
GEC Alsthom Traction
Tour Neptune
Cedex 20,
92086
Paris
France

M.V. McGreevy
Chief Engineer
Ulsterbus/Citybus Ltd
Milewater Road
Belfast
BT3 9BG
UK

R.M. McKinlay, FEng
Chairman
British Aerospace
Airbus Ltd
Comet Way
Farnborough
Hants
GU14 6YU
UK

J. Meredith
IATA Geneva
IATA Centre
33 Route de L'Aeroport
CH-1215
Geneva 15 Airport
Switzerland

Dr L. Miller
Thyssen Industrie AG Henschel
Division Advanced Transportation Technologies
PO Box 80 18 80
Anzingerstrasse 11/V
81671 München
Germany

Professor L. Nördstrom
Handelshogskolan
University of Gothenburg
Box 3016
S-400 10
Gothenburg
Sweden

Commander M.B.F. Ranken, CEng, FIMarE, FIMechE, FRINA
44 Castelnau Mansions
Castelnau
Barnes
London
SW13 9QU
UK

Professor T.M. Ridley, CBE, FEng
University of London Centre
for Transport Studies
Department of Civil Engineering
Imperial College
London SW7 2BZ

P. Rochat
Secretary General
International Civil Aviation Organization
International Aviation Square
1000 Sverbrobce Street West
Montreal
Quebec
Canada H3A 2R2

Dr J. Schäffler
Deutsche Aerospace AG
Postfach 801109
W-8000 München 80
Germany

P.C. Venton, OBE
Managing Director
Siemens Plessey Electronic Systems Ltd
Oakcroft Road
Chessington
Surrey
KT9 1QR
UK

Professor A.H. Wickens, OBE, FEng
Department of Mechanical Engineering
Loughborough University of Technology
Loughborough, Leicestershire
LE11 3TU

C.R. White
Siemens Plessey Systems
Oakcroft Road
Chessington
Surrey
KT9 1Q2
UK

J. Wooton
Chief Executive
Transport Research Laboratory
Old Wokingham Road
Crowthorne
Berkshire
RG11 6AU
UK

Professor I.R. Yates, CBE, FEng
Ivan Yates Associates
4, Fairway
Merrow
Guildford
Surrey
GU1 2XG
UK

Preface

Sir Francis Graham-Smith FRS

The Royal Society discussions on technology in the next millennium provide a meeting point for engineers, far-sighted planners, and hard-headed managers. Transport is an especially important theme. It is a vital part of the infrastructure of any country affecting everyone's lifestyle and prosperity. It is changing so rapidly that its structure through the next millennium is hard to predict and even harder to control.

Transport uses a major part of the resources of all industrialized countries. It affects our environment as a major user of energy, and a major source of pollution. There is an obvious case for central governmental control of overall transport policy, balancing the advantages and the demands of road, rail and air. We need a European policy, taking up the opportunities opened up by the Channel Tunnel: we need local city policies, linked to new developments in city and town planning.

The discussions that follow cover both the developing technologies of transport, and the plans for co-ordinated developments both within and beyond the UK.

Introduction

P. Essig

I have asked myself why you have invited me to give the introductory speech at this meeting which will be devoted to 'Passenger Transport after the Year 2000'. In fact, I am neither a research worker, nor an expert on the future, nor even a general expert on the problems of human behaviour. Nor do I think that it was for my proficiency in the language of Shakespeare!

I believe that you wanted to invite someone who has devoted his entire professional career, for more than 40 years, to transport problems, all over the world, from tropical Africa to the centre of one of the great megopolises, and at the head of one of the leading rail companies in Europe, and to ask him to project himself into the future on the basis of his experience of the past.

You wanted someone who has worked in the field, someone of enterprise, and, I believe I may also say, someone who has given some thought to the relationship between humans and transport:

- what do people gain from a means of transport or a transport facility?
- what are the social and sociological restrictions on transport?

Quite probably, you also based your decision on the friendship network which I have found in the transport world. Indeed, it is a somewhat closed world, a little inward looking, but it has a very family-like, convivial atmosphere, and among the friends I have made throughout my professional career, I would particularly like to greet Professor Tony Ridley, with whom I have worked for more than 20 years in a wide variety of areas, ranging from light rail transit to the boring and operating conditions of the Channel Tunnel, and who will close our final session.

In any event, I consider it a great honour to introduce the proceedings of such a prestigious gathering, and I would like to thank the organizers very warmly for having invited me.

1. The first question that may be asked is a little provocative: will there still be passenger transport in the next century?

You will smile at this question, and yet this is the very question raised by the protests of the Greens. By condemning the pollution produced by transport, and demanding that we do more to protect the ecological balance of our planet, they are, in the end, asking us to stay at home! Why go to the Seychelles for your holidays, when the beaches of Kent are just as welcoming or when a walk in the Highlands holds as many attractions? This is a valid question and, after having lived in Britain for three years, I wonder whether, in many ways, they are not right.

Another attitude may also lead to the desire to reduce passenger transport. This is the attitude generated by a defensive approach to economic crisis, which leads some people to advocate that we should become totally self-sufficient, close our frontiers, protect ourselves; in short, once again, that we should stay at home.

Still others believe that it will be progress in the transmission of information that will affect our social behaviour. Already, the post (Royal Mail) is being increasingly replaced by the dreaded fax, which transmits letters to us in real time from all over the world. Developments in communication facilities enable us to organize tele-conferences, which also cover the entire world. Soon it will be possible to improve them by introducing pictures, which are themselves being continually improved by digital technology. We will end up being able to transmit the smells, sensations and atmosphere of a meeting; you will feel as if you are working in New York or Sydney, whilst remaining peacefully at home in Kensington.

In short, that would settle things nicely; we could bring this meeting to a swift close, and have lunch together in a warm atmosphere of old companions who have been present at the end of a transport era which has lasted several thousand years.

2. In contrast to these somewhat provocative theories, it may be stated that many factors are leading to an increase in passenger transport requirements, possibly even a very fast increase.

Firstly, the population of the world is going to continue to grow. The best specialists believe that it will unavoidably rise from 6 to 10 billion within the next 50 years, and that the only stabilization that can be imagined – unless an epidemic like the Black Death or a third or fourth world war came along to upset things – would lead to a population of around 12 billion by the end of the next century, which, after all, is not so far away. Some of our children will see it.

These 10 or 12 billion inhabitants may perhaps want to know what is happening elsewhere in the world, and I believe that travel agencies do still, in the long term, have some sunny days ahead. Then again, just now I mentioned video-conferences. After having taken part in some of these over the last few months, between France, Britain, America and Australia, I can assure you that what I said cannot be taken for granted, and I would certainly have liked to have been in direct contact with the people I was speaking to.

In the end, the progress we are making in technology calls for the renewal and enrichment of personal contact. But is this not part of a human being's fundamental nature? Remember the first chapter of the Bible. Apart from that lesson which bas been handed down to us since the start of our civilization, it indisputably contains the truth about the nature of humankind: humans are only themselves in the development of their relationships with others. In the development and growth of their brains, which are themselves the result of the increasing complexity of the problems people set themselves. In short, humans are only themselves when they leave their natural space and throw themselves into the adventure and challenge of contact with others.

3. So, let us assume that there will be an increase in transport over the next few decades and, quite simply, I believe that this is the most reasonable hypothesis. We will see later how to answer the questions of our ecologist friends.

At what rate can we suppose this increase will take place? The history of the last few decades shows us that this rate has been greater than the growth in Gross National Product (GNP). Some people are inclined to project this ratio into the future, over a very long period. and have arrived at such high transport figures that, in order to respond to them, it would be necessary to drive dozens of motorways or Rapid Transit lines through the centre of London, and through the centre of Paris, to cover Surrey with airports, and soon. In short, people scare themselves and in this way justify policies of drastic restrictions.

I would like to take the example of forecasts for the consumption of electricity or petroleum products to demonstrate that we must remain reasonable, and that self-regulating mechanisms arise naturally in human behaviour. At the end of the 1960s, the rate of growth of electricity consumption gave the impression that before the end of the century hundreds of nuclear power stations would have to be built in the countries of the West.

In fact, and without much self-denial, we have improved our behaviour, and the rate of growth remains entirely compatible with production capacities. Regulation occurs by itself. We have examples of it every day. You just have to watch the Paris Metro or the London Underground in operation, or, as far as roads are concerned, the M25; when there are too many potential users of these transport facilities, they look for and find other routes, or change their mode of transport.

4. On the basis of this finding, I believe that we should adopt a new attitude

towards the probable growth of transport over the coming decades. We should see it as a contest or as a challenge:

- *the challenge of system capacity*, whether of existing systems or new systems to be created. In both cases, it will be necessary to make the best possible use of reserve capacity, and to create new reserves by improving what already exists, given that the construction of new systems will become ever more difficult in the countries of the West.
- *the challenge of quality*, in all senses of the word: quality for the user, performance, reliability, regularity, safety.
- *the challenge of environmental protection*, without going to the extremes of some of the criticisms made by the ecologists, it is none the less true that responsibility for the protection of the environment is even greater today because humankind is now capable of inflicting irreversible damage. But I do not believe there is a dilemma. On the contrary, I believe that we can reconcile transport and the environment for the benefit of people.
- *the challenge of the economy*. In the Western world, which, despite the present depression, is overflowing with wealth, we must be careful not to waste our economic resources. We must share them sensibly between all the needs of our contemporaries. Transport is one of these needs; it is not the **only need**. Transport must not be transformed into an idol to which we would sacrifice absolutely everything else.

I believe that we are ready to take up all these challenges, because they correspond to an ideal, the ideal of **the service of humankind**. They will lead us to launch new research on new bases, and the success of this research will now be the underlying theme of the analysis I am about to present of the various modes of passenger transport.

5. There are many aspects to the transport problem, which makes it all the more complicated to analyse. You will not be surprised that, in order to solve this complex system, I have used the Cartesian method, which consists of dividing the initial problem into parts which are small enough to solve.

Transport can be classified by (a) modes; (b) system of management; (c) area of application.

(a) Modes
- Land   road
         rail
- Sea
- Air   aeroplane
         helicopter

(b) System of management
- Public
- Private

(c) Area of application
- local, especially large towns
- regional or inter-regional
- long distance

What a combination for the organizers of a working meeting devoted, like ours, to transport problems after the year 2000. And it may easily be imagined that there are just as many lobbies promoting one or other aspect of the problem, to the extent of totally ignoring the others.

I would like to re-examine the problem on the basis of area of application, as is, moreover, suggested by the agenda of our session, by distinguishing local transport from regional transport amd intercontinental transport. And firstly I would like to note that each of these categories of transport very probably presents comparable financial choices and technical difficulties.

In France, for example, we are now contemplating spending as much money over the next 20 years on improving transport in the Ile de France region alone, as on providing the entire country with a complete network of high-speed rail links. Not to mention the technical difficulties. It is probably just as difficult to make metro trains run at less than 90-second intervals, as it is to make a train travel at 300 km/h.

This reminds me of an incident which happened a few years ago, when I was talking with a transport specialist about the difficulty of the problems he had to solve. He told me that, for him, the most difficult thing was to transport millions of people over short distances and even at low speeds. He cited as an example, the problem of the pilgrimage to Mecca, where the future hadji have to perform three rites in places a few kilometres apart. There are millions of them every day and no satisfactory transport system has been found to deal with this problem. You will remember the disaster which cast a tragic shadow over one of these pilgrimages not so long ago.

I would also like to note that one problem has not really been solved; this is the problem of transportation over a few hundred metres. Apart from the moving walkway, which is very slow, there is nothing really satisfactory in existence, and it is strange that this problem is not even mentioned at our conference, although the need is there. You just have to look at the distances we have to cover in our major airports, at Gatwick or at Heathrow, and in railway stations or car parks.

I could continue my comments on each of the fields of transport I listed earlier. However, I will not do so: firstly, so as not to exceed the time allotted to me by the Chairman of the meeting, and also so as not to take the freshness out of the subject of the fascinating debates that we are going to hear over the next two days. However, perhaps I will make an exception and mention sea transport, which has had its share of glory, for centuries, as the only means of transport that could cover long distances within acceptable periods of time. Today it seems like a poor relation compared to its land and air competitors.

Nevertheless, we must not forget the place of the water route on our planet. Sea covers two-thirds of the surface of the globe and our continents are crossed by a multitude of streams and rivers, to which our skill has added just as many canals. In this way, the sea and river system penetrates deeply into the land.

The technology itself has not remained static, as might have been feared, and the progress made in many fields is absolutely dazzling, whether in keel design, techniques for rising above the water line, or systems of propulsion. We probably will not talk much about this over the next two days. I think this is unfortunate, and I hope you will bear in mind that river and sea transport can make an effective contribution in many special geographical situations.

6. I would now like to spend a little more time over the relationship between transport and the environment, from the point of view, as I indicated earlier, of a challenge to be met. I will do so particularly on the basis of my experience of land transport, where rail is often opposed to road.

It is said that rail is clean, efficient and safe; that roads create pollution and cause congestion. To tell the truth, we should always beware of simplistic pictures and should realize that both methods are equally costly, but perhaps not in the same way.

We will take the pollution aspect to start with. Transport is accused of being one of the major factors in atmospheric pollution, and it is true that transport's share in this form of pollution is continually growing, if only because of the progress which has been made in other industrial and domestic areas. Therefore, the idea of electrically driven vehicles is defended, and this leads to the advocation of railways. But the real question that should be asked is this: is electricity a clean form of energy? Yes, but subject to one major condition, which is the acceptance of nuclear power! Otherwise, the efficiency of a thermal power station will always be less than that of any diesel engine used correctly. The truth is that the pollution generated by a power station is generally less visible and reserved for a few unfortunate people '. . . not in my backyard'.

Starting from this argument, we will approach the problem of pollution from another angle, and we will attempt to reduce it whatever the power source in question, in power stations when necessary, but equally at the level of the internal combustion engine. The treatment of exhaust gases is probably one of the areas where some of the greatest progress can be made over the next few years. Reducing pollution from 10 to 1 is probably a target which we can reasonably set ourselves.

The same is true with regard to other nuisances, such as noise.

Apparently, people adapt more easily to the noise of a train than to that of a lorry. Possibly, but I don't think the researchers spent much time talking to people who live along our major rail routes around London or Paris. Moreover, the problem emerges again when we want to build a new rail line, whether in Kent or in Provence. Here again, progress must be made.

There are considerable prospects in the field of road transport. The lorry of today may be said to be less noisy than the private car of 20 years ago, and the process may continue at the same rate over the next few decades. In the field of rail transport, things will be more complicated, since the major progress made by the introduction of welded rails. Now we have to tackle the problem of the wheel itself. To tell the truth, people have already been pondering this problem for 10 000 years. Perhaps there is still more that can be done.

Now we come to the problem of the congestion of existing transport systems. Nowadays people talk of nothing else. Delayed commuter trains, overcrowding at Heathrow, jams on the M25, and people start proclaiming the need for new infrastructures, new systems of transport to respond to situations which are described as intolerable. To tell the truth, I do not believe that these situations are as intolerable as people say, since we get by very well, quite simply because congestion is not synonymous with zero efficiency. Congested transport systems continue to provide a considerable level of service, even if they are not as comfortable as they might be.

At the start of this working session, I would like to invite you to re-examine the problem of congestion in another way, and to redirect your thoughts and research along avenues which would make it possible to deal with present problems more cheaply, and in a way which is more considerate towards our environment:

- for rail transport, this will mean the development of automatic operating systems, which will make it possible to provide greater capacity, greater safety and a more regular service;
- for road transport, this will mean the development of an 'intelligent' motorway, which we will discuss tomorrow;
- in the field of air transport, air control must be totally overhauled on a European scale, not to mention the considerable progress that could be made if the military would return to the civil sector part of the vast air space they set aside for their exercises. Hasn't the Berlin Wall come down? Our air space resources must be shared in a more sensible manner between the civil and military sectors;
- as for access to airports, at the risk of shocking and surprising you, it will prove easier to handle this problem by specific infrastructures rather than creating long-distance land transport systems.

And this line of thought brings me to my conclusion. The transport problems of the year 2000 can be dealt with if we keep an open mind, if we accept that we must question our conventional schemes, if we refuse to confine ourselves to one mode, or to confine one mode to one function. This is a challenge for each of us and for the institutions we represent here today.

And finally, I believe that the best way to keep this openness of mind is to open up greater competition between aircraft, the TGV, long-distance coaches, sea transport, competition between private and public transport, etc. It is in this way that we will be able to achieve the efficiency which is demanded by our fellow citizens now and for the future.

Part One

Local Transport

1

Three years of S-Bahn Zürich

W. Finkbohner

1.1 INTRODUCTION

When the former British Transport Minister Sir Malcolm Rifkind visited the S-Bahn, the Rapid Transit Railway System of Zürich, he was utterly impressed. After his return to London he said at a press conference: 'Switzerland is the land where a train delay is considered a national tragedy.'

This statement, of course, is an exaggeration, yet there is a grain of truth to it. The success of the Swiss Railways is due to a close confidential relationship between the population and the railway. For the last 90 years, the railway has not been the railway of the government, but the railway of all the Swiss. It has built up its reputation by reliability, a solid service to customers before and during journeys, as well as for good commercial husbandry.

That does not mean that its performance is always blameless, but staff and management are constantly and sincerely trying to improve services to compete with road and air traffic.

When the S-Bahn system was put into service in May 1990 with its 380 km lines in the area of Greater Zürich, it meant a big step in the improvement of service quality. When the S-Bahn was inaugurated, the dead-end terminal station of Zürich became virtually at one stroke a transit station with a whole series of new direct diagonal connections.

Contrary to Germany and France, this was not achieved by conversions of individual lines, but by introduction of a completely new timetable plan right after the inauguration of the new large diameter tunnel line, of some 12 km, below the city of Zürich.

At the same time, a traffic community with force of law was introduced for the whole territory of the Canton of Zürich with its 1.1 million

Passenger Transport after 2000 AD. Edited by G.B.R. Feilden, A.H. Wickens and I.R. Yates.
Published in 1994 by E & FN Spon, London. ISBN 0 419 19470 3.

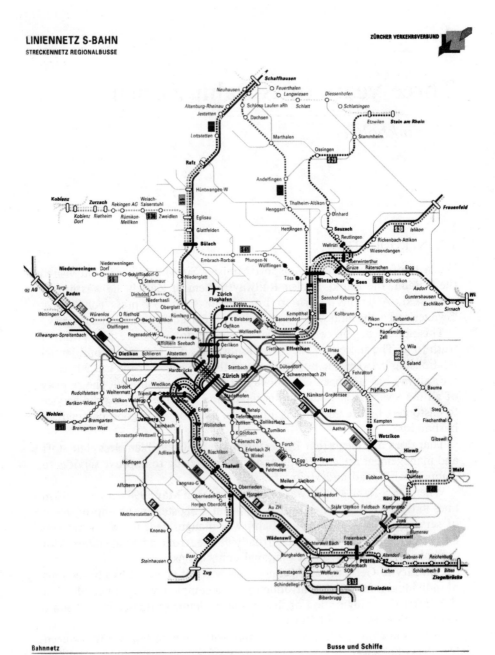

Figure 1.1.

inhabitants. Traffic community means the integration of 34 local private railway, tramway, bus, boat and cableway lines into the S-Bahn network, in order to offer a unified system to the traveller. Clients can profit from the simplicity in the ticket offer: ordinary tickets, day-cards, General Season tickets are valid on all modes of transport.

Also a financing system was introduced which is new to Switzerland: each local municipal government has to pay for the services the system offers, on the basis of the number of stations and stops, and the frequency of travel services on offer, on its territory.

The role of the traffic community in regard to the individual autonomous transport company is to order services, but also to pay the company for their costs.

Now, exactly three years after the opening of the system, the question arises as to whether the goals that were set with the construction and improvement of the S-Bahn have been achieved.

Forecasts for the third year of operation concerning numbers of passengers have been surpassed on nearly all lines. On some lines, even the figures forecasted for the year 2000 have been reached. In principle, the increase in number of passengers was biggest on those lines where the offer and its quality also was notably improved. What the clients appreciate most are big cuts in travel time, followed by the creation of direct connections, improvements in the timetable, and not least the improvement of travel comfort with new cars and increased number of seats on offer.

Contrary to other national railways, it is the designated target of the creators of the S-Bahn, to be able to offer a seat to each passenger. Standing will be accepted on very short sectors and as an exception only. For an S-Bahn system, this requirement is rather extraordinary, but it reflects the wish of the Swiss clientele to enjoy an extravagant, but reasonable, comfort in both travel classes.

Precisely for that reason the increase rates are especially notable in the first class cars with their bigger panorama windows, more legroom, and their carpets. However, it is also an old tradition in Switzerland, that ministers, presidents of banks, careerwomen and members of parliament also belong to the regular users of tramways and S-Bahn. Taking the whole network, the increase in passenger numbers is some 30%. Thus, the objective set for the year 2000, is already reached now, seven years ahead of target.

A political objective was to encourage a shift from the road towards public transportation. It is the task of the traffic community together with cantonal authorities, to follow developments in public transportation and to draw conclusions. As yet, only a few politically motivated statements have come forth.

The city of Zürich, for instance, that had hoped for a relief of its roads from individual traffic, declares that it is disappointed by the results.

According to their research at city borders, the number of motorcars coming into the city has not decreased since 1989. They would have expected, the city authorities wrote, a decrease in road traffic. They conceal the fact that the country-wide private motor traffic increases by 2.5 to 3% annually. In view of the stagnation of individual traffic at the city border it can be said that a shift of 7% from private to public transportation has taken place in 36 months.

Why is it that the city authorities are not satisfied with the present state of affairs? They are arguing for regional roads that lead right into the city centre and which are the responsibility of the regional authority, and that supporting measures are taken to curtail local traffic.

In addition, the city authorities are fighting for a reduction of private and public parking lots on their territory. As anywhere else, political views on this issue differ widely.

1.2 OPERATIONAL RESPONSIBILITY

Operational responsibility for the whole S-Bahn lies with Swiss Federal Railways (SBB) Regional Management III. To monitor the operation according to timetable, and for immediate action in case of disruptions, but also for planning and for bigger variations from timetable standards, a 'Betriebsleitsystem (BLZ)' operation steering centre was installed at the cost of 25 million Swiss Francs.

This centre is operational around the clock and though it mainly supervises lines of the S-Bahn, it also supervises an additional 1000 km of main and secondary lines.

Contrary to similar systems in Germany and France, or even in the the US, only 15 km of double track lines are reserved for exclusive use by the S-Bahn system (the Diameter line of Zürich). All other double and single track lines are used also by Eurocity and Intercity trains, fast trains, goods trains and service trains, with up to 400 trains per day on double track, and up to 120 trains per day on single track lines.

The function of the steering centre is short-term planning, and to order measures to guarantee operation as per timetable. The staff is constantly informed by screens of the real operational situation. When deviations from the timetable occur, the computer calculates difficult situations ahead and thus helps the operator to formulate the right decisions.

Communication with stations is via telephone, and with running trains via radio-display. In order to keep delays at a minimum, two whole trains are constantly ready to be called to service within a matter of minutes. These are the so-called Dispotrains.

The electric power supply, as well as services of rail engines and rail engine drivers, are managed by the respective specialized services in close co-operation with the steering centre.

Another task of the steering centre is the information of passengers by means of the train-radio. Because of technical difficulties, not all trains can, as yet, be reached by radio. The system is operationally directed by means of signals on open lines. In recent years, several regional signal boxes for stations and open lines have been built. Currently, there are still many local signal boxes in operation. The central signal box of Zürich main station (some 1600 train movements per day) is supported electronically and controls, for example, the line of the S-Bahn which is newly built, as well as the approximately 20 km long line with mixed operation on the left bank of the Lake of Zürich.

Works are currently in progress for the installation of ATC (Automatic Train Control). Many rail engines are equipped with ATC units already, and work on the trackside installations has also started. When finished, the ATC computer in the engines calculates the permissable line speed under any given operational or technical circumstances. It warns the driver if necessary and if he/she drives too fast or passes a signal at danger, it brings the train to a stop automatically.

1.3 ROLLING STOCK

Here too, new paths are being followed by the S-Bahn. Instead of using new S-Bahn trains throughout, for commercial and practical reasons only the most heavily used lines received new double-decker coaches of latest construction, for example, line S5 in the heavily populated Glattal where, as a novelty, fast trains are also offered on the newly built line.

The success of this measure was enormous: the presumably most comfortable S-Bahn double-decker coaches of Europe together with the much shorter travel time and the global traffic community ticket, made passenger numbers jump by more than 60%.

In the gradual introduction of double-decker coaches to new lines, those lines with the best traffic conditions come first. Therefore, there are still lines that are operated today with older rolling stock, which has a positive effect on the economy of the system.

After line S5, also lines S7 and S8 were equipped integrally with new rolling stock. In spite of technical difficulties at the beginning, the new vehicles have proven their worth with regard to passenger comfort as well as with regard to on-time performance even with short distances between stops. The new comfortable type of coach is already built in Germany under license. Further railways from Austria and Scandinavia have also announced their interest.

A problem not to be overlooked lies in the relatively high entrance platform above the bogies. Since building a low platform was resisted because of small radius curves, and also in the interest of passenger safety (better view into the body of the coach), all the platforms of stations

Figure 1.2.

served by trains with double-decker coaches have been elevated to a level
of 25 cm.

The distance between the lowest stepboard and the platform amounts to
about 44 cm, which is considered too high especially by elderly people. By
means of simple and easy to install auxiliary step-boards of metal, this
nuisance can be counteracted. It is planned to equip all stations of the
380 km long network of the S-Bahn with 55 cm high platforms.

Figure 1.3.

1.4 CONSTRUCTION OF NEW LINES

The current programme of construction is the implementation of the '2nd amendment' approved by public vote in November 1989. This includes constructive measures for the improvement of the offer (better timetable, more comfortable stations), but also measures to stabilize the current timetable offer.

What is urgent is the introduction of the 30-minute interval on the line Zürich–Oerlikon–Regensdorf–Baden, as well as the extension works needed for the 15-minute interval service on the line of the right bank of the Lake of Zürich, which is partly single track.

The financing is effected jointly by the Canton of Zürich and SBB, with cost-shares between 50 and 80%, depending on the degree of usage of the S-Bahn, long-distance and goods traffic. The original plans foresaw completion of all projects by the years 1993/95. This must be now extended to 1998. The reasons for this are not so much the financial difficulties in

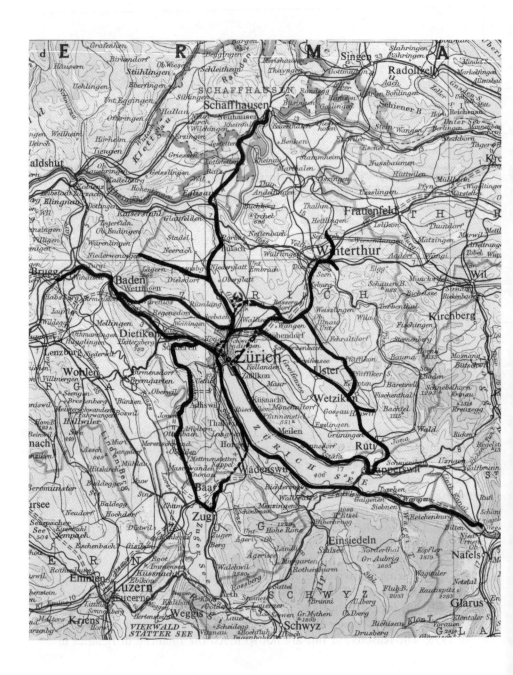

Figure 1.4.

public budgets, but the new law for building permits for railways. This added an average of two years to the procedure of obtaining building permission.

In the plans for the realization of the concepts 'Rail and Bus 2000', as well as for Alptransit, there are further big construction works that are planned in the Zürich area. A double track will be reserved exclusively for EC and IC traffic between Zürich and Thalwil, and between Oerlikon and Altstetten. Thus, more capacity is liberated for S-Bahn traffic, which will in the first years after the year 2000 be entirely separated from other traffic within the city boundaries.

1.5 SUPPORTING MEASURES

To make traffic policy is not SBB's business. It is the task of the traffic community, however, to co-ordinate between rail and bus in regional traffic in accordance with cantonal prescriptions.

In the fields of settlements and land use policy, the SBB co-operate with dedication in many working groups that aim at improving their local conditions of accessibility. They are convinced of the good value of their offers, as long as these meet the following quality requirements:

- availability;
- fast transport from start to destination;
- number of changes as low as possible;
- comfortable and good value.

2

Growth and infrastructure in the Sound region

P.J. Braagaard

2.1 INTRODUCTION

By the year 2010 Scandinavia will have undergone a historical development of full integration with the European continent in terms of traffic and transportation.

The connections across the Great Belt, the Sound and the Fehmarn Belt are the most important initiatives. The road and railway networks linked to these connections have been upgraded following massive investment during the period 1990–2010. Sweden and Norway have effectively been linked to Denmark, Denmark to the continent. Since 1993 transport times have been more than halved. It will be possible to travel by rail in the EuroCityExpress between Copenhagen and Stockholm in three hours, between Copenhagen and Hamburg in two hours or the same amount of time which a trip between Copenhagen and Aarhus requires. International railway trips have increased from index 100 in 1993 to index 315 for this region.

The traffic between the eastern and western parts of Denmark is, correspondingly, expected to rise from index 100 to 200.

From Copenhagen the quickest Catamaran-connections go from the Baltic growth countries, and cruises to the Baltic area are a burgeoning business. By the year 2010 the Copenhagen International Airport, with around 30 million passengers, will be the fifth largest in Europe with a number of swift lines, especially to the Far East and the rest of Europe, and particularly strong for destinations in the Baltic area. The central growth region in northern Europe is the Baltic area with Copenhagen and

Passenger Transport after 2000 AD. Edited by G.B.R. Feilden, A.H. Wickens and I.R. Yates. Published in 1994 by E & FN Spon, London. ISBN 0 419 19470 3.

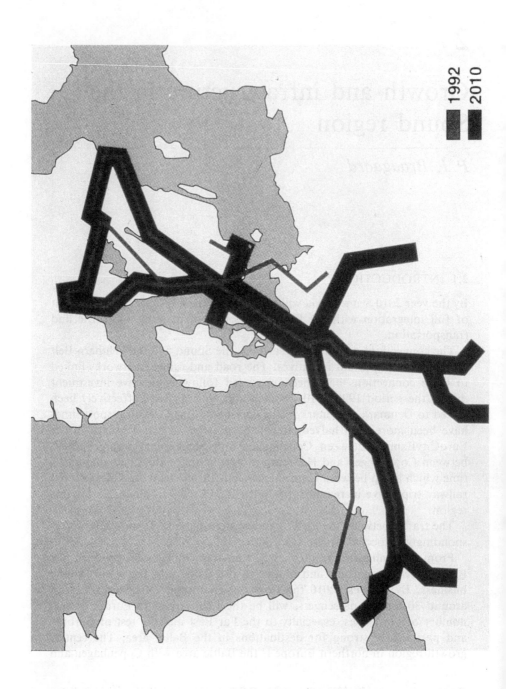

Figure 2.1.

south Sweden as its economic, cultural, and traffic hub. By the year 2000, Copenhagen in Denmark will merge with Malmö and thus with south Sweden when the connection across the Sound is inaugurated.

This is our vision of the future for the year 2010. How can this vision be realized, and how can the transport infrastructures in the Sound region serve to promote this view of the future? Let us turn back to the year 1993.

2.2 A HISTORIC OPPORTUNITY FOR THE SOUND REGION

In the middle of a grave economic and employment situation, Denmark has been given a historic opportunity. Developments in Europe present us with excellent growth perspectives.

Firstly, the collapse of the Soviet Empire has enabled a number of states to develop and contacts to be established with the Western World. Secondly, the completion of the Single European Market is now a fact. With the Danish 'yes' to the Maastricht Treaty on May 18 and similar signals from the British parliament, the foundation has been laid for continued liberalization and harmonization in the Community. For instance, from January 1, 1993, the so-called '3rd Aviation Package' has introduced open competition for all air services between Community member states and a greater degree of competition for domestic air services within the Community. Thirdly, the European Community will be enlarged by Finland, Sweden, and hopefully Norway, too. Their accession to the EEA agreement already means that they are bona fide members of the Single European Market. Fourthly, the German unification creates new dynamism in the former GDR, which largely orientates itself towards the Baltic. For the entire Baltic Basin we are talking about 100 million people and a GNP which corresponds to one quarter of the overall production in the Community.

These landmark events in foreign policy affairs give to the Copenhagen area, as well as to the entire Sound region, a unique opportunity to develop into a regional growth centre, and thus also into a new traffic junction of international importance. The infrastructure in the Sound region may become the foundation of one of those cross-national regional growth centres stimulated into being by the new co-operative conditions in Europe. Thus, Copenhagen will no longer be the most northerly metropolis in the EC, but rather it will be located centrally at the Northern Centre of the European Community. This is a historic opportunity for the entire Baltic region.

2.3 RANKING ORDER IN THE EUROPE OF REGIONS

A number of Danish and Swedish researchers have pointed out the tangible and intangible factors which are considered relevant for assessing the growth potential of a given area. The overall general precondition is that the growth in question has as its point of departure the European system of metropolises mutually competing across increasingly less important national frontiers.

The fundamental prerequisite for growth is that the metropolis must have a certain size and 'metropolitan gross product' in order for a 'critical mass' to be formed. The metropolis Copenhagen with its 1.9 million inhabitants puts Copenhagen at the top of the list of Scandinavian cities and at the 32nd place in the European ranking order. Structures such as Rhein-Ruhr are the largest, followed by Paris, Moscow, and London. If we include the concept of the metropolitan gross product estimated on the basis of data on the size of the population, GNP, 'estimates specific for the metropolis in question', south and east European cities move down the scale, while cities in northern Europe move up. Hamburg will, for instance, overtake Berlin at place no. 13, and Copenhagen arrives at the 16th place. Once again the Rhein-Ruhr area and Paris rank as no. 1 and 2, respectively.

The international contact patterns of trade and industry are, thirdly, considered an indication of growth potential. One way this may be quantified is by registration of the number of telephone calls from one area to another or by taking international passenger traffic into account. The traffic reflects the importance of an airport in the international transport system but can, at the same time, be seen as an indication of the potential contacts of a metropolis.

The Copenhagen Airport found itself at the 6th place in Europe in 1989 with a little over 9 million passengers embarking or disembarking, domestic flights excluded. London – as a whole – was the biggest with 55 million and Paris the runner-up with a little over 27 million passengers. Thus Copenhagen is among the top ranking cities when it comes to international traffic, ahead of cities like Stockholm, Hamburg, and Berlin.

Knowledge, culture and communication are becoming increasingly important as dynamos for social evolution away from the industrial society and towards the information society. Developing and presenting ideas and new concepts are things that occupy more and more people with major implications for product development. Intense regional and global competition means that products must be developed and marketed in increasingly shorter time at higher cost while, at the same time, their market life is reduced, leading to increasing demands for penetration and profitability as a consequence.

Swedish researchers have shown how regional growth will be strongly favoured by the presence of public and private research and development centres which grow synergically with telecommunication and swift transport links. Dynamic, successful undertakings are often characterized either by having an extensive logistic network, or by being small, creative units with a high capability to adjust. Examples of such growth regions which spring to mind are the Cambridge–London–Reading area, the Kansai region in Japan, integrated with the future Kansai International Airport and regional transport system (the 'Shinkansen'), the San Diego/Orange County Corridor, the San Francisco Bay area and the Boston region in the USA, and also the Singapore conurbation in the Far East.

A.E. Andersson (1989) has attempted to measure and rank these areas in Europe by comparing scientific and industrial research and communication capacities. The London–Cambridge–Oxford area is put at an index of creativity equalling 100; Paris equals 70. Then follows Amsterdam–Utrecht–Leiden and Bonn–Cologne–Düsseldorf at index 33, Stockholm–Uppsala at 26; Copenhagen ranking at the 10th place at index 22. To summarize, here in the first half of the 1990s, Copenhagen enjoys a good basic point of departure to assert itself in the competition with other metropolises in the European ranking order.

Copenhagen could become the heart of the north European growth centre in the Baltic Basin in the Europe of regions which, since 1990, has replaced the Europe of nations; this can be illustrated in the following way.

Until 1990 the borders of catchment areas were identical with the national frontiers, and a system of well-functioning cities with an independent function at the levels below that of the capitals had been developed. Especially east of the Iron Curtain the degree of centralization was high. Even such capitals as Berlin and Warsaw were largely dominated by Moscow. From the early 1990s, national frontiers will gradually disappear and be replaced by catchment areas identical with the overall network created on the basis of renewed competition and renewed co-operation. This is the antithesis to the Iron Curtain. The overall hierarchies and catchment areas have changed considerably. The connections across the Sound, will mean that Copenhagen will attain a dominant position not just in Denmark but also in south Sweden. Hamburg and Berlin compete with each other, and the domination of Moscow has been broken as regards eastern Germany, Poland and the Baltic Republics.

2.4 THE OVERALL INFRASTRUCTURE

It is a central condition for growth that the requisite infrastructure has been provided and at a high service level. A number of large-scale construction projects in the billion kroner price range are being completed in the region during these years. The objective is to integrate east and west Denmark by means of the connection across the Great Belt and, in the somewhat longer term, link Denmark to south Sweden by means of the Sound Connection by the turn of the century. In a subsequent phase, beginning at the turn of the century, it is the intention to link Denmark/south Sweden to the continent, primarily Germany, by means of a connection across the Fehmarn Belt. These three main transport routes, each of a length of about 16–18 km, will all be constructed as combined motorway/railway connections and will contribute strongly to the reduction of travelling and transport times in Denmark and between Scandinavia and the north European continent.

The total volume of travel between Scandinavia and the rest of Europe in 1991 amounted to 28 million journeys; 18 million were between Scandinavia and Germany out of which 11 million were short trips across the Danish–German border primarily made by motor car or bus. A doubling of the volume of travel is expected to take place over the next 20 years as a consequence of economic policy developments in Europe.

The rail transport between Scandinavia and the continent has had no major improvements to offer in the period between 1975 and today. Rail transport has not been able to keep up with general developments in transport and has, consequently, lost market shares.

Now increasing volumes are expected thanks to, among other things, the new high-speed trains, modernization of the permanent ways and the new connections consisting of bridges and tunnels across the Great Belt and the Sound after the year 2000. At the same time, co-operation between the national railway companies in Germany, Sweden, Norway, and Denmark has been intensified, one objective being the configuration of a joint railway system that will allow easy passage across borders. In 1993 this is not yet possible as the countries operate with different train concepts and specifications for the power supply and signals systems.

It is expected that by the year 2000 the projects will have reduced the required travelling times by 50% on the main lines Stockholm/Oslo–Copenhagen–Hamburg. For example, we can expect to see the travelling time for Copenhagen–Stockholm/Oslo reduced from 7 to 4 hours, Copenhagen–Hamburg from 5 to 2 hours, and so on.

ECE (the EuroCityExpress) high-velocity trains running at 250–300 km/h will primarily run between the Scandinavian capitals and the continent departing at hourly intervals. The level of comfort and service must be very high.

The EuroCity–Intercity high-velocity train running at 200–250 km/h will stop between capitals. The trains are very comfortable and will depart every two hours and run between regions and, finally, ER trains (EuroRegion trains) running at 160–200 km/h will link regions and will stop every 30 and 50 km.

In the goods field similar improvements are expected, for instance 7 hours between Malmö in south Sweden and Hamburg, compared to 16 hours today and 3 hours by the year 2010, when it is expected that the Fehmarn Belt connection will have been completed. Until the connections are ready, transportation of goods between Sweden/Norway and the continent will continue to be dominated by sea transport between, for instance, Gedser–Denmark and Warnemütinde–Germany (i.e. Dan Link),

Ystad–Sweden and Swinoujscie–Poland, Trelleborg–Sweden and Sassnitz–Germany.

In tomorrow's Denmark, too, the connections and the above mentioned routes to the continent will be supplemented by modern passenger ferries and catamarans between the many Danish islands and our neighbouring countries. The world's largest catamaran, which carries motor cars, has for example just been taken into service between Frederikshavn in northern Denmark and Gothenburg on the west coast of Sweden. It takes this vessel half the time it takes conventional ferries to cover the distance, i.e. 90 minutes.

The decline expected in shipping by the year 2000 caused by the new connections between regions, will partly be offset by the renaissance which shipping is expected to have in the Baltic region. A major reason for this can be found in the meagre infrastructural provisions in the non-Scandinavian Baltic countries. It is, for example, possible to halve transportation time between Copenhagen and Estonia or Latvia by shipping goods instead of sending them by train or road. The road transport time from Copenhagen to Tallin in Estonia is 120 hours, but only 48 hours by sea; it takes 96 hours to go to Riga in Latvia by road, but only 60 hours by sea. A large number of companies are applying for sailing rights for direct lines to the ports of the Baltic republics, especially Riga.

Three of the five largest Scandinavian harbours are located in the Sound region and, for example, the Copenhagen port authorities have expanded the free port in recent years in order to be able to meet the growing demand. Copenhagen was also chosen as domicile of the co-operative organization, the Baltic Port Organization formed in 1991 by ports in 9 countries on the Baltic rim. It is the objective of the organization to develop and co-ordinate shipping in the Baltic area.

2.5 THE SOUND REGION AND LOCAL TRANSPORT

By the turn of the century, the capital of Denmark, Copenhagen, will merge with the towns in south Sweden – Malmö, Lund, Hälsingborg when the connection across the Sound has been completed. The area will be one of the most important metropolises of northern Europe and will be the hub of a financial, cultural and transport network. The metropolis on the Sound will be able to challenge rivals like Berlin, Hamburg and Stockholm.

Within a radius of 50 km from the Copenhagen International Airport we find a population of 2.3 million people. Seen as a whole, this conurbation will rank as number 20 in Europe and by far the largest in Scandinavia. In terms of economy, the Greater Copenhagen Area will leap from a modest 16th place to become no. 8 as regards metropolitan gross product ahead of, for example, Berlin, Hamburg and Stockholm. The Sound region hosts those high technology workplaces which will be decisive for the ability of

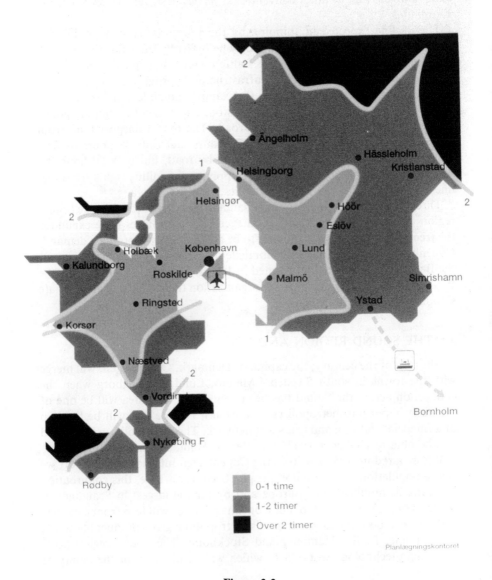

Figure 2.2.

the region to continue to grow and attract investors; similarly the positive trend in the pharmaceutical and health industry, in the service and tourist industries will be able to grow on either side of the Sound.

In terms of creativity, the Sound City will overtake Stockholm–Uppsala, presently in fifth place, by means of having access to the south Sweden research and development units, which will bring it on a par with the creative centres of Amsterdam–Utrecht–Leiden and Bonn–Cologne–Düsseldorf.

Together with the advantages proffered by the region in terms of a strong economy with a record low rate of inflation, and a very active cultural scene, the ability of Scandinavian companies to develop new ways of managing and organizing work by applying the emergent information technologies makes it very attractive for international companies to move all or part of their operations to the Sound region.

The metropolis on the Sound will increasingly be able to benefit from its geographic position with the very best preconditions for integrating transportation by road, railway, sea and air, which will allow it to generate a 'traffic machine' at the largest 'intersection' of the north.

In the field of communication, already today Copenhagen is becoming a focal point for telecommunication to and from Eastern Europe.

Seen in isolation, the harbour of Copenhagen is the largest in Denmark, but seen in the international context it is far smaller than that of Gothenburg, which is the largest in the Nordic countries. However, if we count the harbours on the Sound as one, they catch up with Gothenburg. Considerable growth in the volume of sea transport in the Baltic is expected, as is improved co-operation between ports to effect product refinement and exchange know-how. The deregulation taking effect from 1993 allowing a third party duty-free bonded warehousing in any place of their choice will increase flexibility in Denmark as a transit country for goods to and from the countries on the Baltic rim. The Sound region is centrally placed for 'just-in-time' deliveries.

What do we expect the traffic and transport trend to be in the Sound region beyond the year 2000?

In 1993, contacts across the Sound are dominated by Swedish shoppers coming to Copenhagen and Elsinore, not by business contacts between commercial enterprises. In 1993, 23 million passengers crossed the Sound of which the majority, 18 million, crossed between Elsinore and Hälsingborg. However, to this must be added a relatively well-operating network between university researchers in Lund and Copenhagen.

Apart from this type of traffic, the border of the catchment areas of Copenhagen and Stockholm, respectively, are identical with the Sound. Every time one phone call was made between south Sweden and Denmark, 16 were made between south Sweden and Stockholm. In terms of service contacts the ratio was 1:8 and the goods contact ratio was 1:10.

Sweden's prospective entry into the EC with freer movement for goods, information, services, people and financial flows will, in conjunction with the completion of the connections across the Sound, however, move the present border of the catchment area northwards up through Sweden and will thus dramatically change the contact pattern across the Sound.

'Örecity Train ' (SoundCity Train) is the local 'ER regional' train uniting the region. Within one hour, a professor of Lund University can be with a colleague from Roskilde University Centre west of Copenhagen – from the easternmost edge of the region to its westernmost edge. The Swedish EuroCity-snabbtog (EuroCity-fast train) and the Danish EuroCity–IC3/IC4 meet up in Copenhagen.

Travelling times will be reduced considerably by the connection across the Sound and will be less than 30 minutes between the centre of Copenhagen and Malmö, or 10 and 20 minutes, respectively, from Copenhagen and Malmö to the new railway station at Copenhagen Airport. With frequent and convenient departures of regional and intercity trains, respectively, on the Swedish and the Danish side of the Sound, an obstacle seriously hampering growth in the region will have been removed.

It is expected that the connection across the Sound will mean an increase in the number of passengers from 23 million in 1993 to 32 million in the year 2000. But this will very much depend on the type of rate policy for motor cars and trains which will be adopted. Currently it is the intention that rates are to be comparable to the present price level for ferry fares, i.e. DKK 160 (£16) for bringing a motor car across, but it is not inconceivable that the shipping line operating between Elsinore and Hälsingborg north of Copenhagen will take up price competition once the connection has been completed by the year 2000. For example, one study estimates that a reduction of the fare to 1/4 (DKK 40) would mean 32 million car passengers in the year 2000 with the corresponding train fare costing DKK 30.

The overall transport system between Denmark and Sweden will be supplemented by local light rail which will, for instance, connect the centre of Copenhagen with the airport area and a new development area, known as the 'Ørestaden' (Sound City) planned for the western part of the island of Amager, immediately to the south of Copenhagen. The newly developed urban area which takes up about 3 km² (300 hectares) will be able to accommodate 50 000 workplaces mixed in with houses, teaching and cultural institutions. Based on the expected earnings made on the sale of building sites by the Ørestads-company, loans will be raised to finance the building of an urban railway along the Ørestaden and under central Copenhagen going to downtown (Nørreport Station). The new urban railway line between Nørreport in Copenhagen and the Ørestaden and the airport will mean a reduction of the present travelling time of 30 minutes to 12–15 minutes. During rush hours, these light rail trains will run every

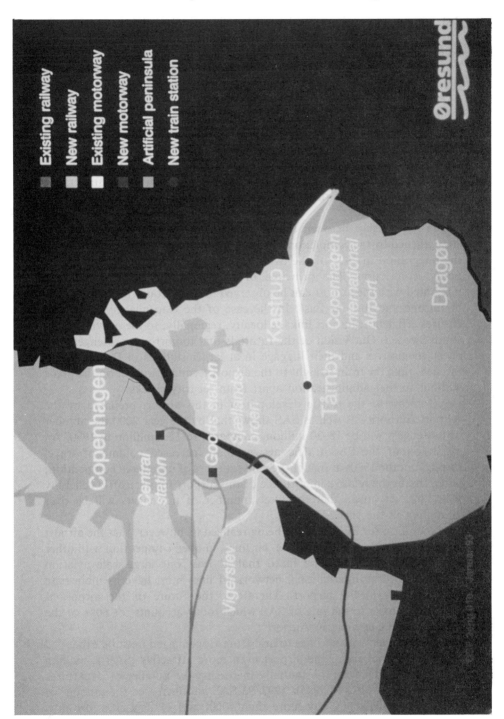

Figure 2.3.

2-3 minutes along the central routes. It is estimated that approximately 30 million passengers will travel on the new urban railway every year. Total construction costs have been estimated at DKK 3.7 billion (*c.* £350 million).

The pivot of future infrastructural investments should, however, be the Copenhagen Airport, as a well-functioning international airport is an important – perhaps the most important – catalyst for growth in the entire region.

Today Copenhagen Airport is the heart of travel to and from Scandinavia and has the potential of becoming the most important centre for traffic to and from the entire Baltic Basin. Furthermore the geographic location enables Copenhagen to become an important pivotal point for traffic between large parts of the rest of Europe and North America/north and southeast Asia.

The relationship between the airport and the nearby markets will be strengthened by the completion of the connection across the Great Belt and the integration in 1997 of the overall road and railway network with the Sound connection. The principle of having a railway station closely integrated with the airport can be observed in many countries, particularly in Europe and the Far East. In the case of the Copenhagen Airport, it ensures efficient transport linkage locally, regionally, to the provinces and south Sweden. Our vision of the future is that tomorrow's passengers can check themselves and their luggage in at larger stations in Denmark and Sweden, take the train straight to the airport terminal and get on the plane without further administration apart from security checks.

A forecast of the traffic development in this airport prepared by the Airport Authority as well as SAS shows that by the year 2000 the number of passengers will be 18–20 million, compared to 12.8 million in 1990. An expansion of the SAS traffic network, an increased volume of travel throughout the 1990s as one of the consequences of unfettered competition, and a rise in the relative importance of this airport for air traffic generally will, however, mean that the likely number of passengers will be over 20 million in the year 2000.

A condition for this objective being realized is, however, that the airport is capable of attracting traffic, i.e. air lines, in open competition with other airports. The fact must be faced that at least one large-scale aviation company with an international network of lines must have its main base of operations at the airport. Therefore, the future of the airport is intimately linked to the fate of SAS which today accounts for 60% of the traffic at the Copenhagen Airport.

The traffic network of lines to and from Copenhagen must be expanded and improved to make the airport even more attractive. SAS is making a major stake here by substantially increasing the number of departures and new destinations. Thus in 1992/93 SAS had increased the number of international departures by more than 5000, and 11 new cities are now

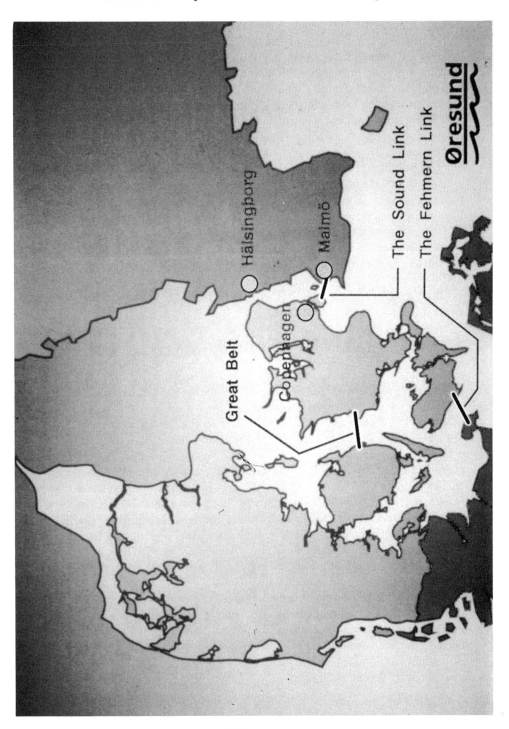

Figure 2.4.

directly linked to Copenhagen. SAS undertakes these expansions because Copenhagen is the most important traffic junction for the company, and because we wish to turn the entire Baltic area and large tracts of Eastern Europe and the former Soviet Union into our domestic market, thus creating 'SAS Baltic Hub'. These efforts also attract other companies, which then go on to create the additional requisite growth.

It is worth noting that this traffic build-up has taken place in the trough of the most serious recession suffered by the international aviation industry and concurrently with negotiations between SAS and potential new partners for co-operation in Europe.

More than 50% of the passengers in the Copenhagen Airport are transfer passengers, who, in principle, could change planes at other, rival, airports like Frankfurt, Hamburg, Amsterdam or at a future up-to-date airport at Berlin. Convenient, quick transfers and a high level of service with a frequent and extensive network of lines is, therefore, a central competitive parameter for the Copenhagen Airport and for its most important operator, SAS. We must realize that the battle in the air will be won on the ground. Without a well-functioning hub, it will be difficult to survive in the context of growing and open competition.

SAS wants the necessary extension of the Copenhagen Airport to include a terminal reserved for SAS and partners, which will place SAS on an equal footing with the company's major competitors abroad. Here experience shows that this is a crucial factor for the setting up of an efficient transport system. It is in SAS, the large national company, that transport development originates. The more SAS expands, the more obvious will be the incentive for other airlines to bring traffic to the centre in Copenhagen.

In a society as highly developed as the Danish one, the service sector is essential. Tourism, and more particularly, business tourism, is becoming more and more important. A well-functioning airport in combination with sufficient hotel accommodation is a decisive factor if Copenhagen and the Sound region are to fight successfully in the international marketplace to get conferences, congresses and fairs to the area. Integrating hotel and conference facilities with shopping malls and other commercial initiatives could create an international 'Sky City' environment close to the airport and 10 minutes by train from downtown Copenhagen and 18 from the central station of Malmö.

By continuing to promote business growth and development strategically and by establishing the requisite infrastructures and transportation systems, not only Copenhagen, but all of the Sound region, has the potential to become the dominant growth centre in northern Europe at the beginning of the new century. It is a historic opportunity for the entire Sound region and not least for Scandinavia.

3

Waterborne passenger transport

M.B.F. Ranken CEng FIMarE FIMechE FRINA

3.1 INTRODUCTION

Earth is a water planet; over two-thirds of it covered by sea water, yet more
by fresh water or ice, surrounding or surrounded by the irregular land areas
of continents, countries and myriad islands, large and small, inhabited or
visited by humankind.

The most economical transport mode between these many land areas now
comprises a huge number of ships and craft of widely differing sizes and
types to suit the diverse requirements of thousands of unique crossings and
the cargo or passengers to be carried between selected terminal points. Prior
to the invention of aircraft, the only alternatives to waterborne craft were
road or rail bridges, which usually eliminated the ferries – e.g. Forth, Tay,
upper Clyde, Lille Bælt (Kolding/Middelfart) – and tunnels, so far limited
to little more than 50 km, i.e. the length of the Channel Tunnel or that
between Honshu and Hokkaido Islands in Japan, both competing with
major ferry services. On very many routes, aviation does not so far offer
any viable alternative to ships or craft affordable by most regular or daily
travellers. A few locations can only be served by sea, for want of an airstrip
or far beyond the range of helicopters; the Falkland Islands was one of
these pre-1982, St Helena, Tristan da Cunha and Pitcairn Islands are
others, all of them UK Dependent Territories.

3.2 THE EVOLUTION OF PASSENGER SHIPPING

Aircraft only displaced passenger liners on intercontinental routes less
than 30 years ago. There was vast evolution and developing of passenger
shipping in the previous 130 years, driven initially by the demands of vast

Passenger Transport after 2000 AD. Edited by G.B.R. Feilden, A.H. Wickens and I.R. Yates.
Published in 1994 by E & FN Spon, London. ISBN 0 419 19470 3.

immigration attracted by rapid economic development and great opportunities in North America. Revolutionary changes have taken place in
shipping since the 1960s, particularly in the methods of handling cargo,
road and rail vehicles and of the ships themselves; latterly these have
extended too to new types of craft and hull forms – hovercraft, hydrofoils,
catamarans (including washless), SWATH (Small Waterplane Area Twin
Hull) – some of them very high speed, and more are to come within a
few years. New propulsion and manoeuvring methods have also been
introduced, and more likely, such as superconducting magnetohydro-
dynamic propulsion, now under trial in Japan. Meanwhile water-jet systems
have great potential and their efficiency increases the higher the speed.

Automation is widespread throughout modern ships, and already allows
the reduction of crew sizes to very low minima, it makes possible the
unmanned ship, which Japan has demonstrated, but it is doubted whether
crewless ships will become acceptable except on very restricted routes.
Automation extends also to the terminals and passenger processing,
accelerated by such disasters as the *Herald of Free Enterprise* capsize in
1987. With very high speeds, automation is essential to safe navigation in
congested waters. We are concerned here with passenger ferries on regular
routes, but cruise liners have become a major growth industry over the
past few years, with a number of very large ships, though generally content
with quite modest (economical) speeds – much lower than the *QE2's* potential 32 + knots available following her recent re-engining with diesel-electric
propulsion.

3.3 VITAL LINKS

Rivers, lakes and inland waterways allow maritime transport to penetrate
far from the sea in North and South America, Asia, parts of Africa, Europe
and the former Soviet Union. The West European waterways' network
extends to 19 000 km, but this now has access via the Main–Danube canal,
opened last year, to the Black Sea and thence to the 250 000 km within the
former Soviet Union, at least during summer and autumn months, for
barges up to 2500 tonnes capacity, 190 m long by 12 m beam (larger or much
larger in various sections on either side of the cross-connection). It was
said a few years ago that 95% of all trade crossing frontiers is waterborne.
Some rivers and estuaries remain natural obstacles in most countries, often
not meriting bridges or tunnels; many retain ferry links, often of great
antiquity, some 'powered' by the flow of the river.

We must not forget the fast ferry traffic and tourist barges on numerous
sections of the network, sea-going vessels of considerable size on the
Danube, Rhine, Seine and other large rivers (large ocean-going vessels,
too, on the Amazon (to Iquitos in Peru), Yangtze, Mississippi, some
ex-Soviet rivers both north and south flowing). There is also much

passenger traffic on rivers, lakes and inland seas, some of it serving commuters, e.g. Zürich, Lucerne, Geneva, Constance; Athens/Piraeus, Sea of Marmora/Bosphorus, Hong Kong, New York, Rio de Janiero, Stockholm, Sydney Harbour, Venice; the Greak Lakes; the Elbe, the Clyde, the Thames (including over 25% of passengers between the City and London City Airport), also across many estuaries.

Transport is a dynamic process, nowadays essential to meet economic, demographic, political, leisure, military, (humanitarian) and other demands to move people or goods. The mode chosen to suit each link (and the frequency of service), is dictated by its length and demand patterns, by geography, sometimes by topography (or hydrography), maybe also by prevailing weather, by congestion and bottlenecks (narrow straits), and by safety considerations. The locations of terminals should relate to their convenience to the connecting links (and modes), as well as to the infrastructure available at either end. The political cohesion of numerous archipelagic states depends greatly on convenient and frequent cheap transport links, especially for passengers, between and around the individual islands (often with distinct ethnic groups in each) and connecting all of them with regional and national government centres, including the state capital. Good examples are Indonesia, the Philippines, the Solomon and other islands states in the Pacific, the Maldives, Seychelles and Andaman and Nicobar Islands in the Indian Ocean, various Caribbean islands, Greek islands in the Aegean and Ionian Seas, numerous islands in the Western Mediterranean, the UK's Hebredian islands, Crown and Dependent Territories – Isle of Man, Channel Islands. If airstrips exist, that mode will be used by those who can afford it, e.g. government officials, business people or individuals, but ships and craft are essential for cargo, and will surely by used by many intent on saving money, e.g. when taking their families on holiday, especially, of course, if using their cars.

3.4 THE FUTURE

World population was 5.5 billion in 1990, rising to 6.1 billion in the year 2000 and 8.5 billion in 2025 (UN Report). 99.5% by weight of world trade is carried by sea in ships. This was 4025 million tonnes in 1991, 17 390 000 m tonne-miles, i.e. average distance carried 4320 nautical miles (OECD Maritime Transport 1991; Paris 1993). World trade could exceed 8000 m tonnes by 2025 and the trading fleet perhaps 80 000 ships of 800 m GT, probably over greater distances as world interdependence increases, driven partly by the demand of still-growing world population.

Today's trade is carried in about 41 000 trading vessels of 421 million GT (out of a world fleet of almost 80 000 ships of 445 GT). Included amongst these are 415 passenger/general cargo ships (max. 12 passengers) of 765 000 GT (average age 27 yrs); 2055 passenger/RoRo cargo (Roll-on/Roll-off)

Table 3.1 International ferry capacity by region (January 1993)

Operator	No. of Ships	GT	Pax	Berths	Cars	Lane length (metres)
English Channel–Irish Sea						
Eastern Channel	26	426 715	33 418	5 501	9 165	28 885
Western Channel	17	239 365	22 966	10 745	5 592	13 382
Irish Sea	9	85 497	14 999	4 259	3 204	5 480
Total	52	751 577	71 383	20 505	17 961	47 747
% of world total	18	23	21	15	22	24
Baltic–North Sea						
N and E Baltic	26	577 782	41 423	30 783	9 597	19 161
S and W Baltic	57	645 521	68 042	22 016	14 861	40 609
North Sea	27	418 633	28 545	21 434	9 469	28 960
Total	110	1 641 936	138 101	74 233	33 927	88 730
% of world total	37	50	40	53	42	45
Mediterranean–Black Sea–Red Sea						
W Mediterranean	37	245 541	44 750	14 160	10 515	13 685
E Med/Black/Red	71	475 378	70 195	25 820	16 269	33 746
Total	108	720 919	114 945	39 980	26 784	47 431
% of world total	36	22	33	29	33	24
Rest of the world						
North America	7	59 343	6 348	3 001	1 165	4 064
Japan	7	47 590	4 083	106	653	4 896
Other	12	73 776	8 651	2 107	955	2 786
World total	296	3 295 141	343 511	139 932	81 445	195 654

Source: G.P. Wild (International) Limited.

Table 3.2 Baltic ferry traffic

Passengers	Cars	Buses	Trucks	Voyages	Routes
10 476 258	234 323	8 219	30 158	5 342	Fin/Swe
3 597 719	597 719	3 361	82 772	6 042	East/Euro
16 420 622	2 175 862	85 088	593 019	67 405	Scan/Germ
470 330	87 520	2 080	7 155	2 436	Norw/Swed
26 344 682	2 801 360	103 160	431 547	158 014	Swed/Denm
3 580 275	461 312	18 512	103 637	2 756	Norw/Denm
61 160 886	6 358 096	220 420	1 248 288	241 995	Totals
19 400 259	4 671 006	48 256	655 639	118 318	Domestic
83 290 145	11 029 102	268 676	1 903 927	360 313	Grd totals
756 168	114 245	1 226	1 940	854	North Sea

Note: Number of voyages not complete on some routes.

ships of 7 840 000 GT (Av. age 18); 2310 Passenger ships of 4 974 000 GT (Av. age 18), which include both cruise ships and ferries. (Lloyd's Register World Fleet Statistics December 1992). In addition there is a vast number of small and miscellaneous vessels and craft around the world providing essential passenger transport links, both domestic and international over distances as short as a narrow river crossing up to several days trip amongst the islands and archipelagoes around the world. In very many cases passenger transport is associated with car, bus, lorry, trailer, container and general cargo carriage; the modern ferry is a highly sophisticated vessel, but many small vessels are little more than short-sea or coastal cargo tramps, usually elderly, pressed into service because they were affordable and reasonably economical to operate.

In contrast to full information covering all ships over 100 GT, passenger statistics are very sporadic. One study finds that the international ferry market comprises some 296 ships of 3.3 m GT in service in January 1993, with a single-voyage capacity of 344 000 passengers and 81 500 cars (Table 3.1). It will be seen that Europe dominates with 270 of the ships (95% GT), of which 110 (41%) serve the Baltic–North Sea. Norway, the Baltic and its six littoral states north of Germany and Poland, with a population of about 31 million occupy an area of 696 000 square miles. Baltic Traffic in 1992, including domestic, involved well over 360 000 voyages, carrying over 83 million passengers, 11 million cars, 269 000 buses and 1.9 million trucks and trailers, all within the Baltic and Kattegat (Table 3.2).

4

Buses

W.P. Bradshaw and M.V. McGreevy

4.1 INTRODUCTION

In many parts of the world the bus is the means of transport used by the poor, the elderly and those without access to a car. In some, but not all places, the bus suffers from a problem of image. In the developed world bus use has declined as car ownership has risen. The rise of car ownership has brought congestion, particularly along the urban corridors where potential bus use is highest. Congestion interferes with bus operation, engendering unreliability, longer journeys, less efficient use of vehicles and crews, higher fuel consumption and lower profitability. In Britain, bus travel is in a cycle of decline where slower, older vehicles become less and less attractive, causing even more people to use cars and exacerbating the problems of congestion. Inter-urban bus services have faced similar problems. As the number of people using buses has declined, frequency of operation has been reduced, making the service less attractive. Inter-urban bus routes face congestion at either end of their journeys. The growth of car ownership has been particularly marked in rural areas, where bus services have become very sparse indeed in most regions and where public subsidy of one kind or another is required to sustain any sort of service (Figure 4.1).

Large urban areas with radial roads around which are clustered dense housing are ideal bus country. Such roads can support frequent services and provide good load factors. For various reasons there has been a decline in population in many such areas, particularly close to city centres. At the same time there has been a move of employment, shopping, entertainment and even education to greenfield sites at the periphery of urban areas.

Because these new locations are peripheral, they tend to generate

Passenger Transport after 2000 AD. Edited by G.B.R. Feilden, A.H. Wickens and I.R. Yates. Published in 1994 by E & FN Spon, London. ISBN 0 419 19470 3.

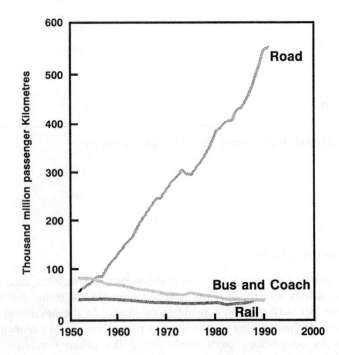

Figure 4.1 Growth in travel in Great Britain (from Wooton, Mitchell and Poulton 'Transport in Europe. Demand, Environment and Energy', Institute of Energy Seminar, London, 1992).

journeys of a widely dispersed nature rather than along the radial corridor. It is usually uneconomic to provide frequent, convenient bus routes to serve greenfield sites. New developments tend to be close to ring roads and motorways and to be laid out for the benefit of the car user. Some developments cannot easily be accessed by pedestrians or public transport. As activity moves from the centres of cities, the bus routes which serve the city become less well used, frequency is reduced and revenue declines. Housing near city centres becomes more and more the place where the poor and unemployed live. These people travel less than the previous inhabitants. The better off move to less densely populated suburbs and tend to use cars, making bus operation in such areas unattractive, particularly in the evenings and at weekends.

We start from the position that the bus, in many places, needs considerable help if it is to make a worthwhile contribution to the transport needs of the future. In democracies, while the use of cars may be constrained in some respects for environmental or other reasons, any attempt to limit or price people out of the cars onto public transport must be accompanied or even preceded by substantial improvements to the overall

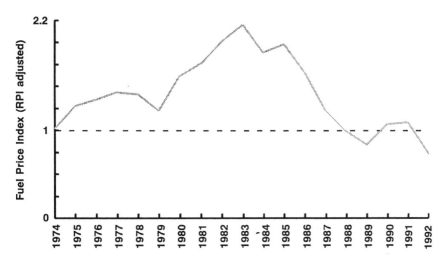

Figure 4.2 Fuel Price Index (RPI adjusted – nett of tax).

performance of alternative modes, including the bus. This paper considers the potential for an increase in the use of buses which may be achieved from the viewpoint of:

- technology;
- design, i.e. its attractiveness;
- payment systems;
- off-bus systems and infrastructure, such as bus stations, bus stops, information systems;
- the road.

While these features all have technical implications which are the principal interests of the Royal Society, reference is also made to the economic and regulatory framework within which bus operations work, because this is as important in creating the climate in which technological advances are likely to be introduced as is the contribution which may be made by engineers and scientists.

Before addressing the issue of vehicle technology, it will be useful to consider how the present cost of operation of a bus is broken down. This will indicate which elements are most significant and establish a relationship between the age of the vehicle and maintenance costs, which is critical in the determination of replacement policy. Strategically, it is sensible to work from the assumption that world fuel prices may rise in real terms, although this has not been the case for the last 40 years (Figure 4.2). We should consider whether different fuel sources may offer advantages both to cost and diversity of source of supply. Increased environmental concern is bound to lead to demands to reduce emissions and noise and both these features must

Table 4.1 Present cost of operating a bus

Cost per mile	New good quality vehicle (pence)	15-year-old vehicle (pence)
Depreciation	22.0	0.0
Maintenance	5.0	30.0
Fuel and oil	7.0	8.0
Tyres	2.0	2.0

Costs based on 40 000 miles per annum.

be anticipated. Interaction between an intelligent vehicle and intelligent highway is almost certain at some time in the future and guidance may be applied to the bus for the whole or part of the journey either by a guideway or some other control system.

All these measures have the object of reducing cost, increasing the acceptability of the bus, particularly within the centres of busy towns and cities, and ensuring that the present high levels of safety are further enhanced.

It should be noted that with new vehicles the major cost component (depreciation) is fixed, whereas with older vehicles the major cost item (maintenance) is often optional (Table 4.1), i.e. some operators may choose to substantially reduce the figure by accepting a lower standard of maintenance and running inferior quality vehicles.

While investment in a high quality vehicle provides some savings in running costs and good design may attract more users, it is less likely that such investment will take place on a route where there is direct competition, because anyone investing will face higher costs than other operators but will not be able to charge sufficient premium to offset these costs.

One of these differences between competition in the bus travel market and other competitive markets is the fact that in most circumstances the customer is not presented with the choice between two or more products at the same time. In facing a choice between a poor quality bus which is at the bus stop and the uncertainty of a better bus arriving shortly afterwards offering a better quality journey, the customer almost invariably chooses the certainty of transport offered by the first vehicle to appear. This dilemma faced by the consumer might partly be overcome by a system of information showing when the next (better) bus might arrive. It would also make any waiting more acceptable if bus stops presented warm and comfortable and secure places at which to wait.

Finally if traffic conditions permitted buses to run very punctually, it would encourage people to develop brand loyalty to companies willing to invest in high quality, reliable vehicles operated to a strict timetable.

That people will pay more money to travel on high quality public

Table 4.2 Grenoble: use of public transport (millions of journeys)

Year	1984	1985	1986	1987	1988	1989	1990	1991
Bus Systems	36	33	34	37	42	45	48	50
LRT Systems				4	13	14	16	22

Source: Cetur Statistics – November, 1992.

transport has been amply demonstrated in Britain in the case of the Chiltern Railway Line from London Marylebone to Aylesbury and Banbury. This line was completely modernized in 1992 with new signalling and new trains and improvements to stations in a process described by Network SouthEast as 'total route modernization'. The trends in numbers of people using the service when contrasted with other services provided by Network SouthEast provides striking evidence of the effect of quality on the willingness of customers to use public transport and to pay higher fares for better services.

From the bus industry our experience in Belfast has been that when high quality vehicles are provided on a route giving a faster, more comfortable and more frequent service than previously, ridership grows significantly and people are attracted from cars.

Experience in Grenoble is that its well known LRT system has been extraordinarily successful in attracting additional passengers to public transport from other modes (Table 4.2 and Figure 4.3).

In all these examples new vehicles, representing a step change in comfort, have been used in combination with other improvements to infrastructure to offer a much enhanced public transport product. Low fares have not

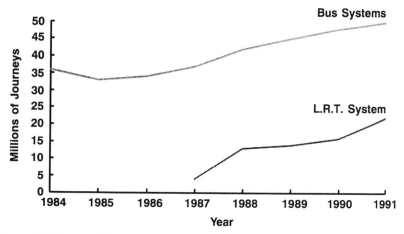

Figure 4.3 Use of public transport in Grenoble (Source: Cetur Statistics, November 1992).

been the key element in the package; improved quality has been. Improving quality has required substantial investment.

Two major questions arise so far as bus transport is concerned:

1. Is major investment compatible with unfettered competition in the market?
2. Will public authorities be prepared to allocate an adequate share of highway capacity to allow buses to operate at optimum efficiency so that investment is worthwhile?

4.2 TECHNICAL DEVELOPMENTS OF THE URBAN BUS

Through the late 1980s, and probably through most of the 1990s, monetary costs and financial competitiveness have been the driving force in the provision of public transport by the urban bus in Great Britain. To date, however, the real impact of environmental costs in terms of atmospheric pollution, noise and road space congestion of our public and private transportation systems have not been fully assessed and have not been taken into account in any financial assessment. As each year goes by, however, public awareness is bringing these environmental costs more and more to the fore. Within the next decade nations will start to take into account the financial penalty arising from the environmental costs which we have thus far conditioned ourselves to bear with a mounting degree of unease. The emergence of environmental accountability will provide the real impetus to the development of a highly energy efficient urban bus of the future, in addition to arresting the general shift away from public to private transport.

For the last 40 years large buses have been powered almost exclusively by diesel engines. Extensive trials have been successfully carried out using modified vehicles and engines running on alternative fuels, such as compressed natural gas, hydrogen, alcohols, bio-fuels and synthetic fuels. Many of these fuels offer the advantage of being clean, producing little or none of the pollutants which contribute to acidification of our atmosphere, and in many cases may offer strategic advantages.

Such fuels can make substantial contributions where emissions limitations are particularly stringent. However, in general, they can add significant complexity to the vehicles and they tend to be less thermally efficient than the modern diesel engine, resulting in the generation of higher greenhouse gas levels.

Western Australia imports 75% of its crude oil requirements for diesel fuel production whilst large reserves of natural gas exist in the northern areas of the state. For strategic reasons Transperth, the public transport operator in the city of Perth, have initiated an extensive trial with 43 modified Mercedes Benz buses out of a 900 strong fleet running on compressed natural gas (CNG). Ultimate operating costs for CNG buses are likely to be similar to diesel fuel when infrastructure costs are taken into account. However, due to the gas compression process, the buses require 6 hours to refuel and have a limited range. (Source: C437/019 I.Mech.E. 1992).

In Sydney, Australia, Scania Ltd. are currently supplying 250 buses powered by CNG, again principally because of a generous local supply of natural gas. CNG engines offer potentially zero particulate emissions and low nitrogen oxide emissions. However, comparable emissions performance can now be achieved by state-of-the-art diesel engines.

Bio-diesels (fatty acid methyl esters), such as those which can be produced from rapeseed oil, are very easy to use and can be employed in unmodified diesel engines. Reading Buses have recently completed a 6-month trial with a number of their buses running on such fuel. For reasons of primary fuel costs, however, the trials have not been extended.

Alcohol-based fuels (methanol or ethanol diesel) can be synthesized from natural gas or coal. Suitable engines require only minor modifications and produce no soot in normal operations.

When reviewing comparative fuel performances we must, however, compare primary energy consumption for the production of these alternatives. Considering the fossil-derived fuels, standard diesel oil results in the smallest release of carbon dioxide (a primary greenhouse gas) to the atmosphere. On the other hand bio-diesel consumes substantial energy in the processing/conversion phase. However, because this is a renewable fuel source, carbon dioxide is fully re-absorbed in the growth cycle producing no net contribution to greenhouse gases. It is the authors' view that biofuels will achieve limited success in the future due to their net zero greenhouse gas release. However, we concur with the views of most major European engine manufacturers that principally for economic reasons fossil diesel fuel will continue as a primary energy source for many decades to come (Figure 4.4).

Already we recognize that today's modern urban bus is some 5 to 10 times more efficient per passenger kilometre than the average private car. Today's modern bus however is, with minor exceptions, not very far removed from that of 30 years ago. Multi-speed automatic transmission systems offering improved passenger comfort are now commonplace. Using modern design techniques vehicles can now be built lighter whilst retaining desired structural strength (operating experience shows that a 10% reduction in vehicle kerb weight equates to a 3% to 5% improvement in fuel efficiency). Improvements in tyre technology and the adoption of modern radial ply tyres has yielded a 2% to 3% improvement in fuel efficiency. Turbocharging, charge cooling, high pressure injection and engine management systems have all contributed to improvements in fuel conversion.

The developments described thus far all contribute to single figure percentage fuel improvements. However, they are cumulative, with a net result that today's vehicles are at least some 25% to 30% more fuel efficient

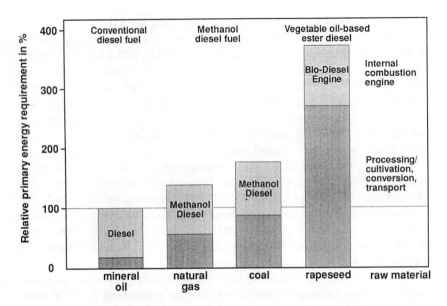

Figure 4.4 Primary energy consumption for alternative fuels.

than those of 30 years ago. To achieve further major improvements will require a radical change and the abandoning of the traditional engine–transmission–axle–roadwheel drive system.

Today's drive system is a once-through system. Energy is provided in the form of diesel fuel and then bled off as heat at several points along the path. The radiator, charge cooler, exhaust stream, transmission cooler, axle lubricants, tyres and brakes all take energy from the fuel and dissipate it. A primary requirement of an improved drive system is that it dissipates as little heat as possible; recovery of 'waste' energy is the prime objective.

Regardless of the primary source of energy, any novel technology drive system would of necessity include an energy storage cell for recovery of energy normally lost through braking (Figures 4.5 and 4.6).

A number of energy storage systems are now available. Hydraulic accumulators and fly-wheels have both been used in prototype designs to capture regenerative braking energy, and most notably the Cumulo hydraulic system by Volvo/Flygmotor has been extensively tested in urban service during the 1980s yielding improvements of 25–30%.

These, however, are purely mechanical systems and are fundamentally limited by relatively low amounts of stored energy in relation to weight of the devices. Chemical batteries have the potential of storing much greater amounts of energy for a given weight than any currently developed mechanical system. Furthermore, the energy is stored in a readily convertible form and a much greater degree of freedom in locating the energy store is achieved.

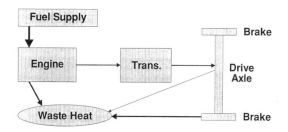

Figure 4.5 Once-through system.

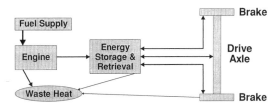

Figure 4.6 Regenerative system.

Development of an advanced high capacity energy storage cell would unlock the opportunity for an additional area of substantial fuel efficiency gains. An urban bus with frequent start/stop operation could be powered by a much smaller internal combustion engine, typically 30–50 kW, in comparison to the 200 kW plus which is commonplace today. This smaller engine would run at constant speed connected to a generator which would provide electrical energy either to the batteries or to electric traction motors, depending on the driving conditions. Under direct drive conditions the engine would be capable of sustaining 50–60 km h^{-1} for a fully laden vehicle on level terrain. Power surges required for smooth rapid acceleration and hill climbing would be supplied by the battery cell. This hybrid would, of necessity, feature a complex electronic control system, monitoring the flow of primary energy from the thermal engine/generator set to the energy storage cell and the dual directional flow of energy between the energy storage cell and the electrical traction motors/brake regenerators.

Iveco Ford is one of a number of European manufacturers actively developing along this route with their Altrobus project. 1993 will see the first of these vehicles operating in Exeter, i.e. 2 Iveco Daily Minibuses. Operating trials are already well advanced in Genoa using full-size 12-m Altrobuses utilizing a diesel engine of only 2 l capacity as the primary power source.

By adopting this type of control and power distribution method, the thermal engine is not subject to either load or speed variations. This permits the engine to operate at the condition of optimum specific fuel consumption and minimum exhaust emissions. In addition, such an engine could be expected to operate at noise levels some 12–15 dB less than those being achieved by today's 200 kW plus, 10 l capacity equivalent engines. During periods of over-supply the engine would simply shut down. Using advanced electronic control systems the driver need not be expected to operate controls different from those in daily use today.

Operational advantages of such vehicles are currently limited by the performance of lead-acid traction batteries, which result in power to weight disadvantages and packaging problems. To fully unlock the potential of hybrid urban buses we eagerly await ongoing developments in chemical battery technology, in particular prospects for zinc air and nickel cadmium batteries, which will result in the power density performance of such systems moving much closer to that of current state-of-the-art diesel engines.

The technologies required for such a vehicle are either already with us or within our grasp. Currently the cost of such systems are seen as prohibitive. Estimates for an optimized 'hybrid' bus range from double the cost to as much as 4 times the cost of a standard bus. Ultimately, however, it will be environmental sensitivity and environmental regulation which provides the impetus for development of such a system.

4.3 IMPROVING THE DESIGN OF THE VEHICLE

Not only must buses become more passenger friendly and eco-friendly, but their external and interior appearance must be such that it differentiates future vehicles from those of the present and the past. Passenger perception of new standards of customer care and customer service must be reinforced by modern, perhaps even futuristic, styling and design.

Bus exteriors have improved markedly over the last decade. However, current impact is being diluted by a very low rate of replacement. This shift in design and styling must continue and indeed accelerate into the next century. Traditionally passenger seating has been basic, with cost effectiveness uppermost in the minds of the providers. A move to individual seating rather than shared seating offering improved levels of comfort is now starting to emerge. This must continue. Similarly interior designs, and in particular front bulkheads and driver cab areas, are now starting to benefit from the contribution of stylists and designers. All these developments will contribute greatly to improvements in passenger perception and acceptability of public transport.

Perhaps most significant of all, however, is the development towards low floor buses. Low floor buses can substantially remove the physical difficulties experienced by mobility-impaired passengers. In this context, mobility impaired does not just mean passengers with physical disabilities, but refers to any passengers whose movement ability is restricted. This includes any passenger, young or old, who is heavily laden with shopping, or mothers with young children or babies in pushchairs. It should be clear that low floors will improve the quality of service available to a substantial proportion of users. Floor levels of some 300 mm have already been achieved over half the length of the modern vehicle through the repackaging of chassis items, i.e. engine and transmission, air cylinders, fuel tanks, batteries, radiator, etc, to the rear of the vehicle. Application of the potential technological developments already described with much smaller engines, independent traction motors instead of a heavy duty rear axle and the flexibility to locate battery packs virtually anywhere will make further substantial contributions towards the concept of the ultimate low floor bus.

4.4 IMPROVING REVENUE COLLECTION ON THE BUS

Delays at bus stops while fares are collected cause longer journey times and delay other traffic using the road. An ideal design of vehicles has two doors to allow those leaving the bus to do so simultaneously with those joining. In the developed world the economics of bus operation do not usually allow the employment of conductors, although there are exceptions to this rule. Ideally passengers should not have to pay the driver on entry but should have paid for their journey before travelling. With prepurchase, not only is delay at stops minimized, it has the added advantage that the driver has no money on the bus, which constitutes a target for thieves.

Technological design is therefore moving to a system where passengers pre-purchase tickets for travel using a system where 'value' is stored in the ticket which they hold. This ticket is a 'Smartcard' which contains a microchip. The Smartcard remembers the last 20 transactions, so an inspector can read the card using a handheld machine to ensure that the journey taken has been paid for. No money changes hands on the bus and no ticket is issued.

While in ideal circumstances self-cancellation of prepaid journey tickets by passengers themselves is preferable in terms of transaction time, even when backed up by vigorous inspection and a high level of penalty fares, it is found in some places that the level of fraud is high. On the other hand, the Smartcard can be supported by a photograph laser printed onto the surface, and the numbers of stolen or lost cards can be entered into the system to prevent abuse. It is therefore likely that in most urban applications we will see the Smartcard used to buy bus journeys as well as many other services, avoiding fraud and reducing the risks and delays associated with cash handling.

4.5 PROVISION OF INFORMATION AT BUS STOPS

Research among passengers shows that the uncertainty of waiting time is the biggest deterrent to bus travel. Except on the most frequent routes, passengers want to know when the next bus is coming. Timetables are difficult to read, are often missing and do not relate in most cases to a particular stop. Traffic congestion interferes with reliability. The Countdown and Automatic Vehicle Location System now operating on Route 18 of London Buses Ltd. is one of the methods being developed to provide real time information to passengers. Information regarding Countdown has been provided by London Transport Planning (tel. 071 918 3889).

Small roadside microwave beacons are mounted on lamp posts at key locations. These battery powered units transmit their identity to buses as they pass. The bus mounted Automatic Vehicle Identity (AVL) equipment is linked to the London Buses Band 3 radio on the bus, which then transmits the location information and the bus identity code back to the control room at the garage. Messages are sent to the bus stops by land line. A 3-line LED display shows details of the next 3 buses due as well as other messages transmitted by the controller. At two stops on Route 18 an audio unit 'speaks' information when a button is pressed. To provide a London-wide system incorporating 100 routes and 4000 stops would cost £35 million. It is clearly conceivable that such information could be called up at home in the future.

4.6 IMPROVED TERMINALS AND WAITING ACCOMMODATION

Most bus passengers wait at the roadside where shelters are often primitive. Traditionally bus stations have been places for buses to load and unload and for drivers to take a rest. Attractive design and passenger comfort have been much less important in the consideration of designers than technical considerations like vehicle turning circles. It is now recognized that better design of bus stations and shelters is an essential part of the marketing package of the bus industry.

4.7 THE ROAD

Even though it is possible to look forward to a wide range of technical improvements in the design and performance of buses and associated equipment, the fact is that in most places the infrastructure on which the bus operates is the public highway.

There have been a couple of notable examples of guided busways having been built in Essen and Adelaide. There are proposals to provide guided systems in Leeds and Bristol, the latter using a more sophisticated guidance system which is more compatible with the general purpose highway. Both systems may be described as a cheaper version of the Light Rail System. Construction work on the Leeds guided busway will commence in November 1992, with the first scheme becoming operational in 1995. It will cost £2.8 million and cover 9.96 km of guideway in several

	Population in Transport Area	Trips per Annum	Trips per Person per annum in Transport area
London	6.7 million	1,941 million	290
Wein	1.52 million	612 million	403
Amsterdam	680,000	220 million	320
Stockholm	1.5 million	432 million	288
Düsseldorf	1.1 million	170 million	160
Hannover	540,000	127 million	235
Köln	1.1 million	179 million	162
Stuttgart	570,000	147 million	258
Greater Manchester	2.6 million	375 million	147
Tyne and Wear	1.1 million	347 million	340
West Midlands	2.6 million	343 million	170
Zürich	550,000	310 million	560

Figure 4.7 Zürich's commitment to public transport.

short sections on either side of key congested interchanges. The busway may be used by up to 6 bus operators. Bill Cottham, Chairman and Managing Director of Yorkshire Rider, the principal operator in the area, forecasts journey time improvements of up to 50% in the peak, coupled with a quieter, smoother ride (*Local Transport Today*: March, 1993).

The advantage of guided bus over light rail is that it is cheaper and the bus can join and leave the guidance system to offer better penetration of the street network than is feasible with light rail. Guided bus systems can share the same corridor as trams and light rail systems, which is an advantage, particularly in the core of cities.

Guidance systems may be developed until they represent nothing that can be seen on the road surface. However, delineating a portion of the road for the use of buses, and more importantly ensuring that it is reserved for bus use, represents the most likely and available means of improving the attractiveness and economics of bus services.

The humble bus lane can do much to assist the bus, but stretches of bus lane often run out at critical places and abuse of bus lanes is widespread. Zurich is outstanding in its commitment to public transport (Figure 4.7). The use of bus lanes in the centre of the road helps to avoid these being obstructed by parked vehicles, although it presents some problems when the bus stops to allow passengers on and off. The problem of obstruction of bus lanes can be avoided by the use of projecting pavements known as 'bus boarders', but this means that while the bus is stationary other traffic is often held up. This puts a high premium on quick boarding and alighting. Another useful device is to fit transponders, which activate traffic signals to give priority to buses. Selective vehicle detection at traffic signals will increasingly give preference to buses.

A 'Balanced Transport Policy', as practised in Oxford, can do a great deal to promote the use of the bus. This policy has the following features:

1. free park and ride facilities on major radial roads served by frequent bus services;
2. very restricted and expensive city centre parking (charges range from 90p for 1 hour to £12 per day; on-street parking is strictly limited to those staying for a short period of time);
3. use of revenue from parking to improve public transport, particularly the park and ride facilities. The buses which service the park and ride have been subsidized during the development phase but are likely to become commercial shortly.

The use of the 'Park and Ride' in Oxford has grown steadily from its inception in 1974 with daily use now approaching 4000 vehicles per weekday. Most important, the diversion rate of inward-bound morning commuters' cars is averaging nearly 20% of the traffic flow into the car parks, with a high rate of 37.5% on the southern approach. Additional car park capacity is being provided with 550 extra spaces to be added to the existing 3100 by the end of 1993. Oxford is, as yet, not well provided with bus lanes in the most congested streets. Properly policed bus lanes with some strategic additions to the present network; further pedestrianization; close supervision of the car parks to deter thieves and vandals; further expansion of existing sites; the opening of a further large car park which will increase capacity to 4700 cars and withdrawal of more city centre on-street parking places, are all policies which will substantially increase the use of the 'Park and Ride' system. This will make all the bus services fully commercial with a fare level of 70p return – a real bargain in public transport terms (Figure 4.8).

For the purpose of this paper we propose examining the more radical solution to the effects of traffic congestion on the bus which is provided by the Red Route.

The first Red Route in London, which was introduced as a pilot scheme, runs along parts of the inner ring road and the A13 running from Harringey in the north through Islington to Hackney and Tower Hamlets, south-east of the city centre, and came into operation in 1991 (Figure 4.9).

Along a Red Route no vehicles are permitted to stop except at places and times which are specified, and then usually the period of waiting is severely restricted. At rush hours, virtually no stopping is allowed, except by buses within marked bus stop areas. A very high level of enforcement is provided both with traffic wardens on foot and police on motorcycles, and with crews available to remove any vehicle which is left unattended. Clearly, in the future, the use of camera and equipment to automatically read

Radial Road (and Car Park)	Direction	A.M. peak (0800-0900)			12 Hour (0700-1900)		
		Use of Car Park (In Only) (a)	Inbound Radial Flow (b)	Attenuation Rate (a/bx100)	Use of Car Park (In and Out) (a)	2-Way Radial Flow (b)	Attenuation Rate (a/bx100)
Abingdon Road	South	406	1,082	37.5%	2,567	17,091	15.0%
Botley Road	West	159	765	20.8%	982	17,650	5.6%
Woodstock Road	North	263	742	35.4%	2,162	12,473	17.3%
London Road	East	76	649	11.7%	859	15.972	5.4%
All Routes (Measured at edge of central area)		904	5,070	17.8%	6,570	90,911	7.2%

NB 1. All flows measured accross the inner cordon except London Road which is the flow across the outer cordon

Figure 4.8 Traffic flow attenuation rates on the Oxford radial routes, 1992 (source: Oxford City Council).

number plates of offending vehicles and issue penalty tickets has much to offer in the way of effective enforcement. Some basic facts about the first Red Route in London are as follows:

- the effects of the Red Route on bus operation has been dramatic and this has led to increased patronage;
- overall traffic speeds have improved and accidents have decreased;
- the cost of enforcement on the first Red Route amounts to about £900 000 per annum.
- Table 4.3 illustrates the effects of the Red Route Scheme on buses.

In June, 1992 it was announced that a network of over 500 km of Red Routes was to be extended throughout London. The job of setting up this network is that of the newly appointed Traffic Director for London, Derek Turner. It is estimated that the cost of implementing the scheme will amount to £120 million over the 5 years to 1997/98 (Turner, 1993).

The evidence suggests that given unobstructed access to the highway, buses can perform a more useful job in urban transport and that this contribution can be made quickly and with very modest capital investment compared with alternatives, such as light rail or metro systems. Because the bus competes for road space with the private car, significant investment will need to be made on law enforcement to keep roads clear for buses. This is the real cost of giving the bus priority which has to be compared with

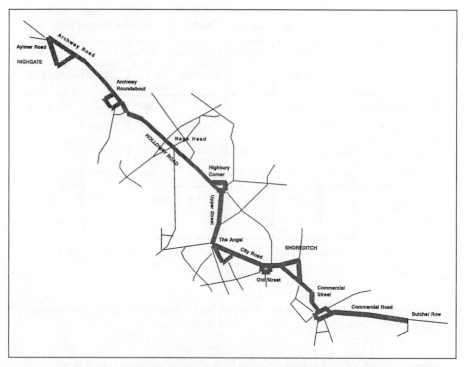

Figure 4.9 Red Route pilot scheme.

the costs associated with building the separate infrastructure required by other modes. Effective enforcement means that offenders must face a high probability of being subjected to penalty payments and enforcement based on technology rather than manpower. This is clearly the way ahead.

It has been demonstrated that the design and technology of buses will advance to enable them to offer an attractive and competitive mode of transport in urban situations for the foreseeable future. Two major obstacles exist to this development. The first is access to a highway infrastructure where the bus can move freely and operate at a high level of cost and fuel efficiency. The second is whether bus operations can earn sufficient revenue to be able to invest in vehicles, information systems and other passenger amenities which are attractive to those people who at present choose to use the car. The difficulty in achieving this condition of profitability is partly bound up with the conditions of entry into the market for supplying bus services. In conditions of free competitive entry into the market, it is likely that short-run competitive pressures will make it unattractive to invest in the best designed buses or infrastructure. This does not mean that competition cannot be applied to the supply of bus services (Bradshaw, 1993). Competition for franchises, the terms of which

Table 4.3 Pilot Red Route scheme: some effects on buses

Introduced January, 1991
2.9 km of bus lane increased to 5.02 km

Decreased journey times
Southbound (inwards) – 30 min to 27.5 min
Northbound (outwards) – 37 min to 28.5 min*
             (*10 min saving in evening peak)

Increased passengers
Route 43 – 3% additional by autumn, 1991
        9% additional by spring, 1992
        (against drop of 2.6% in London as a whole)

Tighter schedules
Because of faster running times and lower allowances for variability, the
schedule of Route 43 northbound in the evening peak has been reduced from
66 min to 50 min.

New Express Service 43X introduced on route

---

can specify the highest quality features, probably offer the benefits of
competitive supply without the disbenefits of a competitive free for all.
Alternatively high quality thresholds before entry is allowed to the market
would encourage investment.

REFERENCES

Bradshaw, W.P. (1993) The Limitations of Competition in Developing the Market
for Bus Services, ALBUM Conference, Douglas, Isle of Man, May.
Turner, D. (1993) *How London's Red Routes Get Buses Moving*, ALBUM
Conference.

5

Surface access to airports

J. Meredith

"Any consideration of passenger transport after AD 2000 will have to take particular account of the major increases in passengers expected in the coming decades. The air transport industry plays a major role in world economic activity and is one of the fastest growing sectors of the world's economy. In 1989 the industry's impact on gross world output amounted to at least US$700 billion and its impact on the labour market was estimated at more than 21 million jobs. By 2010 the economic impact is expected to exceed US$1500 billion and over 30 million jobs.

5.1 GROWTH

Current studies show that the demand for air transport, which averaged 6% p.a. during the 1980s, has only been slightly affected by the Gulf War and economic recession. Growth forecasts from both aircraft manufacturers and the International Air Transport Association (IATA) still show growth rates of over 5% per annum up to the year 2005, by that date the number of passengers travelling by air is expected to have doubled.

As an indication of the forecast massive rise in the number of passengers travelling, a recent IATA study estimated that traffic in Europe would rise from 394 million passengers in 1990 to almost 1010 million by the year 2010.

5.2 THE COST OF CONGESTION

Unfortunately, we have already become very well aware of the consequences of major passenger traffic growth in air transport. The growth in the aviation infrastructure needed to support this increase has been woefully inadequate, and the cost of the resulting congestion has extracted a heavy

Passenger Transport after 2000 AD. Edited by G.B.R. Feilden, A.H. Wickens and I.R. Yates. Published in 1994 by E & FN Spon, London. ISBN 0 419 19470 3.

price from the economies of the USA and Europe. It was estimated in 1990 that congestion and delays were costing the airlines almost US$5 billion p.a. in USA and a similar sum in Europe. These costs took no account of the additional commercial losses and increased fares. Alarming signs are appearing that a similer problem will occur in the Asia/Pacific region if drastic action is not taken urgently and, on present estimates, over 50% of the major airports in the region will be capacity constrained by 1995.

5.3 THE TOTAL JOURNEY

Aviation infrastructure can be divided into three main areas: airspace capacity; airports; and surface access to the airports. A great deal of work is now underway to improve airspace capacity and to build or expand airports, but until recently the provision of surface access capacity has received relatively less emphasis and attention.

It is important to remember that for the passenger the journey does not begin or end at the airport. At both ends of the journey a passenger will have to go through an often lengthy and arduous process involving travel between the airport and the points of origin and destination of his/her journey. If the passenger's journey is to be rapid, efficient and comfortable then it is essential that the links to and from the airports are improved so that they can match the increased capacities planned for airspace and airports.

In some areas, growth has already been constrained by a failure to ensure adequate surface access. Whilst some airports have been linked to city centres and the surrounding regions by efficient rail and road facilities, there are still many locations where these links require major improvements. In Europe, an Association of European Airlines' Study in 1992 showed that out of 69 airports handling more than 2 million passengers per year, 35 have no existing or planned rail links. Even in those locations where good links already exist, they must continue to be improved as the airport infrastructure itself is upgraded. Failure to make these improvements will mean that the congestion in the skies, on the runways, or in the terminals will simply be transferred from these bottlenecks to new ones on the roads and rail lines serving the airports.

5.4 THE AIR TRANSPORT ACTION GROUP

Resolving infrastructure problems between airports and their surrounding areas has been a major aim of the Air Transport Action Group (ATAG), a coalition of organizations that has joined forces to press for urgently needed improvements in aviation infrastructure capacity throughout the world. Its members include airlines, aircraft manufacturers, airport operators, chambers of commerce, consumer groups, travel agents and tour operators, trade unions, tourism associations, investment banks and car hire companies. In co-operation with the Airports Council International (ACI) ATAG established a special Task Force to consider ways of overcoming surface access problems, and the guidelines it produced have just been published.

This paper draws on many of the Task Force's recommendations, and I am most grateful for the invaluable advice of rail and road experts, airlines and airport operators, travel and tourism experts, chambers of commerce and construction experts who have contributed to the guidelines developed by the Task Force.

In the time available I want to consider some important areas which must be taken into account in the development of surface access requirements.

5.5 POLICY CO-ORDINATION

Fundamental to all developments in surface access is the need for policy co-ordination. As measures are taken to improve and expand airport facilities, runways and terminals, access links to the airport must be upgraded in parallel with other developments.

It is, therefore, essential that there is close co-operation between airport operators and local, regional and national authorities at every stage of planning, financing, construction, and maintenance. In the past, the piecemeal and unco-ordinated development of surface facilities has often produced very unsatisfactory links at airports. The rail links at Washington National Airport or the present bus link at Paris Charles de Gaulle are good examples.

5.6 ESSENTIAL STUDIES ON PASSENGER TRAFFIC FLOWS

The need for studies may seem self-evident, but is often given inadequate attention. Each airport is unique in its layout and traffic demands, and before any steps are taken to plan improvements, a comprehensive study of existing and forecast traffic flows and traffic management must be undertaken. A road network for example, will need a traffic model to assess the many types of vehicles likely to operate, their routes and their peak hours of usage.

Failure to take full account of likely traffic growth can result in facilities which become congested almost as soon as they become available – the London M25 is a good example of this failure.

5.7 OBJECTIVES

To forecast required improvements, all parties must have a clear idea of their objectives. Road planning, for example, will be critically affected by the forecast requirements for other forms of transportation. Critical decisions may need to be made on the proportion of public rather than private passenger travel, and the particular types of transport needed in relation to the expected passenger demand. Heathrow Airport, for example, has decided to plan for an increase in the use of public transport from the present figure of 35% to 45%. A main element of this strategy is, of course, the Heathrow Express – the high speed rail link from Paddington to Heathrow – which can be expected to draw passengers from cars and taxis. The Narita express in Tokyo is an excellent example where this type of development has drawn passengers from private to public transport, although it is also a sad example of the long delays which occur before urgently needed links are brought into operation.

With major investments at stake it is essential that all those involved work towards the same overall objectives, and a common understanding of the required transport mix.

5.8 ENVIRONMENTAL FACTORS

In planning surface access, full account must also be taken of environmental factors. Increasing environmental concern has been a major cause of delays in providing adequate aviation capacity. The last major airport completed in Europe, Munich 2, took over 30 years from original conception to completion, mainly due to environmental objections. Whilst the most publicized concerns have been aircraft noise and emissions, it has also been evident in recent years that major environmental pollution can be caused by failure to provide suitable public transport access to airports. Provision of mass travel access by train, for example, can reduce the pollution caused by private road vehicles. Equally, as road access will always be necessary, it is important that it is designed in such a way as to reduce the impact of noise and emissions which become particularly evident if inadequate roads lead to congestion and traffic jams.

In future evaluations of airport expansion, the environmental impact of the surface links may well be regarded as equally important as the airport itself. IATA and the UK Airfields Environment Federation are developing a model to evaluate the balance between increased capacity requirements and environmental problems. This model is now being assessed for feasibility by the European Commission. I believe the surface access parts of the balance will become increasingly important.

5.9 FINANCIAL INVESTMENTS

It is quite clear that the forecast growth of air transport, and the important economic benefits this brings will be in serious jeopardy if adequate aviation infrastructure is not provided for the tremendous increase in passengers.

However, in the many discussions on the need to finance improvements to airspace and airports, relatively little attention in given to ways of funding the integration of various transport modes at key transport hubs. Far too often, high speed rail links are thought of as a competitive form of transport whereas in many cases there are major benefits in linking the high speed train with airports. High speed trains can often be comple-mentary to long-distance air travel, and in at least two airports in Europe, Paris Charles de Gaulle and Amsterdam, provision is now being made for TGV links.

Whilst substantial plans are being developed for improving airspace by the introduction of the satellite-based Future Air Navigation System (FANS), and there are numerous plans for the development of increased capacity at airports, the integration of surface access investments is often overlooked. A startling example of the failure to recognize the need for investment in multi-modal links is the European Commissions' December 1992 plan to provide financial support for projects that promote the integration of transport modes. Air transport is totally overlooked in this proposal in spite of its massive importance to the economies of Europe and in spite of the fact that one of the main objectives of the Community is to build up trans-Europe transport networks to secure effective mobility. Such a goal can only be secured if all forms of transport are fully integrated. The Association of European Airlines, is now pressing for European Community funds to be made available to permit the integration of air transport with other modes of surface access.

Investment decisions on the provision of surface access cannot be considered in isolation. Apart from the estimated effects of noise, road con-gestion, pollution and accidents, detailed cost benefit analyses need to be undertaken to show whether surface access links can be a worthwhile invest-ment for the community as a whole. Long-term potential for traffic growth is particularly important since investments that appear doubtful in the short or medium term can often produce major benefits when long-term pas-senger growth forecasts are considered. As an example here in the United Kingdom, London's pre-eminence as an important world centre has always depended on its worldwide transport links.

5.10 PLANNING SURFACE ACCESS DEVELOPMENTS

I would now like to consider in rather more detail some of the key factors that will need to be taken into account when planning surface access developments.

5.10.1 Rail access

As already discussed, environmental concerns are becoming increasingly critical at many airports and the role of public transport is becoming more important. Consideration has to be given, therefore, to the best way of persuading many users of private transport to switch to public transport. In many airports this has been achieved by introducing rail links into the heart of the airport. Switzerland is an outstanding example of linking rail travel with its major airports. Rail travel is generally considered as relatively fast and reliable and it is unaffected by road construction and traffic accidents. Equally the price of rail travel is usually low when compared to taxi fares and long-term parking charges.

However, if rail travel is to carry a significant amount of airport users then it must meet some critically important criteria.

- There must be frequent services to and from city centres and other key hubs of activity.
- Fares must be competitive.
- There must be quick and easy access to the air terminals from the airport rail station.
- There must be dedicated services between the airports and city centre stations.
- Baggage transfer services must be available either from security controlled city centre check-in or by provision for easy transfer of baggage between trains and airport check in facilities.
- Ticketing agreements between airlines and rail operators should provide for a combination of rail and air tickets to ensure through-ticketing to ease the transfer between air and rail.
- Wherever possible, rail links should include national and international services and not just services to the city centre.

5.10.2 Road access

In spite of the increasing development of public transport links, particularly by rail, every airport requires a well planned network of access roads. These links have often proved totally inadequate in the past and future planning needs to take account not only of expected passenger volume but also the large number of other visitors to the airport. As airports encourage shopping centres to cover increasing costs, airport visitors are growing because of the availability of seven-day-a-week shopping with long opening hours.

Road access must be linked into the national road network in addition to direct access to secondary roads for the local population, and these links must be clearly sign-posted.

5.10.3 Water access

As environmental pressures and shortage of land limit the availability of suitable space for new airports, there has been an increasing tendency for airports to be built offshore. The new Kensai airport for Osaka and Chep Lap Kok in Hong Kong are two examples of this trend and further proposals for offshore airports are being considered in Japan.

In these circumstances, water transport can provide an alternative means of access and can reduce congestion on access roads which have to rely on expensive bridges and tunnels. However, it is essential that water services remain competitive with other means of access both in time and cost, and they must provide a frequent and regular schedule. Like rail transport, water shuttle terminals need to be within short walking distance of airline terminals with adequate facilities for moving baggage.

One unique consideration that can provide problems is water transport's vulnerability to bad weather. If rough weather is a potential danger, a reliable alternative is essential.

Even when the close proximity of water does not provide an adequate alternative for passengers and other users, it can prove extremely useful in transporting fuel, freight, construction materials, and supplies to and from the airport.

5.10.4 Other forms of transport

There are sometimes relatively simple forms of access to airports that need to be taken into account. As an example, in recent years, congestion, environmental pressures and costs have led to a substantial increase in the use of bicycles both within and to and from airports. Heathrow Airport is one of several airports which are looking at the provision of cycle roads in and around the airport. This is particularly useful for staff working at the airport, although Heathrow has also noticed a surprising number of cyclists arriving as passengers. Back-packers are increasingly using air travel!

5.11 EASE OF INTERCHANGE

Surface access to and from airports works most effectively when the interchange between the surface and air parts of the journey is made as easy as possible. Assuming planning provides close proximity for each transport mode, the most important factors in smoothing the interchange are adequate information displays and through-ticketing.

With passengers of many nationalities and an increasing number of first-time travellers, it is essential that signs and information displays are easy to see and understand. International standards or pictographs will help tremendously, but in view of the increasing number of visually and hearing-impaired travellers, announcements and signs must complement each other to ensure maximum understanding. Signs need to be common to airports, stations, taxi ranks and bus terminals.

Through-ticketing is also extremely important in making the transfer between different modes of transport easier. Advantages include reduced connection times, the comfort and security of holding a through-ticket, a single payment at the beginning of the journey, potential savings from special tariffs and promotions and the avoidance of language difficulties when transferring at a foreign airport.

5.12 FREIGHT TRANSPORT

Whilst this conference is focusing on passenger transport, it is important to remember that the economics of passenger transport is greatly helped by the contribution of freight revenue to flight economics. It is, therefore, essential that access to freight facilities receives attention in any plan for airport access.

Freight facilities can often be located at off-airport sites, particularly when airport space is limited. Surface access must, therefore, be designed to cater for these off-airport locations. Whenever possible, access to airport freight facilities needs to be kept separate from roads for passengers, particularly in the approach to the airport. Heavy freight loads can rapidly cause congestion at busy periods if they are mixed with passenger traffic. As environmental objections to heavy road transport vehicles grow, it will also be important for rail access to be made available for freight facilities.

5.13 CONCLUSION

In the time available it has only been possible to consider the general requirements for surface access. However, it is clear that in a world where passenger traffic will grow dramatically, critical attention will have to be paid to making the complete passenger journey as easy as possible. Some of the criteria I have described may sound obvious, but it is surprising how often they are ignored.

As passenger traffic grows dramatically in the next century, politicians and planners will have to recognize the need for multi-modal transport links to make the airport passenger's journey comfortable, efficient and fast. Considerable investment and thought will be required to ensure that all parts of the passenger journey are catered for and that the links provided are as seamless as possible.

It will be particularly important to ensure that the surface links to airports do not fall behind the development of airspace and airport facilities. It will be no good solving air traffic or airport congestion if, in the next century, we then move the problem to the beginning and the end of the passenger journey. Surface access must not become one of the worst parts of an air traveller's journey after AD 2000.

BIBLIOGRAPHY

ATAG (1991) *The Economic Benefits of Air Transport*, Air Transport Action Group.

ATAG (1992) *European Traffic Forecasts 1991–2010*, Air Transport Action Group.

RAS (1992) *Access To and Within Airports*, Heathrow Airport Ltd., Royal Aeronautical Society, October.

RAS (1992b) *Access to Airports by Road and Rail – The Role of Airports in an Integrated Transport System*, German Airports Association, ADV, Royal Aeronautical Society.

ATAG (1992) *Air Transport and the Environent*, Air Transport Action Group.

IATA (1989) *Airport Terminals Reference Manual* (7th edn), International Air Transport Association.

ICAO (1990) *Annex 9 (Facilitation) to the Convention on International Civil Aviation* (9th edn), International Civil Aviation Organization, July.

ADV *Flughafeninerne Verkehrsmittel (Internal Airport Transportation)* (Report of an ADV Study Group), Association of German Airports (ADV) (available in German and English).

IATA (1990) *Airport Automation – The Way Ahead*, Airports Council International and International Air Transport Association.

IATA (1990) *Airport Capacity/Demand Management*, Airports Council International and International Air Transport Association.

IAT (1991) *Rail/Air Complementarity in Europe: The Impact of High-Speed Train Services*, Institute of Air Transport, December.

AEA (1990) *Impact of High-Speed Trains on Air Transport in Europe*, Association of European Airlines.

IATA (1981) *Incapacitated Passengers Handling Guide*, International Air Transport Association (available in English and French).

ACI (1991) *Airports and the Disabled*, Airports Council International.

ICAO (1984) *International Signs to Provide Guidance to Persons at Airports* International Civil Aviation Organization, Document 9430.

ADV (1974) *Pictographs for Orientation at Airports*, Association of German Airports (ADV).

ATA (1985) *Guidelines for Airport Signing and Graphics*, Air Transport Association.

FTA (1983) *Designing for Deliveries*, Freight Transport Association, Tunbridge Wells.

CCC/IATA (1988) *Joint Customs/Airlines Electronic Interchange Manual*, Customs Cooperation Council and IATA, June.

CCC/IATA (1986) *Interfaces Between the Automated Systems of Customs and Carriers (Air Mode)*, Customs Cooperation Council and IATA, September.

IATA (1988) *Community Cargo Information Interchange Systems*, Airports Council International and International Air Transport Association.

ACI (1988) *The Air Cargo Ground Handling Process – Information and Logistics Flows*, Airports Council International.

IATA (1992) *Aviation Security, Joint Position Papers*, Airports Council International and International Air Transport Association.

ACI (1992) *ACI Africa Regional Annual Conference* (compilation of presentations delivered at Libreville conference 1992), Airports Council International.

ADV (1993) *Surface Access to Airports* (Final report of an ADV Task Force), Association of German Airports (ADV) (German only).

ADV *Anlage and Bemessung von Parkplätzen und Vorfahrten an Flughäfen* (Final Report of the ADV Parking Facilities Committee) Association of German Airports (ADV) (German only).

IVTB (1984) *Kosten-Nutzen-Analyse der SSB Flughafenlinie Zürich HB* – Zürich Flughafen, Institut für Verkehrsplanung und Transporttechnik Bericht Nr. 84/3, 1984

AG (1987) *Raccordement ferroviaire Genève Aéreport (Geneva Airport Rail Link)*, Aéreport de Genève.

Mckinsey & Co, (1989) *Kiezen voor Openbaar Vervoer: 'OV maal Twee'* SAMOVE, August (Dutch only).

DMT (1991) *Handboek woon-Werkverkeer* (a Dutch Ministry of Transport report), Commissie Ontwikkeling Bedrijven vab de sociaal Economische Raad, April 1991 (Dutch only).

Part Two

Inter-urban Transport Systems

6

The European high speed network

R. *Kemp*, BSc, CEng, FIEE, FIMechE

6.1 INTRODUCTION

Since Victorian times there have been international train services in Europe. The golden age of these services was between the two World Wars and many of the names of international rail services have passed into legend – *The Orient Express* conjures up images of style and intrigue rather than a mere means of transport.

For most of the post-war period the structure of international rail services has been based on the traditional pattern. Table 20 of the *Thomas Cook European Timetable* still shows the *Austria Nachtexpress* leaving London Victoria at 11.40 in the morning and arriving in Vienna at 10.58 the following morning. Table 28 shows the *Sud Express* leaving Paris Austerlitz at 09.30 and arriving in Lisbon at 10.49 the following day.

While these long-distance international services provide useful domestic connections between intermediate stations and are popular with students during vacations, they are peripheral to the transport needs of most modern Europeans. With the exception of short routes between crowded cities (e.g. Paris–Brussels) the majority of international traffic is shared between the airlines and the motorways.

In December 1990 the European Community published a report (EC, 1990) setting out a plan for a truly international high speed rail network covering all member states (and certain neighbours, such as Switzerland). It recognized that, unlike air travel where it is possible to consider international routes without taking much account of domestic services, a European rail network has to be based on the domestic railway infrastructures of member countries. The report and subsequent documents (EC, 1992), therefore, concentrate on creating links between national railways, rather than on superimposing an international network (Figure 6.1).

Passenger Transport after 2000 AD. Edited by G.B.R. Feilden, A.H. Wickens and I.R. Yates. Published in 1994 by E & FN Spon, London. ISBN 0 419 19470 3.

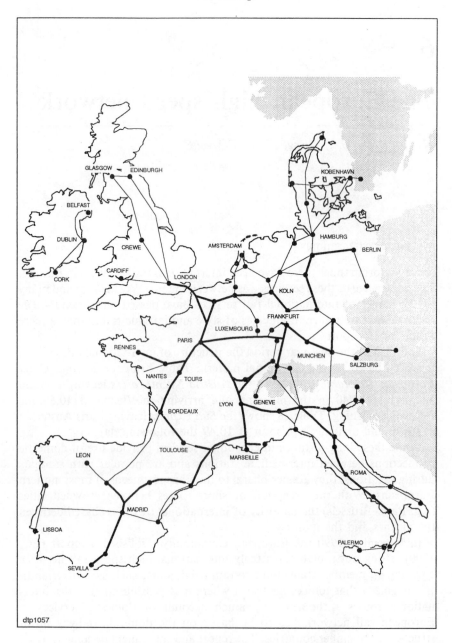

Figure 6.1 European high speed rail network.

6.2 THE DEVELOPMENT OF NATIONAL HIGH SPEED RAIL NETWORKS

6.2.1 France

On the 18 May, 1990 a TGV raised the world rail speed record to 515 km h^{-1} during a high speed test run. The train had been specially modified to run at this speed but every day TGVs operate at speeds of up to 300 km h^{-1} on the major French routes (Kemp, 1991).

In the late 1960s, before the first 'oil crisis', several railways were experimenting with gas turbine propulsion systems. British Rail (BR) produced a prototype train powered by a multiplicity of small gas turbines conceived for road vehicle use, while the French Railways (SNCF) concentrated on applying helicopter engines to rail traction. TGV 001 was built with a pair of Turbomeca Turmo X turbines in each power car. The 4-car train achieved the world record of 318 km h^{-1} in December 1972.

The 1973 oil crisis put an end to gas-turbine traction and the major European networks put their efforts into the construction of new electrified routes.

The work on the gas-turbine TGV-001 had demonstrated that, from the point of view of the mechanical equipment, operation at a service speed of 250 km h^{-1} is feasible and, as long ago as 1955, SNCF had carried out test runs on locomotives that showed it was possible to collect current from an overhead line at speeds in excess of 300 km h^{-1}.

In March 1974 the decision was taken to construct a new electrified line from Paris to Lyon. The technology used on the TGV Paris–Sud Est (TGV–PSE) was essentially conservative. The British approach at the time was to adopt high-technology solutions to achieve shorter journey times over routes that had been designed a century earlier for steam trains; the French approach was to start with a new straight alignment and to construct a high standard line on which all traffic, other than TGVs, was prohibited.

The major area of fundamentally new development on TGV-PSE was the articulated suspension between passenger vehicles. A traditional railway coach has two bogies each with two axles. On a rake of TGV coaches each bogie (with the exception of those at the ends) supports two coaches. This reduces the weight, aerodynamic drag and noise and permits greater isolation of bogie movements to improve passenger comfort.

The new TGV lines are all electrified at 25 kV 50 Hz, the same voltage as BR's electrified lines north of the Thames. In the 1930s the standard electrification voltage on SNCF was 1500 Vdc, the same voltage as on the (now closed) Manchester–Sheffield electrification. Thousands of kilometres of dc catenary exist in France and therefore the TGVs have been designed to also accept this voltage. The Paris terminus of the PSE services is the Gare de Lyon which is shared between the TGVs and conventional trains;

Figure 6.2 The TGV Atlantique (TVG-A).

this is electrified at 1500 V and the TGVs run at reduced performance for the first 20 km until they reach the new line.

6.2.2 The TGV Atlantique

The Paris–Lyon service has been a commercial success; the TGV–PSE fleet of 109 trains serves 30 towns and cities and carries 20 million passengers per year. In February 1985 work started on the second major TGV project, the TGV Atlantique (TGV-A) which serves the Brittany and the Atlantic Coast (Figure 6.2). New high speed lines have been constructed from Paris to Le Mans and Tours; thereafter the trains run on upgraded and/or newly electrified tracks. The maximum speed on the new line is 300 km h^{-1} and, on upgraded track the limit is 220 km h^{-1}.

For the new trains a different type of drive system was introduced (Lacôte, 1986). The Paris–Sud Est (PSE) trains that use dc motors need a motored bogie under the end of the passenger rake. For the TGV-A, synchronous motors were adopted (Cossie, Ragideau and Tisserand, 1986). These have allowed 1100 kW motors, weighing only 1400 kg, to be fitted in the space previously occupied by the 535 kW dc motors. The TGV-A thus has a power of 8.8 MW at the rail with all the equipment contained in the two power cars.

TGV-A went into passenger service in October 1989 and the fleet was completed early in 1992. Following that, TGVs are being built to provide a network service between the provinces of France. This fleet, called TGV-R (*reseau* = network), was ordered in 1989 and starts passenger service in 1993. The 80 trainsets, based on TGV-A but with two fewer trailers, will increase to 300 the number of TGV sets in service in France.

6.2.3 A new generation TGV

The TGV Atlantique and its derivatives will continue in production until the mid-1990s but will then, in international terms, be looking rather dated. At a public signing ceremony in 1990 the Ministers for Transport, Industry and Technology launched the 500 MF development programme for TGV Nouvelle Generation (TGV-NG) (Ministère de l'Equipement, 1990).

To meet the objectives of speed and energy consumption, the train is being designed with a new lightweight extruded aluminium bodyshell, braking systems using novel materials, improved suspensions (with the possibility of tilting to compensate for faster curving on conventional tracks) and a new asynchronous drive system that fully exploits the ratings of modern power semiconductors. The trains will be able to operate at $350 \, \text{km h}^{-1}$ on appropriate tracks.

Independently of the TGV-NG programme SNCF placed orders in 1991 for 100 double deck TGVs (TGV-2N). These will be used to increase the passenger capacity on routes that are saturated (Lacôte and Gléon, 1991). Each 8-car trainset will have a capacity of 545 passengers, of whom 197 (36%) will be first class, compared with 485 seats on the 10-car TGV-A. The combination of double deck trains and the new TVM430 signalling system which permits a 3-minute headway, will boost the track capacity to 22 000 passengers/hour/direction (equivalent to a 6-lane motorway or a classic metro line).

6.2.4 Germany

France is a rural country with a few large conurbations – the Paris region, Bordeaux, Marseilles, the Lille region, Lyon, Strasbourg. Germany, on the other hand, with only 65% of the area of France and 50% more people, is more heavily industrialized and there is no central conurbation as in France. Instead, there are several large conurbations – Köln, Dusseldorf, Dortmund, Frankfurt, Nürnberg, Berlin, Stuttgart, München, Hannover. The railway system (Figure 6.3) reflects this geography and is more akin to a network than to a system of radial routes from a hub.

The majority of Deutsche Bundesbahn (DB) InterCity services are operated by locomotive-hauled conventional coaches which run at speeds up to $200 \, \text{km h}^{-1}$. However, in June 1991 DB launched the IC-Express which was designed to run at speeds up to $280 \, \text{km h}^{-1}$ on the Neubaustrecken (new lines) between Hannover and Würzburg and

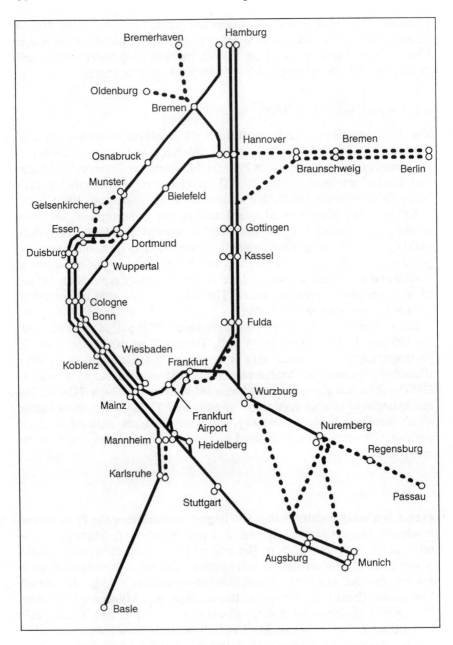

Figure 6.3 Deutsche Bundesbahn high speed rail network.

Mannheim and Stuttgart (IRJ, 1990). The ICE trains are composed of 15 vehicles, a power car at either end of 13 trailer cars, each 26.4 m long. This gives an overall train length of 385 m with 717 seats. The power system uses Gate Turn-off (GTO) thyristors powering squirrel cage asynchronous induction motors.

The ICE train was designed and constructed by the German High Speed Train Consortium; the design and manufacturing plants included: AEG, ABB, Duewag, Krauss Maffei, Krupp, LHB, MBB, Siemens, Thyssen Henschel and Thyssen Waggon Union.

Future development in Germany is based round a second-generation ICE which will be designed for 350 km h^{-1} and which is expected to run in 1995. The 1985 federal transport plan envisaged investment in high speed lines of DM34bn by the year 2000 (Kurz, 1991). DB is planning to expand the ICE fleet from the original 60 to 150 trainsets which will include dual voltage trains capable of running not only on the DB 15 kV 16.7 Hz network but also on 25 kV 50 Hz lines in France or Hungary or 1500 Vdc lines in the Netherlands.

6.2.5 Italy

In the same way that the different geography of France and Germany dictated different approaches to railway development so the 'linear' geography of Italy and the mountainous terrain has encouraged Italian railway development in a different direction. A high speed line (*direttissima*) has been constructed between Rome and Florence and a new design of tilting train (ETR450) has been developed to decrease journey times on the twisting track that is a feature of much of the Italian mountain backbone (Fiat, undated).

Unlike the TGV and the ICE, the ETR450 does not have a power car at each end and trailer coaches between them. The train was designed as a multiple unit with 8 powered vehicles. Each of the vehicles has two powered axles and two unpowered axles. The overall length of the 8-car train is 183 m and it has a seating capacity of 344.

Following the service introduction of the ETR450 a new design of train was launched, the ETR500. Despite a similar name this train is completely different to its predecessor. In concept the train is more akin to the German ICE; it has a power car at each end and twelve 26 m long trailers between them. The total power rating is 8.5 MW, slightly less than the ICE or TGV-A, and uses asynchronous motors with GTO inverters. Like other national high speed projects the trains are built by a consortium; this consists of Breda Costruzioni Ferroviarie, Fiat Ferroviaria, Ansaldo Transporti and ABB Technomasio.

6.3 CHANNEL TUNNEL HIGH SPEED TRAINS

The first high speed trains constructed specifically for international services are those for the Channel Tunnel. Thirty-eight high speed trains are being constructed for services between the UK and mainland Europe. Thirty-one of these will provide the '3-Capitals' services between London and Paris or Brussels. The remaining seven will provide services between major cities north of London and Paris or Brussels (Abrey, 1992; Kemp, 1992).

In 1988 the three railways, BR, SNCF and SNCB (The Belgian State Railways), formed an International Project Group (IPG) to co-ordinate the procurement of trains for the Tunnel. It became clear that, for political reasons, contractors for the trains would have to involve the industries of all three countries. A group was formed in 1987 under the name TMSTG (Trans-Manche Super Train Group) to bid for the trains; this was a joint venture between three national consortia – Belgian, British and French.

The division of work within the joint venture was established to ensure an equitable share both of the design work and of the manufacture. The mechanical design responsibility was given to the French consortium and the electrical design responsibility to the British consortium. A target split of 44:44:12% of contract value between the UK, France and Belgium was agreed.

Since the group was formed there have been many changes in the structure of the European railway industry and of the joint venture and many of the previously independent companies have merged. The 17 main sites involved in the work are now:

- Belgium: Bruges, Charleroi and Manage;
- Britain: Birmingham, Loughborough, Preston, Manchester and Stafford;
- France: Belfort, Le Creusot, Paris, Reichshoffen, La Rochelle, St Ouen, Tarbes, Tours and Villeurbanne.

To meet the Tunnel safety requirements there has been a change in philosophy in many of the train systems. On a traditional train, safety systems are designed to stop the train in the event of any alarms. Although it is not hazardous to stop a train in the Tunnel, the logistics of evacuating passengers, the possibility of panic and the difficulty of sending maintenance staff or emergency services have made the rule 'keep going if it is safe to do so'. To meet this rule control systems and power equipment have been duplicated and special precautions have been adopted to ensure, as far as possible, that a single failure cannot stop the train. In addition the traction equipment has been designed to allow the train to exit from the Tunnel with only two out of six power bogies operating: that is, no traction at one end and one of three 'motor blocs' at the other end disabled.

Mechanically the TMST is based on the French TGV Atlantique (Figure 6.4). However, many changes have been incorporated to make it

Figure 6.4 The Trans-Manche Super Train (TMST).

suitable for running through the Tunnel to London; the most obvious is that, because the British loading gauge is smaller than in mainland Europe, the train has had to be redesigned to reduce the width. This has affected not only the body but also the bogies which have been modified to reduce the overhang of the airsprings and dampers.

Platforms in France are about 500 mm above the rail level and all main line trains have steps – only on the metro or RER are platforms the same height as the carriage floor. TMST has to be designed for boarding either from an SNCF platform or from a traditional 915 mm high British Rail platform. In the Tunnel itself the walkway for emergency evacuation will be further from the track than a normal platform and the train has to cater for this eventuality. With the changed step design and the changed bodyside profile the doors for the TMST are completely new, although based on previous designs.

The power equipment has been completely redesigned in comparison with the previous generation of TGVs. Unlike the French TGVs which were designed to run on 1500 Vdc and 25 kV 50 Hz, TMST has to cope with three different supply voltages – 25 kV in France, 3000 Vdc in Belgium and 750 Vdc on the Network South East lines in the UK. The 750 V supply is a radically new feature for TGVs as it requires pick-up shoes that collect current from a third rail and not a pantograph operating from an overhead line. These collector shoes have to be retracted on other lines, to prevent fouling the gauge, and earthed for safety reasons. Like the TGV Atlantique, the TMST uses 3-phase motors. Unlike the TGV-A they are asynchronous motors fed by GTO inverters rather than synchronous motors fed from thyristor convertors.

The TMST driving cab has to be compatible with 4 different railway systems and is thus one of the most sophisticated in the world. It features a computer console, pre-selection 'cruise' speed control, and in addition, an array of five different cab signalling systems and two different radios. The cab equipment, including the programmable logic controllers driving the on-desk computer screen used for fault finding and predeparture tests, fills 4 floor-to-ceiling 19″ electronic racks.

6.4 PARIS–BRUSSELS–KÖLN–AMSTERDAM (PBKA) TRAINS

In 1992 the four railways of France, Belgium, Germany and the Netherlands placed an order with an international consortium for 27 trainsets with options for an additional 10 sets. These are based on the French TGV and each will consist of two power cars and 8 trailer cars. The power cars use synchronous transmission systems similar to that used on TGV-A and TGV-R but modified to accept power at four voltages 25 kV 50 Hz, 15 kV 16.7 Hz, 1.5 kV and 3 kVdc.

The 200 m long trains, weighing 416 t, will each have 380 seats and, when running over the new line from Paris to the Belgian border, will offer journey times of 1 h 20 min to Brussels, 2 h 50 min to Amsterdam and 3 h 5 min to Köln.

6.5 NEW INTERNATIONAL SERVICES

The TMST and the PBKA projects described earlier were the first international high speed rail projects. How many more projects will be started will depend on profitability of high speed lines, the commercial demand and political pressures. These factors are discussed in the following paragraphs.

6.6 ARE HIGH SPEED RAILWAYS PROFITABLE?

Whether or not a transport system is 'profitable' depends on how you do the sums. The UK Department of Transport has been able to justify new motorways taking account of the value of time saved by the potential users but such accounting devices are not generally allowed when considering rail projects. An investment, such as main-line railway electrification, in which all the costs are incurred in the first ten years and all the profits accrue in the following 30 years is very sensitive to interest rates.

The profitability of a scheme is also heavily influenced by the compensation terms imposed on the constructor: land valuation policies, noise abatement compensation, etc. Traditional accounting completely breaks down if strategic issues are brought into the picture – non-dependence on imported oil, reduction in air pollution, improvement in balance of payments due to technology export, etc.

The only published paper that analyses the results of building and exploiting a high speed line (as opposed to projections about what might happen) describes the TGV-PSE (Berlioz and Leboeuf, 1986). Bearing in mind the above difficulties it is possible to take a simplified look at this project. (units are millions of French Francs at 1985 prices – 10 F = £1).

The investment was as follows:

Construction cost of new line[1]	8300 MF
Fleet of 109 trainsets	7100 MF
Additional electrification	800 MF
Value of investment in non-TGV trains + infrastructure[2]	−6500 MF
TOTAL	9700 MF

In 1985 the TGV-PSE operation showed the following balance:

Revenue	3500 MF
Operating costs	−1200 MF
Interest costs & repayments	−1600 MF
Net contribution of TGV	700 MF

Depending on the assumptions made about the necessity for track capacity improvements had there been no TGV, the internal rate of return on infrastructure (calculated in constant francs over 20 years) is between 12% and 15%.

6.7 THE COMMERCIAL DEMAND FOR HIGH SPEED

When considering the case for a new high speed line the potential demand, and hence revenue, is a key consideration. The most important statistic is the number of full fare (i.e. business) passengers that could be attracted to the service.

In Victorian times the railways had a monopoly in high speed inter-urban transport. This is not now the case and most business travellers are faced

[1] The construction cost was divided roughly equally between the infrastructure (route preparation, earthworks, civil engineering) and the railway fixed systems (track, signalling, power supply). Land purchase and compensation payments amounted to 5% of the total construction cost.

[2] The figure of 6500 MF is the sum that would have had to have been spent on the replacement of 660 traditional passenger coaches and 50 locomotives had the TGV not been built, plus various investments in fixed systems that would have otherwise been required.

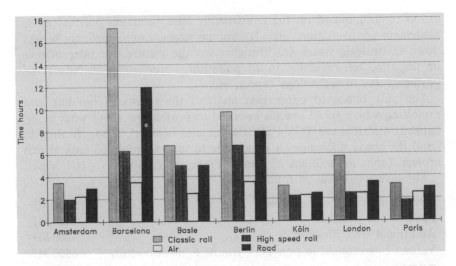

Figure 6.5 Journey times from Brussels. (Note that present and future rail timings are taken from the EC (1990) document; future timings relate to a notional AD 2010 high speed network. An allowance of 45 minutes to reach the station and the final destination has been allowed for present trains and 30 minutes in the future (this assumes improved urban transport systems). Airline timings are taken from current timetables and an allowance of 90 minutes has been added for travel to and from the airport and for check-in. Road timings assume an average speed of 100 km h^{-1} including stops (this is based on observed motorway speeds rather than legal limits).

with the choice of driving on motorways, flying or taking the train. The key deciding factor is usually journey time.

Most transport undertakings acknowledge a barrier of about 3 hours – below this a passenger can make a return trip and still have a productive day, above this threshold the passenger incurs overnight hotel costs. The chart in Figure 6.5 compares journey times from Brussels.

It can be seen that for short journeys (e.g. Brussels to Paris, London, Amsterdam, Köln) high speed rail is time-competitive with motorways or the airlines and is below the 3-hour threshold. The decision on which mode of transport is taken is thus determined by the convenience of the station/airport to home and destination, price, and other factors. Experience during the introduction of the TGV–PSE showed the dramatic effect (Figure 6.6) of the high speed rail service on the parallel airline services (Berlioz and Leboeuf, 1986).

For longer journeys, for example from Brussels to Barcelona or Berlin, high speed rail is unlikely to be attractive to the business traveller. While it may be possible to justify a high speed network extending from Amsterdam via Brussels, Luxembourg, Strasbourg, Lyon and Montpellier

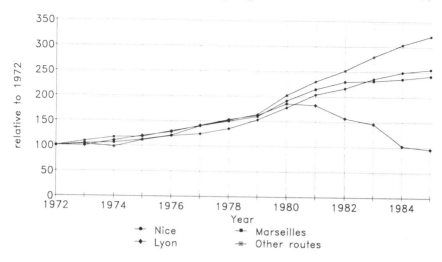

Figure 6.6 Air traffic from Paris.

to Barcelona, the justification would have to be based on the traffic generated on short segments rather than on end-to-end journeys.

6.8 ENVIRONMENTAL IMPACT OF HIGH SPEED TRAINS

In recent years the environmental impact of transport systems has become a major political factor. The three main considerations are:

- visual intrusion;
- noise;
- energy consumption and pollution.

6.8.1 Visual intrusion

Lines constructed in the steam era had to be designed with restricted gradients because of the low power of the locomotives and, in the UK, the steepest mainline gradients are about 1.3%. Even today mixed traffic lines (i.e. for both passenger and freight trains) rarely exceed this figure. However, high speed trains have much higher installed powers (TMST has an installed power of 15 kW per tonne compared with 5 kW per tonne for a conventional passenger train) and thus can cope with steeper gradients. The Paris–Lyon line was constructed with a steepest gradient of 3.5% which greatly reduced both the construction costs and the visual intrusion of the line. The minimum curve radius of a 300 km h^{-1} line is between 4.5 km, proposed by the EC (EC, 1990), and 5.1 km, specified for new German high speed lines (IRJ, 1990). However, the visual intrusion of a 14 m wide

R. Kemp

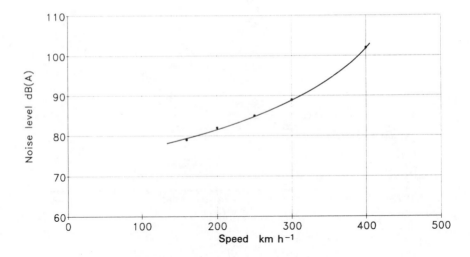

Figure 6.7 Noise of ICE train (at 25 m from track).

two-track railway is very much less than that of a motorway with an equivalent capacity.

6.8.2 Noise

The noise generated by an electric high speed railway can be less than the noise of a traditional mixed traffic diesel-hauled railway. Measurements in Germany (IRJ, 1990) have been made for high speed trains running up to 400 km h^{-1}; these are shown in Figure 6.7. Railway noise is usually measured in open country at 25 m from the track centreline and 2 m above the ground level. Measurements should be treated with caution as the type of track structure and the surface finish of the rail can affect the results by more than ± 10 dB(A) (Moreau, 1991). Civil engineering works and buildings can either amplify or attenuate noise levels.

By comparison, the noise produced by a traditional InterCity electric train at 160 km h^{-1} is around 85 dB(A). A similar noise level is produced by an accelerating motor cycle or a heavy lorry, although the frequency spectra of these three sources are very different. Whether the noise of a high speed line is *subjectively* worse than the noise of a major motorway or a nearby airport depends as much on an individual's associations with different transport modes as on scientifically measurable data.

6.8.3 Energy consumption

Trains have always had a good reputation for energy consumption. A traditional 14 km h^{-1} diesel-hauled train of a locomotive and 8 coaches

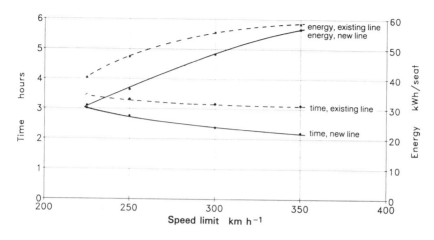

Figure 6.8 Line improvements (London–Edinburgh).

can carry 500 passengers and has a fuel consumption of about 1 mile per gallon. The same passengers travelling 2 per car on a motorway, each car averaging 30 miles per gallon, would use 8 times more fuel. However, the relative benefit deteriorates as the train speed increases and the situation becomes more complicated to analyse if the train uses electricity generated by a mix of gas, coal and nuclear power.

The *North of London* variant of the TMST will run to Edinburgh on the East Coast Main Line. The line is at present signalled for a maximum speed of 225 km h^{-1} but Figure 6.8 extrapolates the journey time for different maximum speeds. Two hypothetical cases are considered: the first maintains the existing track layout but increases the speed limits on straight sections, the second is based on a new high speed line from 20 km outside London to 20 km outside Edinburgh. The graph also shows the energy consumption per passenger for the two cases. It should be noted that the speed–distance profile at 225 km h^{-1} used in this calculation is that used today by the IC225 trains. The higher speed limits on the existing route have been extrapolated by merely changing all limits on straight track. This is not how it would be done in practice and is intended only to show the general trend. Timings are 'flat out' theoretical minima. To convert these to public timetable schedules a margin of around 15 minutes would be added. The 'new high speed line' has been assumed to be the same overall length as the existing line and to have the same gradients; all speed limits have been increased to >400 km h^{-1}.

'Energy' in Figure 6.8 relates to the mechanical energy at the wheel rim. This can be related back to primary fuel (assumed to be oil for ease of comparison). The consumption at 225 km h^{-1} on the existing track can be shown to be roughly 15 kg of oil per seat (the traction energy consumption

Fuel burnt per passenger (lb)

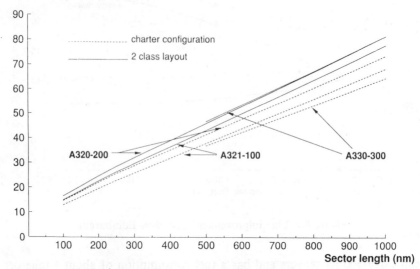

Figure 6.9 Fuel burnt in air transport.

computed for 'flat out' running is 21.4 MWh, 40.4 kWh per seat. This is divided by the efficiency of the train, including passenger auxiliaries (0.8) total transmission losses (0.8) and power station efficiency (0.35). The gross primary energy demand is then converted by the ratio 1 kWh $\equiv 8.3.10^{-5}$ toe (tonne oil equivalent) to give a primary fuel consumption of 15 kg per passenger.) By comparison, the passengers would use about 37 kg of primary fuel if travelling by road, two per car (the assumption being that the average journey is 430 miles at an average consumption of 30 miles per gallon, i.e. 58.6 kg of fuel per car. This is divided by the number of people (2) and 0.8 to account for refinery losses and non-productive mileage.)

Making a comparison with air transport, Figure 6.9 shows that a fully laden A321-100 Airbus would use about 13 kg of aviation fuel per passenger. Referring this back to primary fuel consumption a more realistic 70% average payload gives about 20 kg of primary fuel per passenger. Figures from Airbus Industrie (Figure 6.9) show a fuel burn of 28 lb per passenger for an A321-100 in two-class configuration for a sector length of 300 nm (555 km). Total fuel consumption has been assumed to reduce by 10% if the passenger load is reduced to 70%. This figure is then divided by 0.8 to account for refinery and transport losses and unproductive mileage to relate it to primary energy consumption. It should be noted that, if high density single class seating is used (as found, for example, on many French domestic services) the fuel consumption per passenger is reduced by about 20%.

It can be seen from the above argument that, for the present speed limits between London and Edinburgh, a high speed trains uses rather less energy per seat than air transport, but increasing the speed limit erodes the difference. Comparing the two sets of curves in Figure 6.8, it can be seen that a high speed train running on a new line (built to SNCF standards for TGV) would require far less braking and accelerating and would thus save energy as well as offering a substantial improvement on journey time. It should be noted that braking distances for a 200 m long train were calculated on the basis of a 10 second detection and reaction time for signalling and train control systems, a decelerated rate of $0.7 \, \text{m s}^{-2}$ and a safety zone of not less than 500 m between the front of one train and the rear of the preceding train under all conditions. (This is an over-simplification but illustrates the principle.) To be able to operate a real service a margin of at least 30 seconds would have to be added to the theoretical minimum figures calculated above.

Thus it can be seen that, over a sector length of London to Edinburgh, a modern plane uses about the same amount of primary energy as a train and a car uses about twice as much primary energy. However, if these comparisons were made in France where most electricity is generated by nuclear or hydro-power and there are negligible domestic oil reserves, the conclusions could be very different.

6.9 IS THERE A LIMIT TO 'HIGH SPEED'?

The above section has shown that rail transport loses its energy consumption benefits in comparison with air transport between 300 and $400 \, \text{km h}^{-1}$; the actual value depends on which route is considered and on the efficiency and aerodynamics of particular trains and planes.

As train speed increases so does the track minimum curve radius, both in the vertical and horizontal planes. A line designed for $500 \, \text{km h}^{-1}$ would have a minimum curve radius of 10 km (compared with less than 1 km on UK motorways). To prevent the feeling of a 'hump back' bridge, a $500 \, \text{km h}^{-1}$ line crossing a motorway would have more than 1 km of approach ramps. Such constraints would make high speed lines designed for $>500 \, \text{km h}^{-1}$ difficult to site in densely populated European countries.

Railways have signalling systems to prevent a train running into the rear of the preceding train. As train speeds increase so does the braking distance and thus trains have to run with greater spacing between them. This reduces the track capacity (i.e. the number of trains per hour), as shown in Figure 6.10.

It can be seen that maximum throughput of trains is at about $100 \, \text{km h}^{-1}$; increasing the line speed to $350 \, \text{km h}^{-1}$ roughly halves the number of trains per hour.

A final consideration is the cost of trains for very high speeds. To a first approximation, aerodynamic drag increases as the square of the speed;

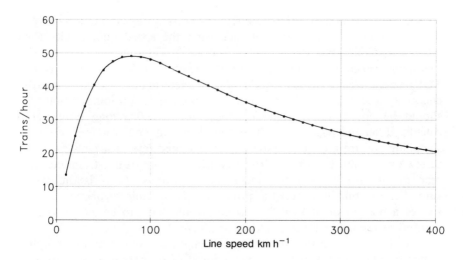

Figure 6.10 Track capacity (trains per hour).

power (equal to speed × drag) increases as the cube of the speed. A train designed for 500 km h^{-1} would thus need 8 times the installed power of one designed for 250 km h^{-1}. In addition the braking systems would have to be capable of absorbing more power and energy, the suspensions and sound absorbents would have to be improved, etc.

The cost of high speed trains varies between about £15 000 per seat for straightforward single voltage trains with a maximum speed of 200–250 km h^{-1} to £30 000 per seat for multivoltage trains capable of operating at 300 km h^{-1}. A train designed for 500 km h^{-1} would probably cost twice as much as one for 300 km h^{-1}. In addition the overhead catenary would have to be designed for higher speeds (higher mechanical tension and more frequent registration), substations would be more frequent and more powerful, the track would have to maintained to a closer tolerance, and so on.

It is always risky to say that technology will not advance beyond a particular barrier. (Twenty years ago the concept of a lap-top computer, as used for preparing this paper, would have been unthinkable to data processing managers.) However, all indications are that the commercial operating speeds of trains will creep up from the present 300 km h^{-1} to around 350 km h^{-1} and are unlikely to reach 400 km h^{-1}. It should be noted that these limits are not imposed by the technology of steel wheel on steel rail and they apply equally to more 'exotic' technologies (e.g. magnetic levitation, jet propulsion, guided roadways, hovertrains); in fact, as steel wheel–steel rail technology is more energy efficient and cheaper than most of the 'exotics', they are likely to be more, and not less, constrained by the factors discussed above.

The recent development of national high speed rail networks in Europe has coincided with the economic boom of the 1980s. The major countries involved (France, Italy and Germany) have all seen major political changes in the 1990s. The realization of the economic cost of German reunification, the decoupling of Italian construction projects from political influence, the election of a non-socialist government in France and the efforts to reduce budget deficits in all three countries may change priorities in railway system development. Capital cost per seat, running and maintenance costs per seat-kilometre and similar parameters are likely to feature more prominently in specifications.

6.10 INTERNATIONAL STANDARDIZATION

It is almost always possible to design a train to meet conflicting requirements. The only question is 'How much does it cost?' The cost is measured not only in the capital price but also in the running costs, the track damage caused by additional weight, the reduced reliability, the increased difficulty of maintenance, etc. On the Channel Tunnel project these costs have probably been underestimated and this may happen on other international projects. An analysis carried out at project inception will generally underestimate the costs of train complexity and will be biased against modifying the infrastructure.

A major source of confusion on international projects is the conflict between the standards of the different countries. This is not a question of technical standards for components (motors, transformers, etc.) which are adequately covered by International Standards, but relates to questions such as the calculation of loading gauge, the methods of testing fire and smoke performance of components, the methods of defining and evaluating reliability, the approach to safety, the provisions that have to be made for disabled people and similar issues.

Safety is a particularly difficult issue. Some administrations have traditionally worked on the basis that a component (such as a track circuit relay) can be 'failsafe' because of its construction or design; the actual wrong-side failure rate is never calculated. Some administrations use quantitative risk analysis that involves putting a price on a human life; to other administrations the possibility of causing a fatal accident is a taboo subject.

Modern trains (including ICE, ETR 500 and TGV-A) use three phase drives. Many older signalling track circuit relays could, at least in theory, be influenced by harmonic currents in the lines if these drives suffer particular (credible but not probable) failures. The Channel Tunnel North of London (NoL) trains will run over track fitted with 50 Hz vane relays, 83.3 Hz relays, coded audio frequency track circuits, impulse track circuits and uncoded audio frequency 'reed' track circuits. Interference Current Monitoring Units (ICMUs) are fitted where a failure could cause interference that might affect the signalling. In total the NoL trains will be fitted with:

SNCF 25 kV lines	83.3 Hz monitors
SNCB 3000 V lines	50 Hz ICMU
BR 750 V lines	50 Hz ICMU detectors on auxiliaries
BR 25 kV lines	Multifrequency ICMU dc detectors.

The proliferation and duplication of equipment means that each train will be fitted with about 20 different detectors, many of them using sophisticated electronic racks containing high precision digital filters, most built and tested to *failsafe* standards. All this adds to the cost and complexity of the product and reduces the reliability, not only because of the high component count, but also because of the possibility of the detectors tripping erroneously due to electrical transients caused by ice on the catenary, arcing at third rail gaps, etc.

European Community committees are studying 'interoperability' of high speed trains with a view to standardizing equipment, systems and interfaces to allow trains to be operated as freely internationally as the Airbus or the Ford Sierra. The costs of redesigning a train designed for one country to meet the standards of others can be prohibitive and the timescales are measured in years. Real standardization will be very difficult and expensive; railway administrations will have to give up long-cherished independence and the freedom to set standards but this has already happened in other transport sectors such as road and air transport. There is a risk that the issue will be 'fudged' and a so-called *standard* will be produced that allows such a wide range of supply voltages, current collection systems, gauges, signalling systems, radios etc. that there is no real standard.

The most intractable technical incompatibilities between railways probably relate to physical infrastructure. An example is the running of TGV-based trains over the BR Network South-East line to London. The routes do not meet the continental UIC gauge, the platforms are at a different height to that which is normal for European inter-urban vehicles and the power supply is third-rail 750 V which is used nowhere else other than for low speed urban railways. Viewed over a 50 year perspective it would make sense to convert the UK railways to accept continental trains; however, because such improvements would be unexploitable until many miles of track had been modified, this will always be seen as an investment with no payback for 20 years. Faced with the conflicting and urgent demands for investment, it is inevitable that the decision will always be to pay extra for the more complicated rolling stock capable of working over incompatible systems rather than to embark on a long-term plan to change the infrastructure.

The 'wish list' of most railway managers and their supporting ministers includes the availability of affordable and reliable high speed trains.

Unfortunately slow progress towards the standardization of infrastructure, common standards, rules and regulations means that, for many years to come, international trains will continue to be expensive, complicated and custom-designed for each project.

6.11 PASSENGER TRANSPORT AFTER AD 2000

This paper has given a resumé of the growth of high speed railways in Europe and the international network which it is planned will be put into place over the next 20 years.

The European network will be based on existing national infrastructures. These have been built to different structure gauges, use different signalling systems and have different power supplies. While it is possible to build sophisticated trains capable of operating over a diversity of infrastructures this cannot be a cost-effective long-term option.

Most of the present high speed lines are being built for $300 \, km \, h^{-1}$. On long straight routes this could be increased to around $350 \, km \, h^{-1}$. However, if speeds are pushed much higher, the energy consumption of rail will compare unfavourably with air travel. Although train speeds in excess of $500 \, km \, h^{-1}$ have been demonstrated, it is unlikely that these will be economically or ecologically justifiable for normal service.

The European High Speed Network will be particularly important for journeys of 150–500 km. For very short journeys it will be difficult for trains to compete with the motorway network, other than for passengers travelling between congested city centres. For business trips over 500 km the journey times are unlikely to be competitive with the airlines.

Whether or not the UK profits from the European High Speed Network, or is pushed into a more peripheral position by it, depends on the investment in new infrastructure and vehicles. The Government's present plans are an order of magnitude less ambitious than those of comparable European nations.

REFERENCES

Abrey, P.R. (1992) TGV-Transmanche begins to take shape. *Railway Gazette International*, April 239–247.
Berlioz, C. and Leboeuf, M. (1986) Performance of the Paris-Southeast TGV. *Revue Général des Chemins de Fer*, December, 127–133.
Cossie, A., Ragideau, J.-L. and Tisserand C. (1986) Self-commutated synchronous traction motors. *Revue Général des Chemins de Fer*, December, 95–103.
EC (1990) *The European High Speed Train Network*, Commission of the European Communities.
EC (1992) *The Future develoment of the Common Transport Policy, a global approach to the construction of a Community framework for sustainable mobility*, Commission of the European Communities.

Fiat (undated) *The future of rail transport is already way down the line.* Fiat Ferroviaria, Public Relations, 12038 Savigliano, Italy.

IRJ (1990) ICE – High Tech on Rail. *International Railway Journal,* Special issue, June.

Kemp, R.J. (1988) *The Class 91 locomotive for British Rail.* IMechE Conference on AC and DC drives, 15 March.

Kemp, R.J. (1991) The Lyon Line, a review of the TGV programme. *IEE Review,* February, 59–63.

Kemp, R.J. (1992) *High speed trains for the Channel Tunnel.* IMechE Conference Proceedings, October.

Kurz, Dipl-Ing H. (1991) Beyond the IC-Express. *Railway Gazette International,* May.

Lacôte, F. (1986) The new generation of SNCF high-speed rolling stock for Atlantic TGV. *Revue Général des Chemins de Fer,* December, 61–72 (available in English translation).

Lacôte, F. and Gléon, L. (1991) Double-deckers launch third generation of TGV. *Railway Gazette International,* September, 593–598.

Moreau, A. (1991) Le contact roue-rail. *Revue Général des Chemins de Fer,* 7–8. July/August.

Ministère de l'Equipement (1990) *Press Release, 31 May,* Ministère de l'Equipement du Logement, des Transport et de la Mer, Paris.

Watts, P.H. (1989) *Mark IV Coaches for British Rail InterCity.* IEE Railway Electrification Conference, York, September.

7

The Future of InterCity rail in Britain

C.E.W. Green

7.1 INTRODUCTION

The purpose of the paper is to demonstrate how human needs and national prosperity can best be served by technology in the 21st century. I can think of no better example than rail passenger travel to demonstrate the exciting potential that awaits us through blending the twin imperatives of people and technology.

7.1.1 InterCity ownership

InterCity is a self-contained high speed business within British Rail which is not allowed to receive any form of subsidy for its operations. It has a £1 billion turnover and it has just completed its fifth year in profit despite the recession and increasing competition from de-regulated air and coach operators.

We should be clear from the beginning that it is now government policy to cease operating a national InterCity passenger network and to fragment the services into seven train companies from April 1994. A nationalized Railtrack organization is being created to own and maintain railway infrastructure from 1994.

This paper will argue that high speed rail services have a good future in the UK regardless of ownership. This springs from the growing congestion in all other forms of transport and the benefits that rail offers for inter-urban journeys in the 150–300 mile zones.

Passenger Transport after 2000 AD. Edited by G.B.R. Feilden, A.H. Wickens and I.R. Yates. Published in 1994 by E & FN Spon, London. ISBN 0 419 19470 3.

Figure 7.1.

7.1.2 InterCity achievements 1983–1993

InterCity has effectively established itself as the surface airline for middle distance journeys in the UK over the last decade. Its market share of UK 'journeys over 50 miles' peaks at 400 km (250 miles) where it has won up to 40% of all travel to and from London. It carries 66 million customers a year on about 780 trains per day.

British transport needs are heavily geared towards the capital, and InterCity's prime strength lies in a series of radial routes out of London which have been raised to high speed standards. Fortunately Britain's major conurbations tend to lie between 240–480 km (150–300 miles) from London in the national rail zone – Bristol, Cardiff, Birmingham, Manchester, Liverpool, Preston, Leeds, Newcastle and Norwich.

Government policy has been for InterCity to develop its 'surface airline' wherever it can do so without subsidy. The result has been to create a high quality, high value operation on existing infrastructure driven by customer demand. No new mainlines have been built in Britain since 1901 but InterCity has taken high speed on existing lines further than most other countries. InterCity is in the top three European countries for the number

Table 7.1 Car Ownership and Usage (Source DOT Statistics, 1991)

	1980	1990	2000 (high)	2010 (high)	2020 (high)
Cars on road (m)	15	20	26	30	35
Vehicle km (bn)	272	408	548	680	816

Table 7.2 UK Airport Passenger Movements

	1980	1990	2000	2005
Domestic (m)	8	13	25	31
International (m)	43	79	138	183

of trains operating over 160 km h^{-1} (100 mph) and is probably in first position for frequency and range of market pricing.

7.2 THE FUTURE TRANSPORT MARKET

It is clear both from the work of institutions such as the Henley Centre and from our own market research that a series of major transport mis-matches will occur by the turn of the century.

Firstly, the demand for greater mobility will continue to rise dramatically and will come into collision with the supply side in the shape of saturated airports, trunk roads and city centres. Car ownership has risen by over 800% since the war and is predicted to rise by a further 200% by 2020. The average speed of travel in London is down to 13 km h^{-1} (8 mph) and is almost identical to the 1893 speed!

Tables 7.1 and 7.2 demonstrate the frightening increase in traffic that is predicted for our congested roads and airports in the next three decades.

Secondly any attempt to increase supply side capacity will increasingly collide with the growing environmentalist instincts of a nation that feels increasingly threatened by tarmac, concrete and pollution. Any remaining doubters need only look at the aggressive public objection to the M3 Winchester by-pass; the proposed London–Folkestone high speed railway and the additional Terminal 5 at Heathrow.

The third mismatch will be customer expectations for quality of life coming into violent collision with even more congested roads, airports and city centres.

This demand for quality is not in doubt and is very evident within InterCity. Ten years ago customer research recorded a straightforward need for punctual, clean trains at the lowest possible price. Today the need is

Figure 7.2.

far more discerning. Punctual, clean trains are taken for granted; the expectations are now for helpful, welcoming staff; a pleasant travel environment; entertainment and catering.

I have no doubt that this trend will accelerate into the 21st pace century. The human needs for transport will be for speed, space individuality and friendly service. National prosperity will be insufficient to meet these expectations through ever more roads and airports – even if the environmentalists would allow it. Technology and good planning may be the only solution.

Road investment is likely to be reduced in the future and focused onto specific by-passes and road widening schemes. Road congestion simply means that the product is under priced with demand exceeding supply and there is already no point in endlessly increasing the supply side. The technology now exists for road pricing and politicians are showing increasing interest in a system that would bring a true level playing field in transport with everyone paying as they go for the peaks they create. Perhaps this is the only way to achieve a true partnership between road and rail.

The challenge to rail in the 21st century is to be the knight in shining armour that resolves these conundrums and allows the nation to recognize transport fluidity. InterCity already has a strategic vision:

'To be the best, most civilized way to travel at speed from centre to centre.'

Let us now look at how this might be accomplished.

7.3 THE FUTURE POTENTIAL FOR INTERCITY

We need to recognize that Britain is as unlikely to invest in a national network of new high speed railways in the next generation as it is in brand new motorways or airports. We are fortunate that there is still considerable stretch in the existing rail network for speed, frequency, comfort and capacity. I believe that the main changes in inter-urban transport in the next century are likely to centre on exploiting the existing infrastructure with fill-in routes where a complete market has been missed.

I believe that we can analyse rail's contribution into the 21st century for our crowded island under three headings:

1. Four new railways to fill the gaps.
2. Going faster on existing tracks.
3. Achieving airline customer service standards.

7.4 BUILDING NEW RAILWAYS

Four new railways are likely to be built in Britain by the early 21st century. Together they will lock InterCity into its two largest pools of untapped demand – Heathrow Airport and the European mainland.

7.4.1 Channel Tunnel route opens 1994

The first new rail market is the huge European mainland rail network. There are an estimated 47 million air trips to/from mainland Europe annually and many of these are in the ideal 2–3 hour rail market as compared to the existing 6 hours for trains and ship. The Channel Tunnel will open in summer 1994 and through operations will start to destinations north of London a year later in 1995.

There is little doubt that the 3-hour Eurostar journey times from Waterloo to Paris and Brussels will take at least half the existing air market. The InterCity network naturally feeds into London and strong joint advertising will promote the new European rail market and bring important new feeder travel onto the InterCity network.

The through trains north of London from 1995 will offer daytime connections with InterCity services at 17 stations and night services to a

Figure 7.3.

further 15. The day trains are likely to appeal to the leisure market but the
Sleepers offer a good chance of attracting business on the longer journeys
to Frankfurt, Basel and Marseille.

Britain will have £500m in the upgrading of the existing route. Brand new
state-of-the-art Eurostar trains will raise the whole perception, quality and
speed of rail travel. Above all, valuable capacity will have been released
at European airports by withdrawing ultra-short distance flights and
making room for longer distance flights.

7.4.2 Union Railway AD 2000

It is already clear, however, that rail's potential to Europe will become
restrained by the demands on the Network SouthEast route from Waterloo
to Folkestone around the turn of the century. This makes the continuation
of the £3 billion Union Railway inevitable if Britain wishes to retain an
efficient link to mainland Europe. The proposal will offer $225\,\mathrm{km\,h^{-1}}$
(140 mph) operation on a brand new track alignment through some of the
most congested parts of the south-east.

The new line is currently being planned in detail for a political decision.

It will offer the opportunity for continuing the excellent TGV Nord to the Thames and will enable the latest technology to be used in signalling, cab control, electrification and train design. It will bring Paris within 2½ hours of London.

It is also intended to operate 175 km h^{-1} (110 mph) commuter trains on the new railway to revolutionize commuting in Kent where average speeds are currently at their lowest.

7.4.3 Heathrow Express 1997

Heathrow Airport is a major city in its own right with 45 million passengers arriving annually – and mostly without cars! This is a huge untapped rail market and a beginning will soon be made with the Heathrow Express link to connect with the Great Western mainline from Paddington. This will offer a 16 minute journey from London to Heathrow every quarter of an hour. The total cost, including BR electrification will be about £300 million; Parliamentary approval was achieved in 1991 and the line should be open by 1997 and conveying 6 to 7 million passengers a year between the country's premier airport and its capital city.

The ultimate solution of diverting the Great Western mainline under Heathrow Airport has not been abandoned and would obviously be of enormous strategic advantage to the nation much as has been obtained at Frankfurt, Zurich and Charles de Gaulle airports. This would change the shape of transport in Britain; domestic air slots at Heathrow could be released by dedicated Airline Expresses and the slots re-used more profitably for long-haul flights. Direct InterCity services could operate from Heathrow International to all the 12 InterCity nodal points.

7.4.4 CrossRail AD 2000

The £3 billion CrossRail scheme for London now has provisional Government support. It will offer a unique chance to improve access radically to the InterCity termini in central London.

CrossRail will provide a brand-new express tunnel under London from West to East (Paddington–Liverpool Street). It will bring Paddington within 11 minutes of the City and 6 minutes of the West End (on a journey that can currently take over half an hour).

Network SouthEast and London Underground will operate through services across the capital, but InterCity and International rail services will gain equally from this long overdue congestion relief, which will radically improve access to InterCity trains in the South East.

Table 7.3 World comparison of passenger usage of rail

Line	Passengers per annum
Tokyo–Osaka	90 million
Paris–Lyons	20 million
London–Manchester	5 million

7.5 FASTER ON EXISTING TRACKS

It seems financially and environmentally unlikely that Britain will build a major new railway through its industrial heart. Were it to do so, it would undoubtedly connect Manchester, Birmingham, London and the Channel Tunnel with a 480 km h^{-1} (300 mph) high speed passenger link offering radical improvements in journey times such as Manchester–London in 1½ hours. The London–Folkestone link is the only part which is likely to be built.

A world comparison (Table 7.3) gives us the reason why Britain is unlikely to need or build a new north–south railway in the next century. Japan and France were able to call on huge passenger usage on their new railways whereas the UK cannot achieve these numbers due to the dispersal of the routes and the shorter distances. As a rule of thumb, it does seem that a new railway needs a minimum usage of about 20 million journeys per annum and a high journey time elasticity.

Studies in 1989 showed that the journey time elasticity is only 0.8 and on this basis the revenue fell short of justifying a new line by a factor of 3. The case remains stubbornly negative even if other destinations on the West Coast route are included.

It is, however, realistic to envisage some radical upgrading of the existing major routes from London to deliver much higher speeds and capacity. The East Coast and Great Western routes are already very straight routes; the West Coast has effectively four track capacity to Manchester but is more curving; the Midland Mainline is under-utilized and has some restrictive curves.

The InterCity vision is to develop 250 km h^{-1} (155 mph) running on all existing main routes in the next thirty years. This can be achieved by harnessing modern technology to extract even more value from the existing tracks. A package of developments is in hand to ensure that 250 km h^{-1} (155 mph) operation is deliverable on existing tracks by the end of the century. These include.

InterCity 250 Train

This is a 25 kV electric push–pull train designed to operate on the straighter routes out of Kings Cross and Paddington. It was designed and put out to

Figure 7.4.

tender in 1992 and the ten vehicle train can be built for about £10m making it good value for money.

50 kV electrification

Engineers are currently studying the use of 50 kV electrification for all future mainline electrification for speeds in excess of 200 km h^{-1} (125 mph). This would distribute power by means of an auto-transformer system and offer the efficiency of distribution at high voltage with collection at the traditional 25 kV.

Dynamic Track Stabilizer

It will be increasingly necessary to switch track maintenance from day shifts to nights for reasons of both safety and productivity as speeds increase.

The Dynamic Track Stabilizer enables the engineer to renew track overnight and restore it to full 200 km h^{-1} (125 mph) operation the next morning without a speed restriction – the traditional speed would have been 64 km h^{-1} (40 mph). This miracle is achieved by a £1m machine which consolidates track in four overnight 'passes' to the equivalent of

100 000 tonnes of traffic. 13 machines now cover most of the InterCity track renewals.

High Output Ballast Cleaner

Technology has also solved the problem of reballasting long stretches of track in a short night possession. The logistics are considerable and can require up to 1000 tonnes of new ballast to be handled in 5 hours.

The new High Output Ballast Cleaner has been designed in the USA and has just started trials in the UK. It has already shown on test that it can work 2.5 times faster than the best existing machines in the UK. It will clean and restore 0.5 km of track in 5 hours and permit $120 \, \text{km h}^{-1}$ (75 mph) operation on the next day. It is so productive in fact that the entire UK needs can be met by just 5 machines. The breakthrough lies in the high percentage of usable ballast that can be returned to the track (up to 75%) to supplement the use of new ballast.

Integrated Electronic Control Centres (IECC)

The revolutionary combination of electronic interlockings with advanced control systems typified by the use of Solid State Interlocking (SSI) and the Integrated Electronic Control Centre (IECC), has become the norm in Britain for all major resignalling since 1988. It provides facilities for automating the production operation.

Trains are now signalled automatically at the height of the London rush hour. Data are provided for the operation of information systems to the benefit of customers and staff. These data also enable performance analysis to be produced in real time, and it is now possible to have a network map of Britain showing the real-time progress of every InterCity train. The next stage is to provide automatic customer information through voice synthesizing.

These developments have dramatically reduced staffing levels and the remaining staff are available for higher level route control.

Let us now look at the application of this new technology to specific UK routes in the future.

7.5.1 West Coast AD 1994–2004

A major £75m track realignment plan has been developed which will allow conventional trains to travel at $200 \, \text{km h}^{-1}$ (125 mph) from London to Coventry and Crewe. This would be introduced selectively initially at the southern end of the route but could be accelerated. Further potential exists for tilt trains to exploit the new track alignments still further at $250 \, \text{km h}^{-1}$ (155 mph) and proven examples now exist in both Italy

Table 7.4 West Coast potential (non-tilt)

London to	Now	Potential
Coventry	70 mins	63 mins
Manchester	160 mins	135 mins
Preston	160 mins	145 mins
Glasgow (non-tilt)	328 mins	310 mins
(tilt)		270 mins

(Fiat) and Sweden (ABB). This would be of special interest for London–Glasgow services where a tilt train could offer 4 hour 30 minute journey time (Table 7.4).

InterCity is currently bidding for new IC225 trains for the Manchester–London route which would enable all West Coast trains to operate at $200 \, \mathrm{km \, h^{-1}}$ (125 mph). They would operate initially at the existing $175 \, \mathrm{km \, h^{-1}}$ (110 mph) limit and would then reach their full potential as track work is completed.

7.5.2 Great Western 2000–2010

The Great Western currently offers the fastest diesel services in the world using the $200 \, \mathrm{km \, h^{-1}}$ (125 mph) HSTs on a mainly straight railway. These diesels fall due for renewal at the turn of the century and offer a unique opportunity for a major step change.

The vision would be to accelerate the existing route to $250 \, \mathrm{km \, h^{-1}}$ (155 mph) by exploiting the straight and level alignment left by Brunel and then to continue the CrossRail electrification beyond Reading to Bristol and Cardiff. Electrification could be undertaken on the 50 kV overhead system. Selective track realignment would be needed and the entire route is due for resignalling in the same time period which enables cab signalling to be introduced at the same time.

Journey times would be dramatically reduced (Table 7.5).

7.5.3 East Coast 2010–2020

The East Coast is potentially a $250 \, \mathrm{km \, h^{-1}}$ (155 mph) electric railway already south of Darlington and initial planning suggests that £1 billion would be needed to straighten out the whole route from Newcastle to London.

As a first stage, the existing $200 \, \mathrm{km \, h^{-1}}$ (125 mph) operation can be stepped up to $225 \, \mathrm{km \, h^{-1}}$ (140 mph) with the existing electric trains as soon as cab signalling and various other lineside safety features are provided. Thereafter it is a question of a series of track realignments and

Table 7.5 Great Western potential

London to	Now	Potential
Swindon	53 mins	44 mins
Bristol Parkway	80 mins	64 mins
Cardiff	118 mins	80 mins

a new tunnel at York if the full $250 \, km \, h^{-1}$ (155 mph) potential is to be realized. The results are dramatic enough to make the construction of a new railway unnecessary (Table 7.6).

Over 80% of the route to Newcastle is suitable for $200 \, km \, h^{-1}$ (125 mph) operations already. The additional investment would enable over 70% of the route to operate at $250 \, km \, h^{-1}$ (155 mph), with a journey time of 3 hours 24 minutes to Edinburgh – a serious challenge to the existing air competition.

Figure 7.5.

Table 7.6 East Coast potential

London to	Now	Potential 225	Potential 250
Leeds	145 mins	115 mins	105 mins
Newcastle	170 mins	150 mins	130 mins
Edinburgh	225 mins	233 mins	205 mins
Glasgow	319 mins	299 mins	255 mins

7.6 AIRLINE CUSTOMER SERVICE STANDARDS

7.6.1 Raising the travel experience

The building of new railways and the upgrading of the old is always exciting. It is, however, equally true that InterCity's future in the next century will depend on its customer interface as well as on its hardware.

InterCity no longer just sells train trips – it has to offer a total journey experience to satisfy the market. This means that it is actually in partnership with the car and to some extent with the bus and plane.

The 21st century will see a period of strategic alliances developing in transport. Inter-urban rail services will increasingly feed airports so that slots are released for more profitable long distance flights. Coaches will increasingly feed trunk rail routes to avoid congestion. The car will cease to be the enemy of rail and will become its partner in the next generation. The car will always provide the beginning and end of most journeys.

Technology can go a long way to providing the main human needs for a seamless multi-mode journey.

Access

The biggest customer frustration lies in the queue for a ticket prior to travel. New Telesales offices are being opened to enable everyone to book their train tickets and seats from home by quoting a credit card number and receiving the tickets in the post. It is only a matter of time before the whole transaction is done by the customers by interrogating their own television screens. This will truly bring rail travel fully into the sitting room.

All reserved trains

The days of random access to long distance trains are clearly over as this inevitably leads to overcrowding and stress at peak periods. Rail must increasingly move towards the principle that buying a ticket automatically buys a specific seat. This guarantees peace of mind and reassurance – both hallmarks of good service.

The new JDS ticket machines currently being installed in booking offices form the first step. It will enable an InterCity ticket to be sold to the top 400 destinations in Europe with the seat reservations printed on the actual ticket. The transaction time will be less than a minute and will ultimately include car parking, meal services and sleepers and other customer requirements such as hotel bookings.

On-train satellite information

The demands for real-time information on trains is forcing the pace on technology. InterCity has just introduced the world's first satellite-linked train on the justification of customer information alone. The train uses the geo-stationary satellites (GTS) used by the US army to enable the train to locate itself continuously and then to give the correct visual information (voice synthesizers can follow) on the time to next stop. This leaves the senior conductor free to concentrate on the customers' needs.

Electronic seat reservation

A micro-chip enables a senior conductor to light up the seat reservations down a train within a minute of joining instead of 20 minutes taken to individually label each seat. This will save customers waiting on the concourse whilst the train is serviced.

On-train entertainment

Demand is increasing for the train to offer some of the conveniences found in the home or office. InterCity is already testing ideas for the 21st century train which include miniature TV sets on each seat back; computer jack-points; fax; photostats and mobile phones that work in tunnels.

7.7 CONCLUSION

I hope that I have demonstrated the huge potential that still exists in inter-urban rail travel for the 21st century.

The future lies in a mature partnership between rail, road and air which recognizes that the nation cannot afford to meet the endless demand for more road space.

The most likely way forward in the UK is for:

- new railways to fill the gaps and open up enormous pools of untapped demand;

- existing InterCity routes to be upgraded to $250 \, km \, h^{-1}$ (155 mph) operation;
- new technology to be used to achieve airline customer service standards.

The nation cannot afford to miss these opportunities. It has few options left if it wishes to keep the nation moving, to retain its prosperity and to meet rising customer needs for civilized travelling.

8

High speed maglev systems

L. Miller

8.1 INTRODUCTION

The increasing volumes of road and air traffic have already led to a significant deterioration in traffic flow, high environmental loads, and severe safety problems. Along with the further increase in population and the future economic development, further aggravation must be expected.

Guided ground transportation systems can be more efficient and environmentally benign, if their attractiveness is sufficient to ensure high acceptability by the users. To meet the growing demand, an improved transport infrastructure operated efficiently and economically with a minimum impact on the environment is urgently needed.

Several novel systems based on the principle of magnetic levitation combined with linear motor propulsion are being developed and investigated to provide such a transport service. It is expected that their integration into the existing transport infrastructure will reduce road and air traffic considerably and therefore improve the quality and efficiency of passenger and cargo transport after the year 2000.

8.2 POTENTIAL OF MAGNETIC LEVITATION (MAGLEV) SYSTEMS

The number and kinds of technologies applied in a vehicle and the required interfaces and their transformation processes determine the complexity and the improvement potential especially with respect to reliability, maintenance, and production cost.

In maglev systems the basic functions are achieved exclusively through

Passenger Transport after 2000 AD. Edited by G.B.R. Feilden, A.H. Wickens and I.R. Yates. Published in 1994 by E & FN Spon, London. ISBN 0 419 19470 3.

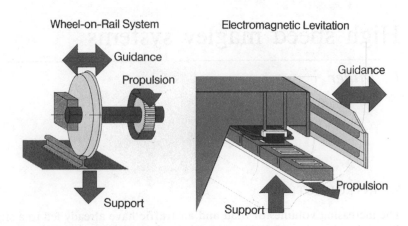

Figure 8.1 Comparison of systems railroad/maglev.

electrical subsystems without intermediate mechanical, hydraulic, or pneumatic conversions.

Thanks to the unchallenged high innovative potential of electrical engineering and microelectronics, maglev technology offers the possibility to design properties into transport systems which are advantageous and contain large technological potential for the future.

In comparison with wheel-on-rail systems, the following performance characteristics can be achieved (most of which been demonstrated successfully already (Figure 8.1).

- Practically no wear and tear on levitation and propulsion systems due to their non-contact operation.
- No friction dependence for propulsion and braking and therefore insensitive to weather and service conditions.
- Operational speeds of 100 to 500 km h^{-1} and great acceleration power. This results in attractive travelling times, especially for medium and long distances comparable to those of air traffic. Because of the great acceleration power, even frequent stops have only marginal effect on the total travel time. The extremely short distances required for acceleration make maglev systems suitable also for short routes and commuter service applications.
- Highest availability can be achieved because the basic concept facilitates a modular design using electric and electronic components with simplified control, monitoring, diagnostics, and handling as well as minimal effort for computer-aided maintenance and repair cost.

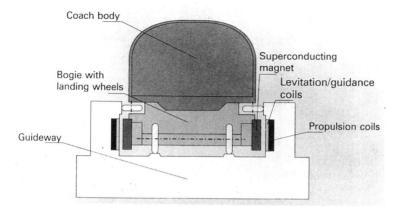

Figure 8.2 Maglev undercarriage (MLU) system: cross-section.

- Maglev guideways can be adapted to the landscape more flexibly because the trains can travel steep gradients and traverse tight curves especially at high speeds.
- Active guidance means no derailing and full adaptability to accommodate the specific loads generated by aerodynamic and centrifugal forces.
- Non-contact operation means low-cost at-grade and elevated guideways with long life-cycle and safe-life design.
- No sensitive link exists between the infrastructure and trains which allows independent management of infrastructure and the operation of trainsets.

8.3 STATUS OF MAGLEV SYSTEM DEVELOPMENT

Worldwide the technical potentialities and specific advantages of the magnetic levitation technology were recognized. Two basic types of maglev technology have been investigated extensively.

1. The electrodynamic levitation system based on the generation of eddy current in track conductors, produced by the moving vehicle magnets. The strength of the magnetic field required is achievable exclusively through superconductivity of the magnet coils. Since relative motion between the vehicle and the conducting guideway is essential for generation of levitation and guidance forces, an undercarriage must be provided for starting and landing the vehicle (Figure 8.2).
2. The electromagnetic levitation utilizes attractive forces between the magnets in the vehicle and reaction rails on the guideway with feedback control to maintain magnet to reaction rail clearance (Figure 8.3).

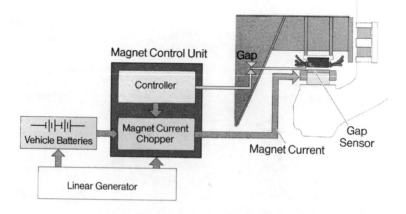

Figure 8.3 Magnet control (Transrapid Technology).

To provide adequate propulsion and braking forces in a non-contact manner, primarily electric systems – short or longstator referring to the linear motor whether the active elements are located on board (short) or on the guideway (long) – have been investigated. To simplify the system structure and to improve efficiency, the magnets are utilized in multi-functional modes in some of the concepts, e.g. levitation and propulsion functions (levitation magnets are used for linear motor excitation) or guidance and propulsion functions (electromagnets guide the linear induction motor and the vehicle itself using the secondary of the motor as the reaction rail).

Development work, basic research, and/or application studies are conducted in various countries, such as Canada, China, France, Germany, Italy, Japan, Korea, Russia, Switzerland, the United Kingdom and the United States of America. In the following section, an overview is given of the state of development in countries dominant in transport technology.

8.3.1 Development in the United Kingdom

Initiated by British Rail, R&D efforts have been largely concentrated on magnetic levitation combined with a short stator linear motor primarily for urban transit applications. First trials started in 1974.

A system with a 620 m long guideway was built to link Birmingham Airport terminal with the National Exhibition Centre/British Rail International Station. It was opened on 1 April 1984. The Birmingham Airport Maglev is the first magnetic system used in regular public transport and, therefore, ranks as a technological breakthrough.

8.3.2 Development in the United States of America

Although pioneering work on basic concepts of magnetic levitation and linear motor propulsion was undertaken in the United States, government support for the activities was withdrawn in 1975.

In December 1989, an interagency maglev co-ordinating committee was formed to co-ordinate maglev efforts within the federal government. At the same time the 'Statement of National Transportation Policy' (NTP) by the Department of Transportation emphasized that in dense intercity corridors there is a need to develop new complementary transportation options. Such options should take into account land use, energy and environmental impacts as well as transportation preferences. One of the options highlighted in the NTP as well as in the National Energy Strategy is magnetically levitated trains, arguing that maglev is a potentially environmentally benign, energy efficient, high speed technology. In response to initiatives within the Administration and Congress the National Maglev Initiative (NMI) was established. Reports of the Federal Railroad Administration and US Army Corps of Engineers concluded that maglev appears to be technically and economically feasible but considerable study is required to determine whether and how maglev should be integrated into the United States transportation network. Studies covering the following subjects are underway: maglev technology assessment, economic and market analysis, right of way and interconnectivity issues, and analysis of public policy issues.

8.2.3 Development in France

Within the framework of a co-operation agreement established in 1977 between the French Ministry of Transport and the German Federal Ministry for Research and Technology, French and German railway administrations, companies, and institutions were successfully engaged in starting maglev application studies and component development.

The outstanding project was the design of a magnetic train with electromagnetic levitation and a so-called U-shaped linear induction motor for commuter applications at speeds up to 200 km h^{-1}. Although technical feasibility of levitation and integrated guidance and propulsion function were demonstrated convincingly on one-to-one scaled test benches in France and Germany at up to speeds of 300 km h^{-1} and the results of a study of fields of application forecast clear advantages compared to modern fully automatic lightweight wheel-on-rail systems, support of railway administrations and governments for this project was withdrawn in 1990.

Figure 8.4 MLU-002 (Japan).

8.3.4 Development in Japan

A further continuously growing demand is seriously expected in Japan and it is broadly agreed on a change in favour of maglev systems to solve the growing environmental problems and to help limit road and air traffic.

Experience has shown that the application of wheel-on-rail systems is limited due to the maintenance efforts required in high frequency operation and the environmental influences on the area along the tracks, especially with respect to noise emission and vibration.

Two systems are being further developed:

- the electrodynamic maglev system MLU designed for long distance application at operational speeds up to $500 \, km \, h^{-1}$.
- the High Speed Surface Transport (HSST) system with electromagnetic levitation on a U-shaped reaction rail and a linear single-sided induction motor on board for propulsion and braking designed for commuter application with speeds up to $200 \, km \, h^{-1}$.

Research and development activities in the field of electrodynamic maglev technology were initiated in 1962 by the Japanese National Railways. In 1979, the remote-controlled test vehicle ML-500 proved the functionality of electrodynamic levitation and a synchronous linear motor (without ferromagnetic circuit) at speeds up to $517 \, km \, h^{-1}$. In 1987, the development of the MLU system was transferred to the Railway Technology Research Institute. The prototype vehicle MLU-002 (Figure 8.4) scaled at half the size of the application vehicle was developed and tested. Based on the results obtained, a system applicable to revenue service was designed.

Figure 8.5 High Speed Surface Transport (HSST; Japan).

In 1989, the Linear Express Project was proposed to connect Tokyo with Osaka. To prove the technical readiness for application in revenue service, the Yamanashi Test Track was approved for construction in the south-east portion of Kofu in 1990 by the Ministry of Transport. Construction began in 1991 and operation will start in 1995.

The development of the HSST system (Figure 8.5) was started in the early 1970s by Japan Airlines. The system was defined from the outset for limited distances to provide connections between city centres and airports. High speeds were, therefore, not required which allowed consequent simplification of the design. The technical feasibility was demonstrated by various test vehicles and prototypes in the 1970s and 1980s. In 1989, the Nagoya Project was started with two objectives:

- verification of technical readiness for application in revenue service;
- analysis of possible fields of application especially with respect to safety and environmental issues.

In a comprehensive study carried out by experienced operators and local authorities, it is underlined that due to higher flexibility and adaptability, the HSST is advantageous for connections between city centres and suburban residential areas and airports. In comparison with conventional systems the following advantages were shown:

- shorter travelling time;
- better ride comfort;
- less audible noise emission;

- higher safety;
- insensitivity to environmental influences.

In an overall assessment, the Ministry of Transport concluded that the HSST system is ready for application in revenue service with operational speeds up to $100 \, km \, h^{-1}$. For connections with an operational speed of $200 \, km \, h^{-1}$ further development and verification of operational characteristics are required.

At present in Japan, the development of both systems – MLU and HSST – is at the final stage prior to application. The realization of first application projects is expected before the 21st century.

8.3.5 Development in Germany

The development of magnetically levitated ground transportation systems was started in 1968 and sponsored by the German Federal Ministry for Research and Technology.

In the first phase of the programme (1968–1971), a demand and feasibility study was carried out. Alternative techniques for high speed transportation systems were conceived and investigated in detail systematically. As a result, it was forecast that for specific transportation patterns, the establishment of a high speed transportation system would mean a considerable economic advantage. Moreover, the study provided momentum and targets for further development. In the following phase, up to 1978, the development and testing of key components, functional qualification and selection of procedures took place. In this phase the research program covered the whole variety of possible techniques: air cushion technique, permanent magnetic levitation, electrodynamic levitation, and electromagnetic levitation.

In December 1977, the Federal Ministry for Research and Technology announced its decision to concentrate its future assistance measures on the electromagnetic system only. Decisive arguments were: low energy consumption, applicability even at low speeds, very low electromagnetic field emission, high cost effectiveness (investment and operational), adaptability to requirements of different applications. Consequently, the further development programme concentrated on the electromagnetic technology – the Transrapid system (Figure 8.6).

In 1979, Transrapid technology was demonstrated for the first time to the public. During the International Transport Exhibition in Hamburg, the Transrapid 05 (Figure 8.7) linked the exhibition halls with the open air exhibition area situated at a distance of 900 m. During the three weeks the exhibition was open, the vehicle with 70 seats carried more 50 000 passengers in scheduled operation.

In 1984, the first part of the high speed Transrapid Test Facility in Emsland (northern Germany), with a length of about 20 km, was

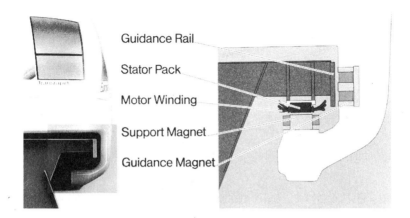

Guidance Rail

Stator Pack

Motor Winding

Support Magnet

Guidance Magnet

Figure 8.6 Vehicle/guideway components.

completed. Already in December 1985 the TR06 test vehicle attained a speed of 355 km h^{-1}.

In 1987, the second part of the Transrapid Test Facility, the south loop, was completed and in January 1988 the TR06 vehicle reached 412 km h^{-1} on the now 31 km long guideway.

In 1990, verification of fail-safe, non-contact operation of the Transrapid system was confirmed by extensive testing of the TR07 (Figure 8.8) vehicle at speeds up to 436 km h^{-1}. The TR07, which is a prototype version of the vehicles planned for revenue service, underwent all stages of certification testing at the Transrapid Test Facility in Emsland under independent technical supervision.

Figure 8.7 Transrapid 05 – IVA 1979, Hamburg.

Figure 8.8 Transrapid 07.

In December 1991, a working group of experts from the German Federal Railway in co-operation with renowned universities approved the technical readiness for application of the Transrapid. That was one of the most important prerequisites for the German Federal Cabinet to include the magnetic levitation system in the new Federal Transportation Master Plan in 1992. The Cabinet also approved the route Berlin–Hamburg to be the first application of Transrapid in Germany, with the condition of private or partially private financing.

8.4 TRANSRAPID – THE MOST ADVANCED SYSTEM FOR GUIDED GROUND TRANSPORTATION

The high speed transportation system Transrapid is capable of revenue operation at speeds of 100–500 km h^{-1}. After successful demonstration of the outstanding technical features of the electromagnetic levitation combined with a synchronous iron-cored, longstator motor, the activities were concentrated on availability, safety, and profitability as dominant factors to be resolved prior to revenue service. In the subsequent paragraphs the subsystems are described, the system characteristics are given, and fields of application are discussed.

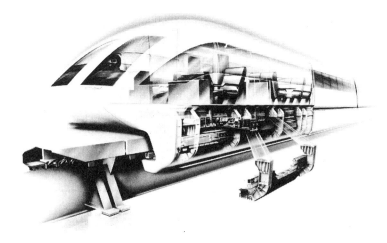

Figure 8.9 Transrapid 07 lift and guide module.

8.4.1 Technical description of subsystems

Vehicle

Transrapid trainsets are composed of up to ten vehicle sections with each section having a length of 25.5 m. They are designed to transport passengers or express goods at speeds of up to 500 km h^{-1}.

Flux-coupled electromagnets arranged in a redundant configuration and controlled in two degrees of freedom are used to levitate and guide the vehicle (Figure 8.9). A safe-life power supply for the vehicles is provided by linear generators independent of any external power supply. These generators convert part of the vehicles' kinetic energy into electrical energy. The safe-life behaviour is achieved through sufficiently high redundancy. At low speeds (less than 80 km h^{-1}), the on-board power supply network is buffered by batteries.

Eddy current brakes using modular design are provided to ensure the safe-life braking function of the vehicle.

Skids are used to support the vehicle on the guideway at standstill after the electromagnetic levitation system is deactivated.

The structure and design of the cabin correspond to the latest technological development. Besides the basic requirements, such as lightweight and low aerodynamic resistance, the following criteria were important:

- good accessibility of built-in components;
- high noise, heat, and fire protection through structure and materials used;
- a low-cost manufacture based on mass production methods.

Table 8.1 Technical data of Transrapid revenue vehicle

Operation speed	100–500 km h^{-1}	
	Empty weight	total weight, allowed
Passenger vehicle	46 000 kg	55 000 kg
Cargo vehicle	42 000 kg	58 500 kg
Vehicle dimensions		
Length	24.770 m	
Width	3.700 m	
Usable Area	78 m^2	
Seats	56 to 113	

As a result of a detailed optimization process, the following properties were achieved:

- small number of different components;
- use of section-optimized profiles, therefore easy installation of components;
- composition of the entire structure with prefabricated units;
- smooth surfaces;
- screw and gluing technology for non-deforming and precise assembly.

In the interest of the approval and acceptance of the transport system, passive fire protection of the interior furnishings have been of particular importance. It was, therefore, based on the currently highest fire protection standard (Air Transport Standard, 1988).

Table 8.1 shows the technical data of the vehicle. Total weight available for cargo transport is limited to equalize guideway loads compared to passenger transport units. If cargo transport is dominant in an application, payloads up to 30 tons per unit can be chosen. In spite of the considerable increase of the vehicle's weight up to 72 tons, only minor design adaptations in the vehicle's and guideway's mechanical structure are required.

Propulsion system

The propulsion system is realized by a synchronous longstator linear motor. It consists of stator packs with a three-phase winding installed under the guideway (comparable to the stator of a rotating motor) and electromagnets mounted on the vehicle (corresponding to the rotor of a rotating motor).

The 'guideway motor' is divided into sections which are individually activated by the appropriate substations as the vehicle enters the respective section. Acceleration and braking capability, which vary locally due to routing and operational requirements, can be accommodated easily by varying the length of the motor sections, the diameter and/or conductivity

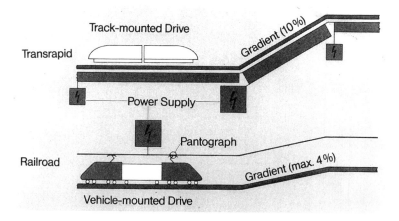

Figure 8.10 Vehicle/wayside propulsion components.

of motor winding and feeding cables, the supplied power capability, and distance between substations. These properties demonstrate the outstanding suitability of the synchronous iron-cored, longstator motor for guided ground transportation (Figure 8.10).

Automatic train control

The communication and control system is fully automated. It maintains the trainset's speed within the operating specifications (safe speed enforcement) and provides a safe and unobstructed travel path (route integrity). The system relies mainly on microprocessors which are designed and verified with fail-safe, fail-active, and fault-tolerant techniques.

Most of the command, control, and communication system requirements for a maglev system can be found in existing fully automated railway systems. It is of considerable advantage that for the Transrapid, up-to-date technology and an optimized system architecture can be chosen without restrictions due to problems of compatibility with already existing infrastructure and equipment.

Guideway

Various types of guideway structures are available for route planning with regard to cost efficiency and environmental concerns:

- Single or double track elevated guideways using steel (Figure 8.11) or prestressed concrete beams mounted on 5–20 m high piers;
- single or double track at-grade guideways for tunnels, cuttings, bridges, and areas where this is required for better general acceptance.

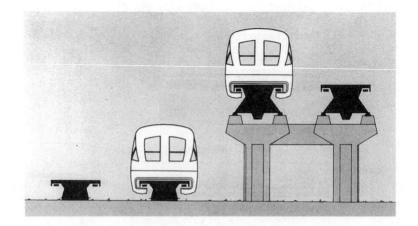

Figure 8.11 Steel-type guideway elevated/at-grade.

For guide switching, bendable switches with maximum vehicle turnout speeds of 100 or 200 km h^{-1} have been developed and tested.

Table 8.2 and Figure 8.12 give an overview of the guideway alignment data and parameters which are technically allowed. The land surface area reflects the foundations required for an elevated or at-grade guideway route. The land required (right of way) and the excavations are based on various representative reference alignments.

Table 8.2 Guideway alignment data

Lateral acceleration	≤ 1.5 m s^{-2}
Vertical acceleration	
Crest	≤ 0.6 m s^{-2}
Trough	≤ 1.2 m s^{-2}
Omnidirectional jerk	
Normal track	≤ 1.0 m s^{-3}
Singular points	≤ 2.0 m s^{-3}
Lateral inclination	≤ 16°
Torsion (change of cant)	≤ 0.1° m^{-1}
Longitudinal inclination	≤ 10%

The sinusoidal transition curves and superelevation ramps are of equal length.

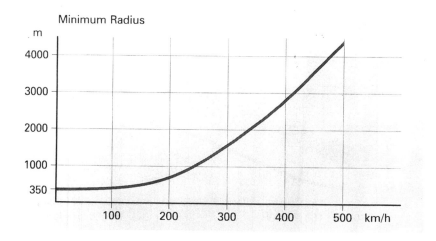

Figure 8.12 Transrapid curvature radii.

8.4.2 System characteristics

Environmental compatibility and performance characteristics

Environmental acceptability has become more and more important for the implementation of transportation systems. Alignment parameters for the maglev train Transrapid are extremely favourable. Due to the vehicle's ability to climb steep gradients and travel tight curves, the guideway can

Figure 8.13 Co-location of maglev and highway.

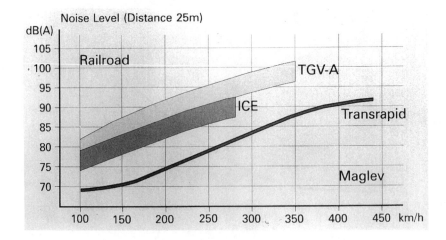

Figure 8.14 Transrapid/railroad noise emission.

be flexibly adapted to the landscape and co-located closely with existing roads and railroad tracks (Figure 8.13).

Transrapid is matchless in terms of quietness, especially within the range of those speeds utilized in densely populated areas or when approaching stations.

The high acceleration and deceleration ability permits the system:

• to serve as a commuter train to and from suburban areas;
• to reduce cruising speed when passing noise-sensitive areas or in tight curves without significant impact on overall travelling times.

The environmental data and performance characteristics are given Figures 8.14, 8.15, 8.16.

The calculation of the vehicle specific data is based on a typical trainset configuration with eight vehicle sections and 702 seats. The secondary energy consumption refers to seat and kilometer when riding at constant speed.

Availability

High availability of all subsystems is essential to ensure that the Transrapid system maintains a high level of operating performance in revenue service.
This is achieved through:

• insensitivity to environmental influences (outside temperature, winter conditions, lightning, crosswind, and earthquakes);
• error-tolerant behaviour, i.e. fulfilment of scheduled stops even in case of multiple component failures;

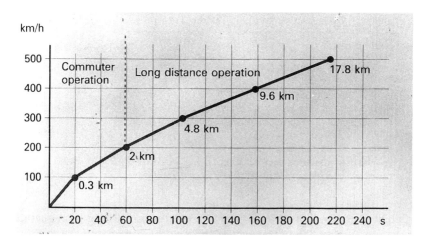

Figure 8.15 Acceleration ability.

- on-line diagnostics;
- automatic deactivation of components in case of failure and on-line self-diagnostics including reactivation routines;
- easy handling and maintainability through computer-aided equipment for preventive and corrective maintenance.

Development models of computer-aided equipment for preventive and corrective maintenance have been installed in the Transrapid Test Facility and undergo continuous testing in daily operation. The target data for

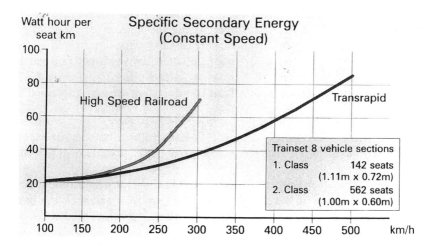

Figure 8.16 Transrapid/railroad energy consumption.

Table 8.3 Operation performance at the Transrapid Test Facility

Speed record	436 km h^{-1}
Total distance accumulated	over 130 000 km
Longest non-stop distance traveled	1 674 km
Maximum daily distance	2 500 km
Long-term test	
average daily distance	1 200 km
portion of distance above 350 km h^{-1}	42%

reliability and availability have been verified during the long-term operation at the test facility. The summary of the operation performance at the test facility is given in Table 8.3.

Safety

The Transrapid high speed transportation system has been subjected to a detailed and comprehensive safety analysis and evaluation. The methodology and procedures in the safety assessment were already based on developed and verified techniques applied to analyse complex systems such as railways, air transportation networks, chemical and power plants. On the basis of quantitative criteria to decide acceptance or refusal of risk, safety measures have been defined and evaluated in a closed loop processing of risk assessment and evaluation. The end of the iterative process results in a final safety specification.

A comparison with other transportation systems demonstrates the high level of safety of the Transrapid. Using the number of fatalities per billion passenger–kilometers as a measure of safety, the Transrapid system is safer than air travel by a factor of 20, than conventional railroad by a factor of 250, and than road travel by a factor of 700 (Figure 8.17). The high level of safety in the Transrapid system can be explained as follows:

- As a new transportation system, the Transrapid profits from the experiences with existing systems by avoiding from the outset known accident risks.
- The technique of magnetic levitation used in the Transrapid system does not introduce any new risks. It guarantees safe operation on the basis of the adopted technical and design measures.

The most prominent features of the Transrapid, namely its elevated guideway and the high speeds, raise two questions:

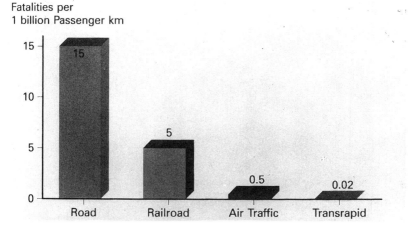

Figure 8.17 Comparative safety evaluation.

- Where and how can people be evacuated from the vehicle in case of an emergency?
- What are the effects of a collision with a guideway element or with an unexpected obstacle?

The rescue strategy with safe hovering ensures that the vehicle only comes to a stop at locations where auxiliary power and evacuation means are provided (Figure 8.18). The distances between these areas are defined so that in case of an emergency the vehicle can reliably coast to the next area, even in the presence of worst-case situations. The passengers, especially handicapped people, can then leave the vehicle at a suitable, i.e. protected location.

To avoid collision, the following measures are applied.

- The construction method for the guideway excludes the possibility of large deformations and takes into account local conditions and possible earthquake loading.
- Guideway structures are dimensioned and qualified according to safe-life standards.
- Piers and beams of the guideway at underpasses are collision-protected.
- In case of overhead traffic, constructional measures have to prevent vehicles and objects from falling onto the guideway.
- Care is taken with trees in wooded sections and operation restrictions are used during periods of extremely bad weather (e.g. wind of more than $35\,\mathrm{m\,s^{-1}}$).

Furthermore, for remote or even improbable cases collision resistance and

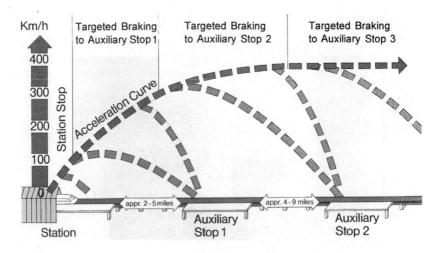

Figure 8.18 Rescue strategy.

crash-worthiness have been investigated. The latest simulation techniques to predict the acceleration level in the cabins and the impact on vehicle structure and components have been applied. Due to the impossibility of derailment (Figure 8.19), the elasticity and damping of the section coupling, the specific characteristics of the levitation bogies, and the design of the nose unit, no injuries from the comparatively low g-forces were experienced by the passengers and less damage to the vehicles occurred in the simulated collisions, than was to be expected.

Figure 8.19 Derailing safety.

Specific requirements for Transrapid applications in the United States were investigated through a US–German co-operation carried out by the Federal Railroad Administration and TÜV Rheinland (safety certification group in the Federal Republic of Germany). In this co-operation project specific data and US statistics were gathered and used as input for the safety analysis and evaluation as well as for the definition of specific regulations for Transrapid applications in the US. Federal Railroad Administration experts realized that the safety has been built into the Transrapid system from the very beginning – designing the accident out.

Economic efficiency

The investment cost corresponds to that required for modern high speed rail systems. The operating cost is significantly lower due to reduced expenditures for maintenance and repair. The non-contact technical concept and aerodynamic optimization of the vehicle lead to lower drag coefficients which result, for example, in approximately 30% lower energy consumption in comparison with modern high speed railroads. From measurements at the Transrapid Test Facility in Emsland, the power factor fluctuates between 0.84 and 0.98 and the efficiency as the ratio of the electrical power required (at the motor terminals) and the mechanical power value varies between 0.91 and 0.95 depending on the speed of the vehicle. These characteristics enhance the opportunity for profitable operation at competitive ticket prices.

8.4.3 Profitability and fields of application

The economic feasibility of the maglev system Transrapid has been verified in the course of a study of profitability and corridors of application carried out by the MVP (test and planning organization for maglev systems, founded in 1984 by the German Federal Railway, Lufthansa and IABG (test organization operating the Transrapid Test Facility in Emsland)).

The tasks of this study were to:

- identify specific applications for hypothetical corridors for maglev and wheel/rail passenger transport;
- establish fundamentals for the operators in order to evaluate and select systems for specific corridors;
- investigate possibilities to co-ordinate, co-operate, and integrate the systems with each other and with other transportation means (Figure 8.20).

The criteria for the comparative evaluation using modern high speed rail systems as a reference were:

- travelling time;

Figure 8.20 Bivalent guideway.

- specific energy consumption;
- required area for guideway;
- adaptability to landscape;
- noise emission;
- investment and operating cost;
- profitability.

The final report presented in January 1991 came to the following conclusions.

- Elevated and at-grade, the Transrapid guideway needs a comparatively small land area (Figure 8.21).
- Transrapid trains are less noisy than railroad trains at the same speed.
- Transrapid trains specifically require less energy.
- Transrapid trains offer, in comparison with air transport,
  shorter travel times at distances up to 500 km,
  similar travel times at distances up to 800 km.
- Cost of Transrapid guideways is relatively low in difficult terrain (hilly corridors).
- Shorter travelling times resulting in a larger demand allow the Transrapid system to be profitable.

8.4.4 Application projects

The readiness for application of the Transrapid maglev system opens the door to a new form of guided ground transportation. At the request of the Federal Ministry of Transportation, investigations into possible maglev routes with and within the new German states were carried out. According

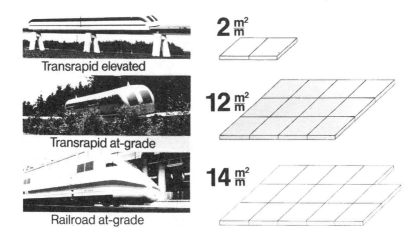

Transrapid elevated

$2 \frac{m^2}{m}$

Transrapid at-grade

$12 \frac{m^2}{m}$

Railroad at-grade

$14 \frac{m^2}{m}$

Figure 8.21 Land consumption (low mountain range).

to the results, the connection between Berlin and Hamburg is preferred for economic and political reasons. With a maximum operational speed of $400 \, \text{km h}^{-1}$, the trip between Germany's two largest cities would be of less than one hour duration. The ridership is estimated to be approximately 14.5 million passengers per year, the operational performance 6.6 billion seat-km per year, the total investment 7.2 billion DM, and the operating cost 210 million DM per year. Based on fares which are similar to those of the German Inter-City-Express train, yearly revenues of approximately 1.1 billion DM per year are expected. The current project plan foresees the construction phase beginning in 1996 and revenue service operation starting in 2003.

For financing the project, partially private models are under discussion. In case these models will be applied, they will break new ground for the realization of future infrastructure projects in Germany and possibly also in other countries. The models offer alternatives which relieve the public budget considerably and in addition provide momentum for the engagement of competitive private companies in the realization and operation of the system and which therefore improve economic efficiency. A preliminary profitability assessment for all models under discussion shows that a reasonable return for the investors and operators can be expected.

On 12 May 1993 a resolution submitted by the parliamentary groups of CDU/CSU (Christian Democratic Union/Christian Social Union) and FDP (Free Democratic Party) with regard to the draft of a law on the improvement of the federal railway network (Federal Railway Improvement Law) was passed. Apart from details relating to different financing models

Figure 8.22 Maglev/airport integration.

and the further procedure, the resolution contains the following basic statement:

> The German Bundestag has recognized that the maglev system Transrapid, due to its innovative technology, can play an economically and environmentally sensible role in overcoming the continuously growing volume of traffic. The German Bundestag welcomes the consideration of the Federal Government in the Federal Transportation Master Plan with regard to the application route Berlin–Hamburg.

Already in the 1980s, a number of application studies have been conducted in the US. The most advanced project is the connection between Orlando International Airport and the centre of Orlando's tourism district on International Drive, 21 km away. With a top speed of 400 km h^{-1} it takes only 7.5 minutes to travel from the airport to the Maglev Grand Terminal. Passenger demand is expected to be up to 10 million per year. On June 12, 1991, the Governor and Cabinet of the state of Florida certified the Orlando-based Maglev Transit, Inc. to construct the first superspeed maglev train in the US on the basis of Transrapid technology.

 8.5 CONCLUSION

To meet the growing demand to transport people and goods safely, efficiently, and economically, an improved transport infrastructure with a minimum impact on the environment is required. In addition to further technical optimization of road, air transport, and wheel-on-rail systems, decisions in favour of guided ground transportation systems based on non-contact, magnetic levitation and linear propulsion can solve the transport problems and reduce the environmental loads.

At present, the Transrapid maglev system is at the leading edge worldwide. Existing technology appropriate to transportation systems has been applied here to achieve the favourable properties of outstanding adaptability, high safety, environmental compatibility, reliable operation, and economic feasibility. Thanks to the unchallenged high innovative potential of electrical engineering and microelectronics the Transrapid technology contains large potential for further improvements.

To minimize adverse effects caused by the construction of any new system, the maglev guideway should be co-located as closely as possible along with existing rights of way. Maglev systems have a great potential for a positive impact, if they are thoughtfully integrated and interconnected with the existing transport infrastructure (Figure 8.22).

It is one of the great challenges of this decade to open the door for the first applications of maglev systems in revenue service and therefore establish the prerequisite for a more efficient, safer, and environmentally benign transport infrastructure in the next decades.

REFERENCES

Glatzel, K., Rogg, D. and Schulz, H. (1980) *The Research and Development Program Magnetically Suspended Suspended Transport Systems in the Federal Republic of Germany*, IEEE International Conference, 763–774.

(1984) *Maglev Transport Now and for the Future*, International Conference, Solihull, England, IMechE Conference Publications, 12.

Marx, H.-J. and Stöckl, R. (1993) Alignment and Surveying of Magnetic Levitation Train Guideways. *13th International Conference on Magnetically Levitated Systems and Linear Drives, Argonne, USA, May*, 201–205.

Masada, E. (1993) Development of Maglev Transportation in Japan – Present State and Future Prospects. *13th International Conference on Magnetically Levitated Systems and Linear Drives, Argonne, USA, May*, 1–6.

Miller, L. (1992) Safety and Availability of the High Speed Transportation System Transrapid. *6th World Conference on Transport Research, Lyon, France, June/July*, 3135–3146.

Miller, L. and Wackers, M. (1993) Transrapid Maglev System – Technical Readiness and Corridors of Application. *Journal of Advanced Transportation*, 27(1), 49–64.

MVP Versuchs- und Planungsgesellschaft für Magnetbahnsysteme mbH (1991) *Einsatzfelder neuer Schnellbahnsysteme (Magnetschnellbahn- und Rad/Schiene-Technologie)*, Kurzfassung, February.

Raschbichler, H.G. and Miller, L. (1991/1992) *Readiness for Application of the Transrapid Maglev System, RTR 33*, 9–14.

Raschbichler, H.G., Miller, L. and Wackers, M. (1993) Analysis of Prospective Transrapid Applications. *13th International Conference on Magnetically Levitated Systems and Linear Drives, Argonne, USA, May* 29–34.

MVP Versuchs- und Planungsgesellschaft für Magnetbahnsysteme mbH/Transrapid

International, Gesellschaft für Magnetbahnsysteme (1984) (eds) *Transrapid Maglev System*, Hestra-Verlag, Darmstadt.

Uher, R.A. (1989) The Role of High Speed Maglev in the Future US Transportation System. *International Conference Maglev '89, Yokohama, Japan, Proceedings, May.*

Department of Transportation/Federal Railroad Administration (1992) *Safety of High Speed Magnetic Levitation Transportation Systems, German High Speed Maglev Train Safety Requirements – Potential for Application in the United States*, DOT/FRA/ORD-92/02, Interim Report, February.

US Department of Transportation/Federal Railroad Administration (1992) *Improving Transportation Through Railroad Research (Period Covered 1988-1991)*, DOT/FRA/ORD-02/14, July.

Wiescholek, U., Mayer, W.J. and Rogg, D. (1993) High-Speed Magnetic Levitation Train Transrapid, Planning of the Development Program until 1995 and Prospects of Utilization in the Federal Republic of Germany. *13th International Conference on Magnetically Levitated Systems and Linear Drives, Argonne, USA, May*, 22-28.

9

Regional airlines in Europe

M.A. Ambrose

9.1 INTRODUCTION

It is generally accepted that the lessons of history help forecast the future. It is, therefore, appropriate that the first part of this paper should be devoted to briefly recounting the factors which have influenced the situation which exists today.

The European Regional Airlines Association (ERA) was formed in 1980 by what was then a very small group of airlines – in those days they were more often referred to as commuter airlines but this is a term which is fast fading into history. In forming ERA the airlines concerned were reacting to early efforts for so-called liberalization of civil aviation by the European Commission. Their move was soon recognized as more far-reaching than that by aircraft manufacturers, airports and many other elements of the industry which offered their support.

It was clear, even more than 10 years ago, that regional airlines were going to have a major role to play in a united Europe. It was, and is, a tough business to be in. In the early 1980s national carriers treated their smaller brethren with disdain whilst simultaneously claiming the protection of their national administrations to ensure that they were protected from the elements of competition which regional carriers could provide. The aircraft operated by the regional carriers were often outdated, uncomfortable and thirsty or hand-me-down aircraft from larger companies which were originally used on longer routes. Regional air transport was, more often than not, the world of the entrepreneur battling to produce a margin against difficult odds.

Many elements of the industry were aware that this situation was going to change and change quickly. Over the years ERA has received more than

Passenger Transport after 2000 AD. Edited by G.B.R. Feilden, A.H. Wickens and I.R. Yates. Published in 1994 by E & FN Spon, London. ISBN 0 419 19470 3.

its fair share of commitment from them. ERA is unique as a trade body with its regular airline members joined by a wide cross-section of supporting Associate members from the world-famous manufacturers complemented by many of Europe's airports and other supplier and service companies.

Today, their far-sightedness has paid off. ERA now has 50 airline members offering fast, regular and passenger-friendly services across western Europe and now extending into the new independent eastern European states. Regional air transport provided by ERA's members is a vital element of the continent's transport infrastructure. More importantly, it is a mode which is self-supporting, with virtually no public investment except in areas of public service need. ERA member airlines annual passengers carried is almost one in 12 Community citizens. All this has been achieved without significant environmental impact – unlike road and rail transport – enormously beneficial effect on regional economies.

9.2 EUROPEAN COMMITMENT

Regional air transport is a crucial power house for jobs and technological development in Europe. Likewise, Europe leads the world in the manufacture of regional aircraft, satisfying 2 out of 3 new aircraft deliveries for this sector of market. Its strong home market means that the regional air transport industry as a whole equates to around 4% of EC Gross Domestic Product. What can regional airline managements expect?

The pioneers which formed ERA in 1980 have been proved to be right, but why should they continue to support regional airline operations for the rest of the century and beyond? It is at this point that it is appropriate to stop looking backwards and step into the future.

At present, half the ERA fleet of aircraft – over 620 – is now about 5 years old. As the youngest fleet of any civil aviation sector it has produced a revolution in passenger perception of the comfort and efficiency of small airplanes. By the year 2000 however, much of the fleet will still be in service but by then will be around 12 years old. The cost of a complete and dramatic replacement programme is simply too high and competition on the relatively thin routes operated by regional carriers too constraining to enable their early retirement. Airlines will have to squeeze every last drop of return out of their investment.

In the same time period, growth in the market will demand a much larger fleet so that the 5-year average age is likely to survive as a statistic. What will have become the out-dated technology of today's modern regional airliner will be matched by the exciting aircraft now rolling out of the manufacturer's hangars. The process of renewal has already begun.

Thanks to the regional sector's healthy growth, even during the year of the Gulf War in which the regional sector was the only part of civil air transport to expand (it achieved a growth of more than 10%), the manufacturing industry has still been able to invest in technological development aimed specifically at the demands of regional airlines in spite of the current European economic recession. In 1992 and 1993, 4 new aircraft types have been produced with at least 3 more in production. All of these aircraft have been custom-designed to the needs of regional sector economics, passengers and the environment.

For example, a European-built regional aircraft, the Saab 340, launched 10 years ago has achieved a 60% market share in Europe. Its new stable-mate, the Saab 2000, has the fly-by-wire technology of the latest transcontinental jets but also has highly advanced propeller design, producing a very quiet and agile aircraft.

A similar step has been taken by Germany's Dornier, whose established regional aircraft is the Dornier 228. Dornier have now stepped into the marketplace with the Dornier 328, a larger, more technologically advanced aircraft with an airfield performance enabling it to operate efficiently and safely from even the smallest airfields.

Fokker, which has been a major player in regional aircraft production for the past 3 decades, has launched a new 70-seat twin-jet (the Fokker 70), Spain's CASA has announced plans to develop the CASA 3000 which is a high speed turboprop operating at jet altitudes. In Britain, the Jetstream 41, rolled out only a couple of years ago as a larger version of the Jetstream 31, has already achieved a high level of market success. All of these programmes, which by no means constitute an exhaustive list of European activities, will help Europe maintain its dominance in the regional aircraft market. Each of Europe's major industrialized nations has some significant share in regional aircraft airframe or engine production.

Even so, the rest of the world is also committing itself to upgrading the regional fleet. The Canadair Regional Jet has recently been introduced with Lufthansa, and the Brazilian manufacturer Embraer is finalizing plans to start production of a competing 50-seat twin-jet, the Embraer 145. Avro (née British Aerospace) is gaining more market share with its latest RJ version.

9.3 A GREENER SKY

The aircraft which will fly the ERA network in the year 2000 will constitute advanced turboprops with an ever-increasing number of new jet types. They will use existing technology but closely tailored and developed to the operational marketplace needs of the customer and operator. Although plans will also be laid during the coming decade for the following generation of aircraft it cannot be expected that the industry will be able to achieve anything more than evolutionary progress. To expect revolutionary changes is unrealistic. Civil air transport in general and the regional sector in particular remains a long way from hydrogen-power or similar advanced techniques for use in anything other than highly specialized applications. Indeed, given the commendable environmental performance of regional sector operations – regional operators contribute less than 0.2% of manufactured emissions – coupled with the major investment necessary to introduce ultra-advanced technology, there are strong arguments against possible environmental legislation which would compel artificially high development requirements.

International regulations led by the International Civil Aviation Organisation and driven by the demands of airports and the public to reduce noise nuisance have been bettered by regional sector aircraft. What has not been apparent is that the industry has received little or no credit for its environmental investment in terms of increased hours of operation and that the regional sector has out-performed all existing regulations.

It is easy to predict that stricter environmental legislation will be applied over the next few years but much of it is likely to ignore the superb environmental performance of existing regional aircraft types. The reason is simple. Much of the industry's self-regulation has resulted in performance levels which have bettered the requirements of international regulations. The achievement of these levels has been driven by the demands of airports to reduce noise nuisance but, more importantly, by the economic necessity of minimizing fuel consumption. Meanwhile, miss-directed governmental investment which has restricted runway capacity development has encouraged the creation of high speed rail and motorway links throughout the countryside of Europe.

Whereas it is easy to show that aircraft emissions of hydrocarbons, carbon monoxide, oxides of nitrogen and smoke have consistently reduced since 1970, road and rail cannot demonstrate parallel and equivalent achievement. Currently, regional airlines in Europe consume less than 7% of the total fuel burn of European aviation as a whole and, moreover, the height at which the bulk of regional aircraft operate means that there is little or no effect on the ozone layer.

During the next few years it is important that the existing and projected environmental performance of regional aircraft should be recognized in the formulation of Europe's overall transport policy. Although existing technology can be further stretched to produce marginal gains in environmental performance it is important to realize that the situation is now being reached in which a gain in one area can often result in a deterioration in another. However, as Europe's transport policies develop it would be wholly unreasonable if air transport were to be subjected to environmental constraints and penalties not imposed on other modes operating with inferior environmental standards.

9.4 AIR TRAFFIC SYSTEM INFRASTRUCTURE

The development of an integrated air traffic control system would, without doubt, enable civil air transport to avoid unnecessary fuel burns as well as going a long way towards eliminating delays causing ground congestion – another form of pollution – and allowing the airlines to produce a better product. Such a system is however a long way away.

For the past quarter of a century the member states of Europe have, with the best of intentions, developed their own systems with comparatively little thought to the way in which these might integrate into other state systems, even where these other systems may be in neighbouring states. Many facilities have been shown to be incompatible and much work and research has been unnecessarily duplicated. The task of transforming these discrete systems into an integrated super-system, devoid of national interests, wasteful practices and with streamlined management is immense. Yet, throughout the past 25 years airlines have had to fund the establishment of these individual empires with little or no meaningful say in the way in which the authorities concerned have conducted their affairs.

When airlines had navigation and air traffic control facilities provided by states free of charge then it was quite reasonable that states should maintain a full authority over the operation and control of the facilities they provided. The move to full recovery of the costs associated with these facilities and services by the imposition of a full charging policy on airspace users changed the nature of the air transport industry/state authority relationship.

If states wish to recover their full costs then it is only fair that the air transport organizations, whether as airlines, business aviation or general aviation, should have a more direct influence in the provision of the facilities and services concerned and the policies associated with them. The relationship should be in the form of a partnership. Sadly, this situation does not exist and many states continue to adopt the principle of 'aunty knows best'. As a result, the overwhelming feeling within the air transport industry is that, whilst having respect for the abilities and skills of individual technicians within the state authorities, no serious attempt has been made to place them on the same levels of efficiency and performance as those which the realities of the commercial world demand must be achieved by airlines.

9.5 TOWARDS SUSTAINABLE MOBILITY

In recent months the European Commission has produced a White Paper on its thoughts concerning environmental protection and the creation of conditions for sustainable mobility. Within the White Paper the

Commission puts forward various ideas which many observers believe are unachievable.

The Commission recognizes that there are imbalances in the present conditions under which various transport modes operate and it seeks to eliminate these distortions. The most obvious distortion is the degree to which rail transport has the benefit of massive and consistent financial subsidy by governments throughout Europe. As simple examples, in 1991 the Italian rail system lost US$6.5 billion and in 1992 the German rail system had an operating loss of US$15 billion. Compare these two sample figures, both of which were recently reported in the *Financial Times*, with the loss reported by IATA for the world's international air services for 1992 of US$4 billion! Comparatively small change in market conditions for airlines can turn the current losses into break even. There is not one national rail system in Europe which could operate without major government subsidy.

When the dimensions of discrimination in favour of rail are so large it is hard to believe that even the European Commission will be able to eliminate this sort of imbalance. The Commission's good intentions are not doubted but the adjustment which would be necessary to rail fares and operating systems to achieve comparable levels of economic self-sufficiency between rail and air would be politically unacceptable. No European government seeking to implement this type of change would survive.

Yet, even with this level of annual public subsidy, it is evident from the development plans for the European high speed rail system that railways will continue to enjoy public funding for well into the next century – if not forever. They enjoy other favourable discrimination. Unlike air transport neither rail nor road is constrained by nightly curfews. Airports are subjected to intense scrutiny by noise-measuring agencies and limitations put on aircraft performance according to population densities in the vicinity of airports. Most transport industry observers will be familiar with the by now 'traditional' noise footprint diagram for airports. Few, if any, will have seen a noise footprint for a high speed train based on the same parameters and requirements as those imposed on civil aviation. Road transport is granted even more freedom.

9.6 REGIONAL OPPORTUNITIES

As regional airport development accelerates to cater for local markets and those markets show continuing growth, the case for shifting emphasis to more regional services becomes very powerful indeed. Passengers who have in the past been obliged to accept travel to their nearest hub airport are now able to use their local regional airport to meet many of their travel requirements. The increasing range of direct services from regional points bypassing national hub airports is a common phenomenon throughout Europe.

Substantial investment by regional airport managements is supporting this trend. In the UK new terminals opened at Manchester and Birmingham and the opening of London City Airport are good examples. In continental Europe, the creation of purpose-built facilities at Stockholm–Arlanda and Amsterdam–Schiphol airports underline the importance of the new range of regional services. A recent study undertaken by the University of Rotterdam confirmed that most regional authorities believe the benefits of regional airport services and facilities to be self-evident. They provide international accessibility, stimulate local industry and commerce and have a job-multiplier effect.

Yet, with such obvious economic and social benefits resulting from regional air services to the regions themselves, it is surprising that so many states within Europe are prepared to focus their attention and policies solely on the needs of hub airports. As congestion worsens at Europe's principal hubs there is an increasing temptation to manipulate the pricing policies for airport charges to eliminate smaller airlines. The result is that a state which has supported the liberalization of air transport for the past decade – for very sound reasons, including regional economic development – can find that the essential air communications to its own regions have been eliminated owing to the pricing policy of its principal national airport. In recent weeks the UKCAA, having recognized this trend, has passed the problem up to the Department of Transport for resolution.

9.7 CONCLUSION

Europe's regional airlines have been one of the principal beneficiary sectors from the liberalization process. In constructing each of the successive stages of liberalization leading up to the so-called 'Third Package' implemented on the 1st January 1993, the European Commission has recognized the economic and social value to Europe as a whole of regional air services.

Similarly, Europe's aerospace manufacturing industry is a major asset. It dominates world supply of new regional aircraft. It accounts for almost 4% of Europe's GDP. About one third of its products are for home consumption.

The spectacular growth in the regional air sector is strong evidence of public demand for local air services. Past protectionist policies requiring travel through a national hub airport have prohibited this demand from being satisfied. The new liberalized regime encourages it.

All the ingredients exist for continuing prosperity of regional air transport operations provided that these are not unnecessarily inhibited by miss-directed environment policies, lack of government and political courage in planning additional facilities and capacity and control over those agencies which impose charges on the airlines concerned.

If adequate airport and ATC capacity can be provided then Europe's regional airlines have the equipment, motivation and skills to continue making a valuable contribution to Europe's overall development.

Part Three

Intercontinental and
Transcontinental Traffic

10

From physics to customers: the Jet Age Phase II

R.A. Davis

10.1 INTRODUCTION

I bet most people can remember their commercial first airplane ride. Mine was in 1951. I was 18 years old. I flew from Spokane to Chicago on a Northwest Airlines Boeing Stratocruiser. Since that first ride I have become an airplane designer ... and have spent many hours flying aboard jet-powered transports all over the world. I have changed, aviation has changed and passenger expectations have changed.

The Jet Age Phase II is shaping up to be quite different from the Jet Age Phase I. The paper concerns this and how it is leading to the reinvention of Boeing.

The Jet Age took hold in the late 1940s with the first swept wing, jet-powered airplane. At Boeing, the six-engine military B-47 and the eight-engine B-52 were followed by the commercial 707. The 707 had four engines and carried as many as 189 passengers. Then came the 727 trijet followed by the 737 twin in 1967, the 747 jumbo in 1970 and the 757 and 767 large modern twinjet airliners in 1982. Along the way, the 737 and 747 have been modernized and the whole family of jet airplanes have been continually improved.

There was something different about the *first* phase of the Jet Age than there is in the *second* phase – the phase we are in today. In the first part of the Jet Age, the emphasis was on

- speed
- distance
- altitude.

Passenger Transport after 2000 AD. Edited by G.B.R. Feilden, A.H. Wickens and I.R. Yates. Published in 1994 by E & FN Spon, London. ISBN 0 419 19470 3.

We accomplished that task very well. A Boeing jetliner now takes off or lands every two seconds. Of every $10 the airlines have paid for jets, $6 have been for Boeing jets. Worldwide, the safety record for modern jetliners is very good. Each new generation of jets has been safer than its predecessor. Last year, over 1.2 trillion revenue passenger miles were flown.

We looked physics in the eye during this first phase. We made airplanes fly across continents and then oceans. We made them bigger and faster. We put on better engines and made twinjets go long distances. We leveraged engineering, especially propulsion and aerodynamics, to dramatically cut fuel burn and increase range and payload. We succeeded in dropping the cost of air travel so that it became commonplace in much of the world.

We have always provided value for the airlines and passengers, but the emphasis is changing. *Now* the biggest leverage is in areas like yield management, cabin flexibility, operations research, maintenance and the cost of ownership, manufacturing and productivity.

In the first phase we looked physics in the eye; now we're looking at the customer.

The air transportation business is in a crisis. Many airlines are struggling financially and operationally. The industry has been hit by enormous operating losses – between five and ten billion US dollars over the last three years, depending on the basis of calculation. This is a lot of money to lose. Airlines are demanding more value and lower-priced airplanes. They want airplanes that are less expensive to own and operate, and ones that are more easily adapted to market changes.

10.2 REINVENTING BOEING

If we continue in the same way as the first phase, we will fail. There will be wonderful flying machines, but they will not be affordable and profitable for airlines. Passengers will miss out on affordable air travel. Things are changing. Just to keep providing safe, affordable air travel in a way that makes the airlines successful means Boeing must change itself. Some say Boeing is 'reinventing' itself. This will reshape aviation.

We are reinventing Boeing to be *more intently customer driven*, and by 'customer' we mean not only the airlines we sell to, but also the ultimate customer, the passenger. The focus is on providing value, producing more cost-effective airplanes that satisfy airlines and passengers. To do this we are focusing on:

- customer needs;
- working together;
- reducing costs;
- shortening product flow time.

Reinvention to be more intently customer driven is causing us to:

- set new standards;
- make enormous long-term investments;
- ensure that technology is applied in ways that make airlines successful and safe.

We are asking our engineers to be masters of change, to apply technology to, and work with, manufacturing and most importantly, directly and intently with our customers.

Manufacturing engineers, design engineers, tool planners, finance experts, maintenance specialists, and customers are teamed together to create our seventh commercial jetliner, the 777. There are nearly 200 design/build teams. These teams include representatives from all major functions, including customers and suppliers, where necessary.

So far, the teams are working even better than we hoped they would. We have essentially completed the airplane design, and every indication is that the 777 is coming together more smoothly than anything we have ever done before. For example, instead of the planned 19 weeks to assemble the first 777 floor beams, it actually took just three weeks.

Here is another example. Compared to our last two models, the 757 and 767, we have seen a large reduction in drawing changes. That means that we are doing a better job of coming up with the right design for every part the first time. When you are dealing with three million parts, that is no small accomplishment.

To be fair, part of the gain is the result of new computer technology. Our digital design system lets our engineers see problems much earlier than before. The computer makes it very clear when one team's conduit cannot fit through another team's spar. That is one reason why we are reducing the number of design changes so dramatically. The computer detects potential mistakes long before they appear in our manufacturing process.

The 'working together' teams are transforming manufacturing and design. Plans are to telescope the traditional steps of design, tooling and manufacturing into concurrent activities. It is happening right now in our factory. On the new 767 freighter program, we expect to cut 25% of the flow time from the development process.

We are having to reduce our cycle times to satisfy better the airlines that do not want to stand in line for three years waiting for a new airplane. In three years, the economy can change dramatically. Airlines may no longer need the airplane, or need a completely different kind of plane. That's why we are cutting cycle time, such as working toward reducing the flow time from 13 to six months for a 737.

Flow time reductions go hand-in-hand with reducing costs – and passing savings on to airlines and funding innovations to further reduce costs.

Airlines are having to be quick on their feet, too. They are faced with a certain reinvention of their own. They need airplanes in which they can rearrange the location of seats, galleys and lavatories, to almost anywhere in the cabin, within a matter of hours. When the new 777 goes into service in 1995, its operators will be able to rearrange it within hours. Within hours! They will be able to re-configure the interior to one, two or three classes. This way the plane can serve one market one day, another the next day. To airlines this is a serious business. It can make the difference between being in business or not.

Becoming more intently customer driven is not easy. Airlines want less expensive airplanes. We are having to sharpen our pencils. Our goal is to reduce our costs by 25–30%. Technology and working together concepts are being applied to reduce manufacturing costs and improve productivity.

Over and over again we are hearing customers say they want lower costs rather than high-tech features. So each time technology is considered we ask: At what cost? What is the benefit to the customer? It was a major consideration in choosing the amount of lightweight composite materials on the 777. Though technically feasible to have more than 10% of the airframe weight in composites, development and manufacturing costs dictated against it.

Reinventing ourselves to be more intently customer driven and agile is causing us to *set new standards* and it is driving enormous *long-term investments*.

- Investments in training: we are re-tooling our people as well as our factories. We are putting our offices, workshops, and research labs figuratively – and sometimes literally – on wheels so we can become more flexible and ready to change to the next project quickly.
- We are spending over a third of a billion dollars on a non-flying airplane. This is really an airplane within a building – a giant Integrated Aircraft Systems Laboratory inside the Lab. There will be seven engineering simulator labs, an 'iron bird' and over 50 functional laboratories. The 777 Systems Integration Laboratory will bring all the 777 avionics and electrical systems together with production wiring harnesses so they can be tested as an integrated system in simulated flight conditions. The Systems Integration Lab provides essentially a 'sixth test airplane' – a *full year* before the 777 first flight.
- Our flight testing and validation test program is going *far beyond anything ever seen before in the industry*. Standard certification flight tests will be supplemented with 1000 flight cycles on each airframe/engine combination to demonstrate reliability in simulated airline operating environments. United Airlines, British Airways and Cathay Pacific will participate in the 1000 cycle 'service ready' testing. In navy terms, it is like a series of shake-down cruises – 3,000 in all.

'Looking the customer in the eye,' has resulted in some new applications of good solid engineering. Human factor engineering is, for example, being heavily applied to maintenance needs. Airline maintenance costs and dispatch reliability are big ticket items for customers. Maintenance people now join the engineers early in the design process – with good results.

For example, face-to-face interaction with a customer taught us that an access handle we had designed was just fine – if you had bare hands. Unfortunately, a lot of this airline's mechanics work in Chicago, in the winter. They were not too excited about taking off their gloves to grab a freezing chunk of metal. We listened, and changed the design, making it possible to open the door and to close it properly without having to take off your gloves. The result? A higher quality product for the customer, with less chance of maintenance error.

Applying technology in a way that helps the airline be successful, while providing safe affordable air travel, is the emphasis in the Jet Age Phase II. This is part of the 'reinvention'. ETOPS is an example. ETOPS is an acronym for extended-range twin-engine operations – long-range flight using modern twin-engine airplanes.

Second-generation jet engines have fewer problems initially and obtain high levels of reliability faster than did early generation jet engines. This, combined with improvements in airplane system reliability, has enabled ETOPS flights to become routine and successful. The safety record is enviable, so much so that some airlines have applied ETOPS standards to three- and four-engine airplanes to improve their reliability.

With ETOPS, airlines have opened international routes between secondary cities, reduced congestion at major airports and given the passenger safe affordable travel – just what is needed in the 21st century.

10.3 PRODUCTS OF THE REINVENTION

Today there are around 10 000 commercial jet transports (excluding the former Soviet airplanes). Another 12 000 new airplanes will be delivered by the year 2010. A third of these will replace older airplanes. Two-thirds – 8000 – will be to accommodate growth.

The airplanes designed and built today are likely to be around for the large part of the next century. Here is a snapshot of these airplanes, and other future products.

I've talked about the new *Model 777* that will roll-out of our factory in March 1994. The design is truly customer-driven. We have worked with most major airline customers for five years. Powered by two 74–84 000 pound thrust engines, it will carry 375 to 400 passengers transcontinental. New airfoils, and the largest wingspan ever for a twinjet give range and performance. It has side-by-side flat panel displays in the flight deck, improved economics, passenger amenities and cabin flexibility features that should please both passengers and airline.

What else lies ahead? We have spent the last two years gathering requirements from our customers for the next generation of 737. Their message is that simplicity and reliabilitv head the list. It is a good airplane – make it better and reduce the cost. Right now we are in the verification step of the *737-X* development process. Teams from Boeing are out listening to customers. The configuration they are evaluating has a modified wing with a larger span and new engines with improvements in noise, fuel burn and thrust. These changes provide transcontinental range and increased speed.

In the medium-size category, some customers see the potential for more range for the 767–300. We are discussing a growth version which would be capable of flying up to 1000 nautical miles further. Interior revisions are being considered to make it more flexible for airline needs by applying the technology and lessons learned from the 777.

The *767 freighter* – mentioned earlier – will provide our customers a medium-sized cargo airplane to complement the existing 757 and 747-400 freighter airplanes. The 767 freighter will certify in 1995.

In response to customers who may need additional seating, we are studying a *stretch version of the 777* that would offer 20% more capacity.

In the large airplane category, customers are asking for even greater capacity than the existing 747. We are studying increased carrying capacity and range with a gross weight of over 410 metric tons (in excess of 900 000 pounds).

For the end of this decade, some airlines have expressed interest in an airplane *larger than the 747-400*. Boeing has been meeting with potential customers to understand their requirements and define possible configurations. These include a stretched 747, or an all-new airplane with initial seating capacity up to 600. Future derivatives could carry possibly even more passengers.

Airlines have asked Boeing to study airplane speed – the next realm of choice for their passengers. Projected Pacific Rim traffic growth indicates that a market for the supersonic *High Speed Civil Transport (HSCT)* could materialize in the next century. At Mach 2.4 such an airplane could carry you from Los Angeles to Tokyo in about four hours, less than half the time needed today. The critical issues facing the HSCT are community noise, engine emissions and economics. Our continued work on the HSCT will posture us to provide the best solutions to airlines.

To ensure airlines get the most value from these products, we are working to 'reinvent' the approach to global systems and infrastructure. We have teams dedicated to developing worldwide standards for airline information systems and a global aeronautical telecommunications network. We are also working toward worldwide aviation standards for data links, airplane type-design certification, maintenance and operations. These are customer-driven. They are needed for safety and for the success of the airlines. The payoff will be most apparent in the 21st century.

10.4 CONCLUSION

You would not expect aviation to look the same from its first century to its second. It will not; and Boeing will not.

You are already seeing changes. The fanfare and curtain rising for a newly proposed airplane has been replaced with discussions and listening, verification talks and more listening – all centred around customers and what they need. This highlights the importance of working together with customers and satisfying them.

Boeing is in the process of reinventing itself, which will reshape aviation. We led the first phase of the Jet Age, now we are preparing for the second. In the first phase we looked physics in the eye – we went higher, faster and further; we leveraged technology. In the next phase of the Jet Age, the focus is more intently on the customer. The opportunities for providing value will come most directly from satisfying customer needs. Technology remains important, but we will make it *even more* responsible for airlines' success and for providing safe, affordable air travel. We are reinventing ourselves to focus more intently on the customer by working together, cutting costs and being agile and responsive.

Things have changed since my first flight. I believe we will see some of the finest transportation products and services to ever grace the face of the Earth.

11

Regional aircraft

J. Schäffler

11.1 INTRODUCTION

There are three segments to the air transport system: intercontinental traffic; continental traffic; and the third segment – commuter and regional operations. This paper is concerned with the third category.

Commuter aircraft are normally turboprops operating on shorter stages, defined here as 15–70 seaters, whereas regional aircraft are jets with higher capacity and longer ranges. Generally stage lengths of less than 1500 km are considered to be regional traffic. Commuter aircraft are competing in USA, Europe and Japan at the lower end of their spectrum with ground transportation systems, such as road and rail.

The structure of commuter/regional air traffic is influenced by:

- politics;
- regulations;
- infrastructure on the ground and in the air;
- structure of the operators;
- structure of the manufacturers;
- advances in technology.

11.2 MARKET AND ACTIVITY

11.2.1 Transport activity development by mode

Figure 11.1 shows the activity of different modes of transport within Europe during the last 20 years. The analysis is valid for Europe, but the picture would probably look similar for the US and Japan. An analysis of

Passenger Transport after 2000 AD. Edited by G.B.R. Feilden, A.H. Wickens and I.R. Yates. Published in 1994 by E & FN Spon, London. ISBN 0 419 19470 3.

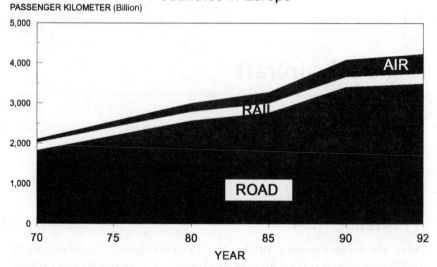

Figure 11.1 Transport activity development by mode.

the traffic activity in passenger-kilometers over this time period shows a doubling of traffic. It should be noted that:

- air traffic is growing at the fastest rate;
- road traffic is providing the bulk of the passenger transport, and is growing by a factor of two;
- rail is stagnant, even after introducing faster trains in the 1980s.

For distances beyond 1000 km air traffic is without competition. In the journey length band of 500–1000 km, rail systems might gain some traffic from air transport, if their average speed can be increased considerably, while maintaining frequency and the necessary minimum load factor.

11.2.2 Current traffic distribution

Figure 11.2 illustrates the share that regional and commuter traffic had of the total world traffic in 1992. From this, it can be seen that commuter and regional operations together made up only about 17% of the total world (excluding the Commonwealth of Independent States) Revenue Passenger Kilometer (RPK) performance. This traffic is performed almost exclusively on journey segments of less than 1500 km.

Taking the commuter market, almost 60% of the productivity is located in North America, followed by 20% in Europe, 13% in Asia/Pacific and the rest in Africa and Latin America. In the regional markets, again North

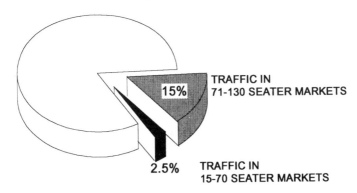

Figure 11.2 Share of regional traffic in 1992, when total world traffic is 2050 billion RPK.

America, including Canada, the United States, Mexico and the Caribbean plays a major role, with 35% of the world productivity. Europe, with 27% of the world productivity, follows the North American market.

11.2.3 Regional traffic flow patterns in 1992

Regional traffic flow patterns can be divided into two general groups: hub-and-spoke systems; and point-to-point operations (Figure 11.3). In the USA, after deregulation, traffic patterns changed significantly and hub-and-spoke systems were built up. Although some airlines have been retreating recently from some unprofitable hubs, the US system is currently orientated strongly towards hubbing. This trend should continue.

In Europe, however, liberalization up to now has actually encouraged point-to-point operations, since restrictions on traffic rights to and from hubs and airport congestion have all helped this development. Despite hubbing efforts of some airlines, there should be some more increase in point-to-point flights.

In Asia traffic flows are divided about evenly between the two groups. The demographic profile supports significant hub operations in this area. Some increase in fragmentation should be expected in the future, however.

11.2.4 Regional aircraft in operation since 1980

Figure 11.4 illustrates the numbers of aircraft in passenger-airline use only from 1980 to 1992. In the smallest commuter category, DHC-6 and Beech 9 aircraft were the dominant type. In the largest-sized aircraft category, the F 27 and BAe 748 were the dominant aircraft types. It can be seen that at the end of 1979, nearly 2000 commuter aircraft were in operation. Of this total, only 120 (or 6%) were in the 21–40-seater categories. However, the

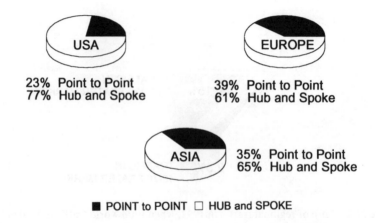

Figure 11.3 Regional traffic flow patterns, 1992 (passenger operations under 1500 km).

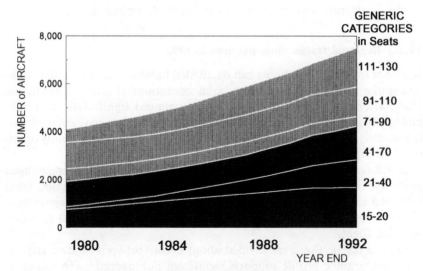

Figure 11.4 Regional aircraft in operation.

development during the 1980s shows a significant market-share-gain of this 21–40-seater size of aircraft. Here, the aircraft DHC-8, ATR-42 and SAAB 340 played a major role. The 15–20-seater category can also be seen to gain through Metro and BAe Jetstream 31 deliveries.

At the end of 1979, the regional aircraft categories were dominated by the 91–110-seater aircraft, such as the DC9 and B737. Although the 71–90 and the 91–110-seater aircraft in operation stayed constant throughout the 1980s, significant deliveries of B737-500 and -300 into the largest-sized

Generic Categories In Seats ►	15-20	21-40	41-70	71-90	91-110	111-130
Aircraft Considered:						
In Production ►	Do.228	Do.328	Fo.50	Fo.70	Fo.100	A319*⁾
	BAe J31	BAe J41	BAe J61	BAe RJ80	BAe RJ100	B737-300*⁾
	Metro	DHC-8-100	DHC-8-300		B737-500	B737-500
	Beech	Saab 340	Saab 2000			MD87*⁾
	1900D	C.212	CN-235			
		EMB-120	ATR-42			
			ATR-72			
			Can. RJ			
Out of Production ►	DHC-6	Shorts	F.27	F.28	BAC1-11	DC9-30
	EMB-110	330/360	DHC-7		DC9-10/30	B737-200
	Beech 99	Gulfstream 1	An-24/26		B737-100	
	L-410	YAK-40	CV-580		B737-200	
						*⁾ partly

Figure 11.5 Generic categories of aircraft.

category during the second half of last decade made the B737 the dominating aircraft by the end of 1992.

11.3 PRODUCT CATEGORY DEFINITIONS

11.3.1 Generic categories of aircraft

Aircraft categories are defined by a number of elements. The seating capacity and spacing between the capacity-bands of aircraft is primarily defined by the market and the operational requirement for serving the market economically. Figure 11.5 lists the aircraft both in and out of production according to their generic categories defined by the seating capacities.

Certification rules for both aircraft and operators define conceptions and many details, while regulations exercise influence on the operation and design. Economics and available technologies are another important element in defining the aircraft categories. Smaller aircraft operating on shorter routes generally use slower turboprops, whereas larger aircraft for longer hauls use jet-propulsion. Currently, there is a trend for higher speed turboprops.

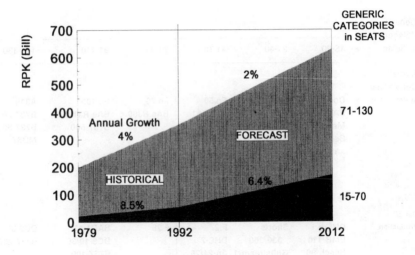

Figure 11.6 Regional traffic development until 2012.

11.4 REGIONAL TRAFFIC DEVELOPMENT

By the year AD 2012, it is estimated that commuter traffic will increase 3.4 times to about 170 billion RPK. The increase in regional markets during this time will be about 1.5 times. The future growth in the commuter market, however, will be lower than its 13-year historical average of 8.5%. An annual average of 6.4% is estimated for the future, mainly due to the stabilization of the market development in the US (Figure 11.6). It should be noted that this historical growth is, however, an average of slower growth in the beginning of the last decade and the double-digit boom of the second half.

Although traffic growth in regional markets has been about 4% in the past, it will be on average only about 2% by 2012. In the US domestic market where, during the last several years traffic growth has been low (indicating a possible maturation), future growth could be even lower than 2%. At the end of the year 2012, the share of the commuter and regional traffic will be 3.5 and 8.5% respectively, down from 17.5%, of the total world traffic today. Thus, the commuter share should grow from today's 2.5%, while the regional share will drop from its actual 15%.

11.5 AIRCRAFT AGE AND REPLACEMENT NEEDS

Aircraft replacement and retirement assumptions play a significant role in the future demand for new aircraft. Unless the replacement plans of an airline are known, it is assumed that aircraft will stay within the present fleets with the following operational lives:

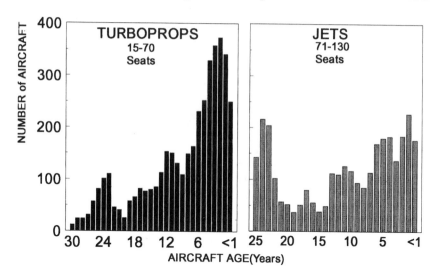

Figure 11.7 Current aircraft age distribution.

- *Commuter:*   20–30 years (depending on aircraft type)
- *Regional jets:* old generation: 22 years
                    new generation: 25 years

Figure 11.7 shows the present age distribution of all the world's commuter and regional passenger aircraft. Whilst the turboprop fleets are very young, regional jet fleet age is distributed relatively evenly with three age peaks.

All jet aircraft which do not fulfil the FAA/ICAO Stage 3 regulations must be out of service or silenced around the year 2000 in most parts of the world. An in-house study of the re-engining and hush-kitting market showed that about 370 Stage 2 twin-engined passenger aircraft will be re-engined or hush-kitted (mainly the latter) and fly after the above-mentioned deadline.

In addition to the ongoing replacement cycle for regional aircraft, significant replacement potentials are expected in 18–20 years for both generic categories.

11.6 MARKET POTENTIAL 1993–2012

11.6.1 Number of aircraft

The total market potential (excluding the CIS) for passenger aircraft between 15 and 130 seats for replacement and for growth is about 9000 aircraft. This will be divided in the following way (Figure 11.8):

- *Commuter aircraft (<70 seats):*   6000 aircraft
- *Regional aircraft (70–130 seats):* 3000 aircraft

1993-2012

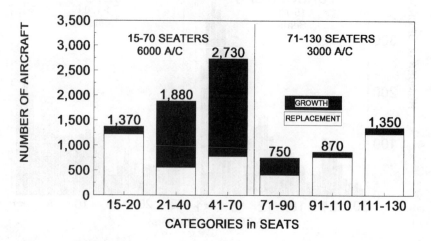

Figure 11.8 The potential for new deliveries of aircraft between 1993 and 2012.

Figure 11.8 shows the distribution of the 9000 aircraft potential into six product segments. In the 15–20, 91–110 and 111–130 seat product categories, the replacement market rather than the growth market is dominant, with almost 90% of the deliveries. The other seat product categories show the strongest potential in growth, rather than replacement.

The 1993 DASA World Market Forecast of all passenger aircraft shows 16 800 deliveries during the next 20 years. Commuter and regional markets make up about half of the total. This is an impressive number, but not in dollars and cents.

11.6.2 Business volume

Figure 11.9 shows the sales value of the world commuter and regional market potential, again divided into six product categories, as in Figure 11.8. The total commuter sales is US\$55 billion (1993). This is about 6.5% of the 20-year world total capital need for all passenger aircraft, which is US\$835 billion. About 63% of the aircraft will be in product categories above 41 seats, so these larger aircraft represent by far the largest part of the world commuter potential.

With about US\$97 billion, the regional aircraft market potential represents 12% of all world passenger aircraft potential in sales value. Commuter and regional sales together make up about 18% of the world business. All sales values are calculated with comparable aircraft list prices at economic conditions in January 1993.

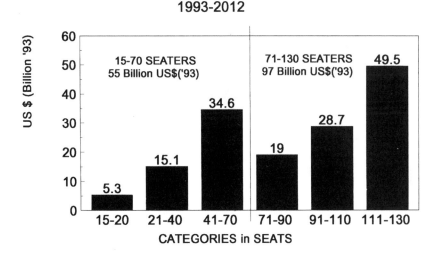

Figure 11.9 The potential for an increase in business volume between 1993 and 2012.

11.6.3 Geographical distribution

Figure 11.10 shows that the largest portion of the 9000 commuter and regional aircraft potential will be delivered to North America. North America and Europe combined will take 70% of future commuter deliveries. In this category, the Far East market is not significant.

It should be pointed out here that in the past, about 25% of commuter aircraft deliveries have been for non-passenger use. These deliveries were distributed differently. However, for the next 20 years, aircraft deliveries for non-passenger use should be 15–20%. Major markets for these will be in the Far East and the rest of the world.

As far as regional aircraft are concerned, North American and European airlines will be the major customers. The ongoing liberalization in Europe and the fleet replacement needs of Eastern European airlines will continue to create opportunities for regional jet aircraft sales.

11.7 FUTURE FLEET DEVELOPMENT

Figure 11.11 shows that the commuter aircraft capacity in SKM at the end of the forecast period is nearly three times that of 1992. However, the number of aircraft increases only by a factor of 1.8, which reflects the continuing introduction of larger aircraft. The 15–20 seaters represent the largest portion of the fleet at present. They will decline to only 24% of the number of aircraft in the year 2012. The stable fleet size for smallest commuters

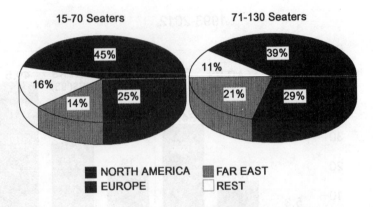

Figure 11.10 The geographical distribution of the potential new deliveries of aircraft.

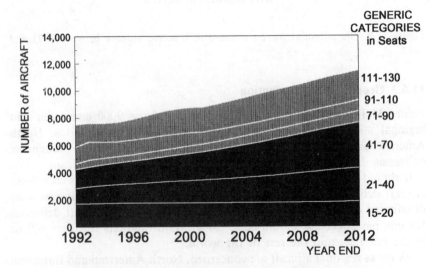

Figure 11.11 Future fleet development.

is a reflection of rapid capacity growth of the markets and also to an extent of increasing restrictions on small aircraft operations from congested airports.

A significant growth in the number of aircraft is occurring in the 21–40 and 41–70 seat categories, despite the increasing number of highly productive fast turboprop aircraft being introduced during the 1990s. Due to a relatively modern fleet, retirements of these aircrafts over the next ten years will be low.

The world regional aircraft fleet size will remain constant at approximately 3300 aircraft, with a slight increase towards the end of the forecast

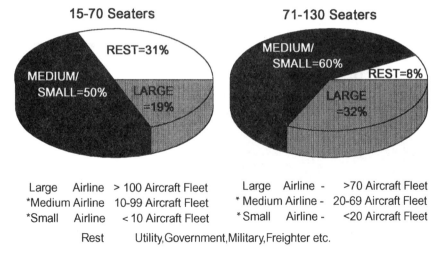

15-70 Seaters

REST=31%

MEDIUM/
SMALL=50%

LARGE
=19%

71-130 Seaters

MEDIUM/
SMALL=60%

REST=8%

LARGE
=32%

Large	Airline	> 100 Aircraft Fleet	Large	Airline -	>70 Aircraft Fleet
*Medium	Airline	10-99 Aircraft Fleet	* Medium	Airline -	20-69 Aircraft Fleet
*Small	Airline	< 10 Aircraft Fleet	* Small	Airline -	<20 Aircraft Fleet

Rest   Utility,Government,Military,Freighter etc.

* Airlines in Code-Sharing with Reservation Systems of large Airlines

Figure 11.12 Customer profile in 1992.

period. Within the regional generic category, 111–130 seater fleets will dominate after the year 2000.

11.8 CUSTOMER PROFILE

Currently, small and medium-sized airlines cover more than 50% of the fleets in commuter/regional aircraft worldwide. This can be seen in Figure 11.12. Large airlines today already control 19% of the market with the 15–70 seater category, and 32% of this market segment with the 71–30 seater aircraft. Reservation systems and code-sharing have increased the influence of trunk airlines on commuter/regional air traffic well beyond the above percentages.

While the ongoing process of concentration in airline structures will increase the influence of large carriers, a considerable portion of commuter/regional operations will stay with small carriers.

11.9 AIRCRAFT FINANCING NEEDS

The capital requirements for regional and trunk operators during the next 10 years is estimated to be US$380 billion, nearly the same as that of the last 20 years (Figure 11.13). There is concern over the financeability of such requirements for the following reasons:

- there has been a significant jump in world capital needs due to political changes in the beginning of the 1990s;

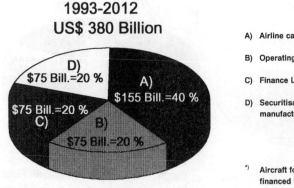

**1993-2012
US$ 380 Billion**

A) Airline cash flow, asset sale, new debt

B) Operating Leasing *)

C) Finance Leasing

D) Securitisation packages, export credit, manufacturer support

*) Aircraft for this purpose will have to be financed by lessors with some of the methods noted in A), C) and D).

Figure 11.13 Aircraft financing requirements in US$ (1993).

- traditional forms of aircraft financing have come under pressure during the last three years due to a dramatic drop in aircraft values and very poor airline financial performance.

In addition to the banking sector financing, which played a major role in the 1980s, new sources of capital such as securization will have to be made more accessible. For this to happen, full airline profitability must return, which is expected in 1994.

Since traffic growth is only one of the parameters in the airline financial performance, others such as lowering of costs and increasing revenues without adversely influencing traffic must take effect.

11.10 MARKETS AND MANUFACTURERS

Figure 11.14 compares how the commuter and regional aircraft manufacturers are addressing the two markets (15–70 seats and 71–130-seaters) with their present and planned products. About three times as many commuter aircraft manufacturers as regional aircraft manufacturers are chasing a market which is half as attractive with three times as many products. Figure 11.14 may seem somewhat complicated, but the message is simple: the commuter aircraft industry is in need of consolidation and this will happen soon.

11.10.1 The importance of family concept

Twenty years ago trunk airlines discovered the advantage of aircraft families (Figure 11.15). With growing fleets and a growing number of operators being subsidiaries of major airlines, the importance of family concepts in commuter/regional operations will grow. Family concepts provide

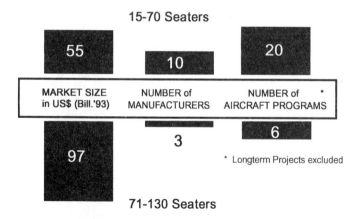

15-70 Seaters

MARKET SIZE in US$ (Bill.'93)	NUMBER of MANUFACTURERS	NUMBER of AIRCRAFT PROGRAMS *

* Longterm Projects excluded

71-130 Seaters

Figure 11.14 Markets and manufacturers.

more flexibility in manufacturer–operator relationships, accompanying growth and cyclic change; improved economy of operations; and improved economy for manufacturers. Operations economies come from only requiring one 'family' of spares, tooling, training for maintaining operations, plus a simplification of crew qualification, training and simulators. Manufacturers gain by reducing costs of development and incurring a lower cost of manufacturing different sizes of aircraft in larger quantities.

11.11 INFLUENCE OF REGULATIONS

Deregulation and liberalization will tend to have a positive influence on commuter/regional aircraft as far as traffic rights are concerned, as they allow higher flight frequencies as a competition tool. In Europe, through liberalization, routes between secondary cities have become available for new competitors, who can enter these markets only with smaller aircraft. The situation in the rest of the world is also favourable for commuter/regional aircraft due to the infrastructural and geographical limitations existing for ground transport means (Figure 11.16).

Slot availability at larger airports should really have no influence on regional aircraft, although smaller commuter aircraft might be banned from some airports. Capacity problems at larger airports already lead to fragmentation of traffic flows (more point-to-point, by-passing hubs) which works in favour of smaller aircraft.

Commuter/regional aircraft usually fly out of the congested airways at lower altitudes and away from hub-to-hub segments. Therefore, future trends are positive. Due to their slower speeds, however, some older commuter aircraft have problems in being integrated into the traffic flow at terminal areas.

Figure 11.15 The family concept of aircraft.

Figure 11.16 The influence of regulations.

Finally, turboprops are not noisy, their emissions are low and they operate at lower altitudes. Similarly, modern smaller jets should not have any technical problems in fulfilling future noise and emission standards.

11.12 HIGH SPEED TRAINS – A THREAT TO REGIONAL AIRCRAFT?

The conventional tracked high speed train has been competing with air travel in Japan since 1964 and in France since 1981. These trains help to eliminate the problem of congestion on some short-distance high density sectors with major origin-destination traffic flows. The future influence of these trains on air travel is forecasted to be mainly in Europe and Japan (with perhaps very few connections in North America and elsewhere); most of the air traffic loss to rail will in the under 500 km segments, where trains have travel time advantages (Figure 11.17).

On a limited number of city pairs, magnetic levitation trains (i.e. from Hamburg to Berlin) are expected to reduce air travel. Studies show that if the EEC railways' three-phase conventional tracked high speed train development were to be realized fully, there will be some traffic shift away from air to rail on a few heavily travelled city pairs, which are currently served by large capacity aircraft. However, influence on regional turbo-props and small jets which usually operate on markets with lower demand will be negligible.

It is envisaged that during the next 20 years, this railway development

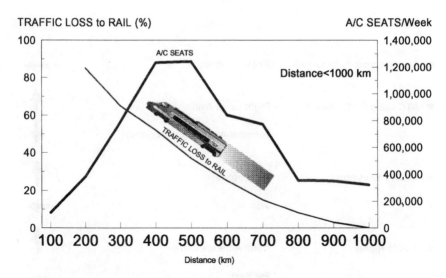

TRAFFIC LOSS to RAIL (%)   A/C SEATS/Week

Figure 11.17 High speed trains and the threat to regional aircraft.

could reduce aircraft manufacturers' deliveries of jet aircraft to European airlines by up to 7% (around 220 aircraft). This would affect generic aircraft categories above 130 seats.

11.13 CONCLUSIONS

Providing there are no sudden and unexpected changes in the political situation worldwide, a number at trends in commuter/regional operations can be identified:

1. commuter/regional operations will remain a vital element of the air transport sytem, even if this segment decreases in importance in relative terms in the future;
2. trends in politics (the integration of Europe), regulations and problems in infrastructure, will favour the evolution of commuter/regional traffic;
3. both point-to-point and hub-and-spoke operations will exist in the future;
4. the influence of large carriers on commuter/regional operations will increase;
5. the financial strength of smaller operators might weaken their position in the fight for financing;
6. the structures of the manufacturing industry will undergo a concentration due to globalization, while at the lower end of the product-spectrum aircraft manufacturers of lesser-developed countries will try to enter the market;

7. major parts of the fleets in 2012 will be aircraft which are on offer today;
8. new technologies which reduce the cost of acquisition and maintenance will be introduced in small steps, while available technology will allow commuter/regional operations to grow without being limited by environmental considerations;
9. no new systems requiring new infrastructures will be introduced in the next 20 years (VTOL–passenger aircraft);
10. commuter and regional operations will not really be influenced by high speed trains.

ACKNOWLEDGEMENT

I am indebted to Mr. Haluk Taysi, Manager Market Analysis Deutsche Aerospace Airbus GmbH, for his contribution to the analysis and perspectives presented in this paper and for his support in preparing it.

12

Airbus and future passenger aircraft

R.M. McKinlay

12.1 INTRODUCTION

The remit for this paper was to take a European perspective on Airbus and future passenger aircraft. Perhaps, fortunately, the term 'future' was not defined and this allowed the choice of a time-span which matches the business cycle of the commercial aviation industry.

In the aviation business we are used to looking ahead since we are in a long cycle business, e.g. from conception to the last aircraft leaving service, a successful commercial aircraft can be around for 50 years. In general, we feel that we can, and have to be, fairly confident of the aircraft and infrastructure developments which will take place over the next 10 years and we are capable of intelligent speculation for a further 10 years.

Beyond that forecasts become of dubious value because of the continuing rapid rate of technological evolution combined with the ever-changing nature of the global economic community, a factor of particular importance as we try to forecast the future from where we stand today. Therefore, this paper limits itself to a 10-year outlook with some thoughts on the most important trends up to 20 years ahead.

To do so, the paper summarizes the Airbus programmes, how they began and how they evolved to where they are today. From this background the paper considers how the Airbus family of aircraft should be developed to respond to the needs of the market and the important political and industrial issues which could materially affect the business over the next 20 years. The paper will also consider the needs for continuing development

Passenger Transport after 2000 AD. Edited by G.B.R. Feilden, A.H. Wickens and I.R. Yates. Published in 1994 by E & FN Spon, London. ISBN 0 419 19470 3.

in technology and touch on some philosophical questions on how future collaboration and competition might be conducted.

In order not to further confuse an already complex picture, the paper limits itself to aircraft with more than 100 seats. No other limits on size or speed have been imposed.

12.2 EVOLUTION OF AIRBUS

Since the launch of the A300 in 1969, the present consortium members, British Aerospace, Deutsche Aerospace, Aerospatiale and CASA have, through Airbus Industrie, successfully launched a family of aircraft such that today Airbus offers aircraft with from 150 to 330 seats and ranges up to 7500 nautical miles. After an initial slow start to establish a new product, the sales of Airbus aircraft have increased dramatically since the first delivery in 1974 and Airbus Industrie has captured some 30% of the large aircraft market making it second only to Boeing. The importance of creating and maintaining a family of aircraft cannot be overemphasized since it is essential to match the products offered by the competition and to do so by offering as much commonality between types as possible to reduce airline investment in both spares and aircrew. The family approach and the use of advanced technology, in combination with the continuous development of each type, has been the hallmark of Airbus success.

The original A300B as conceived in 1969 was the world's first large wide-bodied twin-engine aircraft with seating for 250 passengers and two prototypes were built to this standard, the A300B1, with the first flight taking place on 28 October 1972. However, AirFrance, the first Airbus Industrie customer, wanted extra seating capacity and the fuselage was extended to provide an extra 3 rows of seats; this became the B2 aircraft and was the first to enter service. Later, a B4 variant was introduced, having increased maximum take-off weight and 3000 nautical mile range. A total of 248 B2/B4 aircraft were produced.

Following the philosophy of developing a family of products, in 1979 the 210-seater A310 aircraft project was launched to meet an airline requirement for a medium range aircraft of smaller capacity than the A300B. The change was accommodated by taking 21 ft out of the A300B fuselage length and the opportunity was taken to introduce a completely new, highly optimized wing design to give aircraft performance competitive with the emerging Boeing 767 which was the Boeing response to the A300B. The A310 entered service in 1983.

The next step in the family development was small in investment terms but very important in keeping the aircraft up to date. In 1984, the technology developed for the A310 was fed back into the A300 in the form of a slightly longer version, the A300-600. This gave the A300-600 the flight deck technology and control systems of the A310, including operation by a 2 person crew.

The next major aircraft development was the launch of the 150 seat A320 to compete with the Boeing 737 range and McDonnell Douglas MD80 series. It was decided that the A320 should be an all new aircraft offering significant economic and operational benefits to the airlines and capable of operating and being developed well into the twenty-first century. The A320, therefore, embodies advanced technology in all respects from a completely new wing to the flight deck systems and flown through computer flight management systems. The aircraft cabin is also significantly wider than the competition.

The success of the A320 is reflected in the sales of 657 achieved to date (30 April 1992). The logical evolution of the A320 design was to extend it to provide 180-seat capacity. This aircraft, the A321, is now in production and will enter airline service in 1994. It is also very likely that a smaller version of the A320, the A319, will enter service in 1996.

Airbus Industrie next decided to tackle the top end of the product range to combat the domination of the Boeing 747 and counter the threat of the McDonnell Douglas MD11. The outcome was the twin-engined A330 and four-engined A340 aircraft programmes both of which use the A300 aircraft fuselage cross-section, though with different lengths, and have a common new wing design. The wing design enables a range of options to be provided from high capacity (300+ seats) medium range (4000 nm) on the A330 to lower capacity (250+ seats) long range (7500 nm) on the A340.

Thus the Airbus product range today consists of the A320, A321, A310, A300-600, A330 and A340 with a total backlog of firm orders amounting to 792 aircraft and US$60 billion, as at end April 1993. The aircraft family is shown pictorially in Figure 12.1.

It is now appropriate to consider the impact which Airbus has had on the aviation world and the likely future evolution of this highly successful family.

12.3 AIRBUS FUTURE DEVELOPMENTS

12.3.1 Current family

The expense of designing, developing and producing a modern airliner is such that there is great pressure to keep each successful type in production, basically unchanged, for as long as possible. At the same time, there is a contradiction in that there is increasing pressure on manufacturers to provide upgrade options that extend aircraft life and improve operating effectiveness, introducing new technologies where appropriate and keeping the aircraft competitive with new products.

Thanks to the relative youth of the Airbus family and a policy of progressively up-grading each type, Airbus are not facing major developments in the current product range during the remainder of this century. There will be further developments of existing types, e.g. the stretched version of

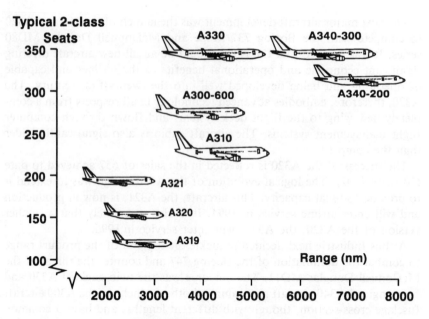

Figure 12.1 The Airbus family.

the A320 – the A321 – has already been launched and the smaller version – the A319 – will likely follow. Increased payload/range versions of the A330 and A340 are under consideration and they will happen when the time is right. Stretched versions of the A330 and A340 are also envisaged by Airbus but they are unlikely to see service this century.

One area, which must always be considered and which has not been touched on so far, is the powerplant. Powerplant developments in their own right can trigger new aircraft ideas or major up-grades. In the medium term it is considered unlikely that developments will provoke significant new aircraft programmes although aircraft will likely benefit from the continuous improvement which takes place on powerplants. With regard to new powerplant configurations, now that thankfully the prop-fan engine seems to be behind us, other engine developments like the Ultra High By-pass fan are more likely to see their way into service next century and probably without major disruption to airframe design.

In terms of aircraft which could be delivered this century – as opposed to those that might be conceivably launched for later delivery – Airbus will compete with the US manufacturers with essentially the family of aircraft which exists today. The primary competition will come from Boeing whose latest entrant, the B777, goes into service in 1995.

In 1995 the line-up of competing aircraft will be as we see in Figure 12.2.

The next 7 or 8 years will be commercially very important for Airbus since they will be competing with the US manufacturers with an established

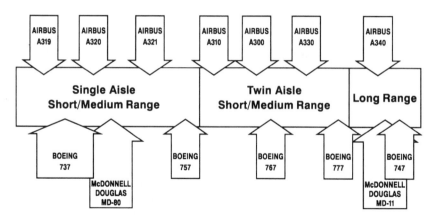

Figure 12.2 Facing the competition.

range of Airbus products. The pioneering days are over and the phase of business consolidation has begun.

Assuming that the current airline financial problems are overcome, forecasts show that there is a very big market available and the quality of the Airbus aircraft family is such that they should be able to hold or improve their position in the market.

12.3.2 Technology needs

Both as part of the continuous up-dating process and preparing for the launch of an all new aircraft, manufacturers must pursue extensive research programmes to develop the technology which future aircraft will require.

The drive for change in commercial aircraft capabilities will come from one or more of the following requirements:

- increased flying efficiency;
- reduced acquisition costs;
- reduced operating costs;
- improved effectiveness of air traffic management;
- enhanced safety standards;
- increased passenger appeal.

Note that achieving an enhanced level of technology does not appear as a driver in its own right. This is because improved technology is the enabling mechanism for the achievement of the improved capabilities and not an end in itself. However, enhanced technical capabilities are essential if new aircraft are to be competitive with existing fleets; advances are required across a wide range of technologies and the appropriate technologies are likely to be provided from research carried out both nationally and in international collaboration.

In a major new initiative, representatives of the UK aeronautics industry, under the auspices of the DTI Aviation Committee, have recently completed a comprehensive review of the future technology needs of the UK civil aircraft industry, including identification of research topics suitable for international collaboration.

The extent of government funding available in support of research is of vital importance and will be addressed further in this paper. To pursue essential research and to minimize the cost of the necessary funds to both governments and industry, a number of international collaborative research programmes have already been set up. These programmes which address critical issues such as overall aircraft efficiency, including energy management and environmental impacts, are a cost effective means of conducting research which must be carried out in order to stay competitive.

12.3.3 Longer-term aircraft developments

While progressive improvements of existing types will serve Airbus well this century, the time will come when new aircraft developments need to be considered, either to replace existing types which have become outdated or to break into new sectors in the market.

In the first category, derivatives of the A320, A330 and A340 will likely see Airbus through the next 20 years but in that time-span the older aircraft, the A300 and A310, will need to be replaced. Recognizing that following the success of Airbus the US manufacturers, particularly Boeing, have become much more aggressive in raising technology levels and reducing costs, the replacement A300/A310 will be a challenge for Airbus to provide a competitive aircraft. There is every reason to believe that Airbus will meet the challenge but it further emphasizes the need for effective research programmes.

While the above represents a formidable challenge for the future it is felt that the second category, that of breaking into new market sectors, will in practice prove to be the more interesting and potentially the most trend-setting possibilities with the second generation Supersonic aircraft and the Very Large Commercial Transport belonging in this category.

Each of these types is being considered separately by the relevant players, e.g. British Aerospace and Aerospatiale have continued their long-term relationship on supersonic aircraft and Boeing and McDonnell Douglas have studied a High Speed Commercial Transport, both privately and using significant NASA funding. On the Very Large aircraft both Airbus Industrie and Boeing have their own studies and McDonnell Douglas continues to pursue its own ideas in this area.

The more interesting aspect of these possible programmes and the more significant for the future is that they are also being investigated by collaborative teams which bring the US manufacturers and Airbus together.

Figure 12.3 The Supersonic Commercial Transport (SCT).

Starting in 1990, a joint team of British Aerospace, Aerospatiale, Deutsche Airbus, Boeing and McDonnell Douglas started investigating the possibility of producing a second generation Supersonic aircraft termed the Supersonic Commercial Transport (SCT). This team has since been swelled by the addition of Alenia of Italy, Japan Aircraft Development Corporation and Tupolev of Russia. In this study the emphasis is on the size of the relevant market and the technical standards which will be needed jointly to produce an environmentally acceptable, commercially viable aircraft.

To some in this country the idea of repeating the 'Concorde experience' is a complete anathema. However, other countries have no such hang-ups and see the Concorde for what it is; a magnificent collaborative technical achievement which *works*. It does the job it was intended to do and has demonstrated that there is a market demand for speed. It is not wise to pre-empt the result of the joint studies but there is a reasonable prospect that there is a large enough market out there to justify the expenditure necessary to produce an acceptable aircraft and such an aircraft could certainly only be produced by international collaboration. The general characteristics of a possible solution are shown in Figure 12.3.

On the Very Large Commercial Transport the studies started in January 1993 and they are between the 4 Airbus Partners and Boeing.

These studies will concentrate primarily on the size of the market, the

Figure 12.4 The Very Large Commercial Transport.

technical challenges of such a large aircraft and whether competitors in one part of the market can collaborate in another. There is no chosen configuration for such an aircraft but possible general characteristics are shown in Figure 12.4.

As might be imagined there are very strong opinions on the wisdom or otherwise of these collaborative studies. It is not easy for the Airbus team who have fought their way up from nothing to sit down with their most bitter rival and talk about collaborating. It is not easy to sit in collaborative discussions with a competitor who seems to be very active in promoting US Administration action against Airbus. There are deep suspicions that the attempts at collaboration are a facade – perhaps on both sides – and the only way to continue is in competition, Airbus versus Boeing, Europe versus the United States.

So why try to collaborate? In 1969 the need to rationalize European activities on large aircraft gave rise to Airbus. Now, 24 years on, there is a looming need to take a step forward in rationalizing global manufacturing activities and the VLCT could be the right place to start. Apparently such a collaboration would be the creation of a monopoly but, if there is to be no collaboration, competition through 2 entries into the very large aircraft market may be simply too risky and too expensive; this would result in there being no very large aircraft and disadvantages to the airlines and travelling public.

The next few months while studies proceed will be very interesting and important. If they succeed – which it is hoped they will, they will change the face of aviation as we know it today.

12.4 LIKELY FUTURE POLITICAL AND INDUSTRIAL ISSUES

Having outlined likely future aircraft developments which the industry would like to see, it is now appropriate to assess the political and industrial climates in which these developments will take place and identify the critical issues that could arise.

The first of the industrial issues to be assessed is the future of Airbus itself. Through its programmes, Airbus has established the European aircraft industry at a level which the Partners could not have attained separately and has created a business which will grow to be one of Europe's largest commercial enterprises, it already is a US$8 billion/year business. But Airbus is not just a business, it is a focus for 'Europe getting its act together' and 'a major example of successful European collaboration'. There is no question that Airbus is here to stay but there is a question of interest for the future as to whether the form of collaboration is the most suitable and whether it should be limited to the 4 current Partners.

The present structure of Airbus is that of a Groupement d'Interet Economique, a GIE. This is a very flexible structure which, while binding the Partners very tightly together in commitment terms, allows plenty of freedom to develop organizational and procedural structures to match the evolving needs of the business.

Through the eyes of the US manufacturers and Administration – and to a considerable extent through UK eyes – it is not a 'normal' business structure and lacks the visibility and accountability which is associated with the more 'normal' corporate structures. From the inside of Airbus it certainly can be argued that there is total visibility and accountability and the Partners are entitled to run their business as they see fit within the available legal structures. However, that is not the issue which is seen to be important for the future. Were it only a question of a difference of opinion on how the business should be organized then frankly the opinion of the owners of the business should and would obtain; the question is likely to be more subtle in that even if the GIE structure is justified it is different from the 'normal' and as such is it supportable in the long term as the global aviation business develops? Time will tell but it is felt that in relation to political issues which will be discussed later, there could be pressures to alter the current Airbus structure.

But in fact it is not the business structure of Airbus as such which is the most intriguing or likely to be the most important for the future. The most important aspect it is felt will be the relationship of the Airbus partnership with Europe as a whole. Specifically, should the Airbus collaboration be expanded by the addition of more members to reflect either:

1. the legitimate wishes of other European manufacturers to join in the business as it grows; or
2. by having more participants than today to be more comprehensively European in the 'battle' with the United States.

On the first point a simple view is taken that when the business expands further by the addition of new types there will likely need to be additions to the number of Airbus participants for straightforward industrial and commercial reasons – and the changes which such additions would engender could be the trigger for an evolution of the structure.

The second alternative is felt to be far the most important issue since it explicitly introduces the concept that Airbus is or should be Europe's champion in the commercial aviation business and forces consideration of the nature of the world market and the developments we have seen since Airbus started some 24 years ago.

Airbus success has been a major shock to the United States industry and administration. It has forced them to re-consider their position in commercial aviation and recognize that while they still have the major market share they are going to have to fight hard to hold their position in the future. Almost inevitably the strains imposed by losing market share to Airbus in combination with the general economic recession has led to polarization of the US versus Europe and claims by each side of illegal subsidies being provided by national governments.

It is not the purpose of this paper to go in depth into the subsidies argument but it is perhaps of interest to consider, as an example of the political issues which need to be faced, the EC/US agreement concluded in July 1992 on national support for aircraft industries.

Taking a straightforward European perspective it is felt that as the US industry saw its market share eroded by Airbus it needed to find an explanation and it seized on Airbus having an unfair advantage because of national government subsidies. The industry provoked the administration to enter into a debate with the EC to establish the facts and seek limitations on direct support for aircraft programmes.

The Airbus Partners, whilst acknowledging the receipt of repayable launch aid pointed out that the US industry receives a much greater level of subsidy through the indirect support provided by the US Government by sponsorship of technology programmes carried out by NASA and the extensive read-across into civil projects of technologies developed under US military contracts. The Europeans contended that the vast majority of the support provided by these methods has a very high subsidy element since it is not repayable. Incidentally, the Europeans also pointed out that the US, particularly McDonnell Douglas, had fallen behind in providing the technology improvements and passenger attraction which the airlines wanted and this was behind much of Airbus success as opposed to subsidy.

The eventual outcome of protracted and difficult negotiations was a bi-lateral agreement to limit government funding of both direct and indirect support.

In future direct support will be limited to 33% of the qualifying development costs and there are strict rules governing interest rates and repayment periods. Indirect support will, in future, be subject to an overall limit of 3% of the annual commercial turn-over of the industry and a limit of 4% for any one firm. This agreement is far from satisfactory with obvious problems in monitoring and identifying support levels, to say nothing of the near impossibility of enforcing the indirect support disciplines.

The above agreement is of great importance to the future in that it impinges directly on the Europeans' ability to fund programmes in the absence of an established indirect support system. This is a subject which is being discussed extensively with governments. However, the long-term significance of the agreement lies in the fact that such an agreement had to be made at all and it is surely the harbinger for a more and more complex regulatory atmosphere as more and more players try to join the aviation industry of the world. This can already be seen in the GATT discussions which are attempting to multi-lateralize the EC/US agreement. Writing the rules of fair play has never been easy and becomes extremely difficult when there is no objective arbitration process available.

There is another danger stemming from the above which could be very important in the future if not avoided. In an attempt to protect national industries the creation of 'rules' could become more important than the recognition that the aviation market truly is a world market and that all players *must* be able to participate in all areas of the market. The current polarization between Europe and the US would be taken *ad absurdum* if the manufacturers were not able to share in both markets, each of which is vital to both the US and European manufacturers. It would also be very foolish of Europe and the US by concentrating on rules to ignore the emerging aeronautics industries in Asia and the expert but currently disorganized capabilities that exist in the CIS.

The challenge for the future is to weld together the different talents, cultures and ambitions of the global players in the aviation industry to their mutual benefit, not to try to write rule books which protect some perceived dominant share in the market, which could, in the long term, be illusory.

Finally, in this section it is necessary to touch on what the airlines might look like over the next 20 years. This is an area where even looking forward the traditional 10 years is very difficult. Currently, the airlines of the world are still in major difficulties with 1993 inevitably being another year of major losses. The situation is at its most extreme in the US where public ownership and the US bankruptcy laws make the situation very visible.

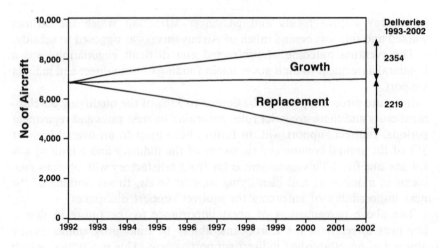

Figure 12.5 Fleet in service 1992–2002 (jets > 120 seats).

However, in the rest of the world, where state ownership is more prevalent, the difficulties are of very similar degree.

The problems which the airlines face are a study in their own right, but for the manufacturers to have a future the airlines must move back into profitability and do so to an extent which allows them to finance the purchase of the aircraft which the predictions say they will need.

Forecasts of aircraft requirements are virtually forced to ignore current problems like today's recession in the airline market and look ahead at long-term growth statistics. That is always difficult to do when the situation is as bad as it is today but there have been recessions before and the long-term statistical approach has fairly well established validity. If we take the normal industry methodology and look forward 10 years the average industry forecast is a requirement, outside the CIS, for some 4600 aircraft deliveries of more than 120-seat capacity. Of these deliveries 2200 are assumed to be required to replace existing aircraft and the remainder will be for growth. These deliveries would be in addition to those already covered by firm orders on the manufacturers. The forecast is shown graphically in Figure 12.5.

Within these deliveries the maximum growth areas would be in the Middle and Far East with a fairly rapidly emerging need for a Very Large aircraft as discussed previously in this paper.

The existence of a forecast traffic requirement which will grow substantially, will not of its own right make the airlines recover. Nevertheless, it is the essential ingredient which must be there if there is going to be recovery. Exactly how and when the airlines will recover is a matter for conjecture and beyond the scope of this paper but it is considered that by a combination of increased globalization of airline operations, decreased airline costs, increased aircraft efficiency and increases in real fares, the recovery will take place and give the manufacturing industry the basis for its future aircraft programmes.

12.5 CONCLUSIONS

In presenting views as they have been in the paper, one conclusion is implicitly drawn which has not been discussed. That is that the next 20 years or so will not see some radically new form of aircraft being developed, i.e. a new shape in the sky. It is always very brave to forecast that there will be no radical developments but it is felt that with the exception of the SCT and the VLCT – both of which will require very radical thinking – aircraft of the next 20 years will look like they do today. After that, when possibilities like hypersonic aircraft become feasible, then who knows?

Within that framework, in the next seven or eight years we are likely to see the continuing evolution of existing families of aircraft featuring the phased introduction of technology developments that will contribute to one or more of the following:

- increased flying efficiency;
- reduced acquisition costs;
- reduced operating costs;
- improved effectiveness of air traffic management;
- enhanced safety standards;
- increased passenger appeal.

The research programmes required to provide the contributing technologies are likely to be carried out nationally and internationally and for the most part are either underway or in an advanced state of planning. In the longer term, further directed research programmes will need to be fulfilled, aimed at finding solutions to the technological problems posed by the projected second generation supersonic aircraft and by the very large commercial transport. These programmes are likely to feature a high international collaborative research content.

The high speed and high capacity trend-setting aircraft projects are likely to be so expensive that the market will be able to sustain only one of each type in the period under review. The programmes are likely to be the first truly global design, development and production ventures undertaken by the aircraft community.

Governments, particularly in the US and Europe will need to strike a careful balance between support for their own industries and the need to maintain the aviation market open to all. Particularly in Europe, governments will need to increase market support funding to match that clearly available through NASA in the United States. In this context, HMG should do all it can to fund the National Strategic Technology Acquisition Plan put forward by the DTI Aviation Committee.

Should a successful balance not be struck by governments the options available for longer-term global projects will be severely constrained.

None of these programmes will be brought to fruition without the world's airlines returning to profitability and credit worthiness, but when they do, the prospect of substantial growth is there.

In the future, the aviation business will be what it has always been – a business activity which stretches human technical and managerial ability to the utmost. This focus may change from time to time from technology to financial or political issues, but the challenge will always be there and the Airbus team are well placed to meet it.

Part Four

Transport Systems 1

13

The intelligent highway and the passenger

L. Nordström

13.1 INTRODUCTION

One of the distinctive features of today's society is the sheer volume of personal travel. Almost everyone moves from one place to another, over some amount of distance, every day. When a country's gross rational product goes up, personal travel increases by a factor of 1.5 in relation to the GNP. This means that travelling, measured in terms of traffic, increases faster than most other segments of society.

This tendency is expected to continue, and, in point of fact, there are no arbitrary constraints on how much people may travel. Time, of course, is the limiting factor, but in most cases this has been compensated for by an increase in travelling speed, i.e. we, as travellers, select faster modes of transport. This, in turn, means that we can cover greater distances in the same amount of travel time.

In 1900, adult Swedes covered an average of 300 m daily using some mode of transport. By 1930, this distance had increased to 3 km, and by 1990, to 45 km. If these tendencies continue, the average traveller in the future will cover up to 60–70 km on a daily basis, using increasingly sophisticated modes of transport. Facilitating this increasingly extensive travelling requires an expanded and more complicated transport system. This transport system, in turn, absorbs much of the GNP in most countries, because travel costs have gone up, and a large part of the private individual's economic resources are invested in travelling.

The person employing public transportation needs to know how journeys will be carried out. This involves information about travel times,

Passenger Transport after 2000 AD. Edited by G.B.R. Feilden, A.H. Wickens and I.R. Yates. Published in 1994 by E & FN Spon, London. ISBN 0 419 19470 3.

connections, prices, etc. This mass of information can be provided in different ways, and has, with time, become increasingly computerized, which makes it easier for the traveller to choose a mode of transport. The traveller, of course, once embarked, relinquishes control of the journey to others – e.g. the train engineer, the conductors, etc.

For motorists, travelling assumes a different character. Often, drivers are alone in the car, which means that they both implement their movement and, simultaneously, are in control of it. Hence motorists play both a passive and an active role, namely being transported and transporting themselves. To make this possible, the modern automotive society has developed increasingly sophisticated cars that are both safer and more reliable than previous generations of vehicles. The driver of an automobile is by and large isolated, and needs information about what is going on outside in order to handle the car well. To facilitate that, the modern automotive society has compiled a large number of static information systems to assist the driver, e.g. road signs, which are most common, but also other types of signals. By and large, this system functions well, even if the demands placed on today's drivers are so numerous that many, and not least elderly drivers, feel that they are incapable of adequately fulfilling their traffic responsibilities.

13.2 THE MOTORIST OF THE FUTURE

The automobile of the future will function somewhat differently. The interaction between the car and its surroundings will be enhanced; a number of sources of information will automatically provide drivers with data about what to do and how to act. In some circumstances, this information will be provided directly to the vehicle. These information sources are intended to automate some parts of the information that is today transmitted more manually or statically. This applies to information about route selection, possible accident hazards, traffic problems, bottlenecks, etc., but it also involves information to help drivers understand the opportunities available to them in deciding on directions and speeds.

Naturally, all of these systems will be expensive, and major investments will be required to extend them throughout a country. Consequently, priority will be given to areas with the heaviest traffic. The technical effort required to develop these new information systems has made great progress in Europe as well as in the US and Japan, but we will be well into the twenty-first century before the automated information system – the intelligent highway – becomes a common phenomenon.

What is happening simultaneously is that the car is taking on other roles than being just a means of transportation. Modern information technology had made it possible for the car to function not only as a concert hall and a workplace, but also as a place where the individual can relax, sit back and make his or her own decisions about how to be informed. In most cases, the playback equipment in today's automobile makes it a better environment for the enjoyment of music than the living room at home. In addition, many cars today are equipped with telephones, which means that the surest way of contacting a person is to call while he or she is driving. Cars are also gradually being furnished with other improvements in information technology – telefax equipment, TV sets, etc.

As a result of all this, the car will be a part of the individual's private life and also, perhaps, the only place where individual human beings can enjoy an interlude from their surroundings, deciding for themselves what music to listen to and how to carry out certain details of their work assignments. Hence the car will be a part of our everyday life and an element in our private life as well.

The development of an automated highway will facilitate this, because the consummate intelligent highway will be able to take over some of the motorist's driving operations, i.e. the car can be 'plugged in' to a highway and then be on autopilot until the driver has to again take over the controls when it is time to leave the highway. During the time the car is being driven automatically, motorists will be able to devote themselves to any number of other matters – or just simply relax.

13.3 TELECOMMUNICATIONS AS AN ALTERNATIVE TO TRAVEL

Hence the intelligent highway enhances the car's function as an important ingredient in the life of the individual as a social being. On the other hand, current developments in the telecommunications field provide an alternative possibility, namely that it should be feasible to substitute telecommunications for a great many of the trips we make at present. It is not always necessary to travel to participate in a meeting, or to be present at a certain workplace, in order to accomplish a work assignment or to be involved in a meeting. The telecommunications system can mean that many tasks can be carried out at home – that transportation is replaced by teletransmission.

Consequently, a lot of travelling could be avoided, and we would thus obtain a less car-orientated society. At present, however, there is no indication that this will affect the need for trips; the likelihood is rather that some kinds of trips will be replaced by others, i.e. we will use our cars more in our functions as leisure time beings and perhaps less as commuters to and from work. At any rate, this factor, too, implies an altered function for the automobile. The simple transport function, i.e. moving a person from one point to another to be able to carry out a certain objective, e.g. work, can be replaced by telecommunications, and the car will be used for those social functions in which travelling cannot be avoided. During the time that the journey is going on, however, cars can in large part be operated automatically, and the travellers in cars will be able to devote themselves to matters other than the driving itself.

This, in turn, suggests a certain correspondence with people who employ public transportation today. The difference, however, is that the car offers a totally different kind of flexibility than any kind of public transport system, while simultaneously providing great intimacy. It is difficult to imagine a public transport system in which every individual passenger can independently select the news program or the kind of music desired, or how to behave in general. Public transport systems always imply showing some kind of consideration to one's fellow travellers; naturally, motorists must also show consideration, but of an entirely different kind.

13.4 CONCLUSIONS

Accordingly, what we can see down the line, assuming technological developments continue in the direction that appears to be manifest today, is an automobile society in which the car will fulfil societal functions different from those it has provided us with in the past. The car will become an increasingly integral part of the overall involvement in life for the individual human being, even as it becomes still more user-friendly, and many of the operations that preoccupy the motorist in today's cars will be assumed by new information systems. Whether or not this will turn out to be the predominant technological approach as we enter the twenty-first century remains to be seen. However, the possibilities are there, and as we all know, things change with lightning speed in the field of telecommunications when new developments are introduced.

14

The future of road transport

J. Wootton

'The freedom offered by the motor car is counteracted by growing congestion, parking deficiencies and rising numbers of accidents. Side effects are also evident: decreasing patronage of public transport and a changing environment.'

These words, written 26 years ago, still express the main concerns about the consequences of traffic growth. Consequences that manifest themselves in the form of congestion, a deteriorating environment and concern about safety. The evidence suggests that the growth, which is the result of economic growth, will continue for the foreseeable future, increasing the pressure on our towns and cities and changing their shape. The solutions must recognize the need to change lifestyles and travel behaviour; the important link between the location of buildings and transport infrastructure; the important but limited role for public transport; and the need for new road construction.

We are also entering an era when electronics, computers and communications will be applied to our transport systems, an application now known as 'Advanced Transport Telematics'. This technology will improve our traffic control systems, provide us with better travel and traffic information, influence our behaviour and change the vehicles we drive. In 50 years time we are likely to have still greater personal mobility, but the changes that have occurred may make it difficult to distinguish between individual (private) and collective (public) transport systems.

Crown Copyright 1993. The views expressed in this publication are not necessarily those of the Department of Transport. Extracts from the text may be reproduced, except for commercial purposes, provided the source is acknowledged. Work described in this paper forms part of a Department of Transport funded research programme conducted by the Transport Research Laboratory.

Passenger Transport after 2000 AD. Edited by G.B.R. Feilden, A.H. Wickens and I.R. Yates. Published in 1994 by E & FN Spon, London. ISBN 0 419 19470 3.

14.1 TRAFFIC GROWTH

Traffic growth is largely the result of economic growth, which encourages the purchase of vehicles and increased travel by all modes of transport. This increase in travel can in turn lead to increased productivity and so feeds the economic cycle.

There were 24.5 million vehicles licensed in Great Britain in 1991, of which 19.7 million were cars. Figure 14.1 shows how car ownership per person in Britain has grown over the last thirty years and contrasts the growth with that of the former East and West Germany, the USA and Poland. Although there are important variations year by year, the trends are remarkably consistent, with growth varying from an average of 8 vehicles per 1000 people per annum for Great Britain to over 10 per 1000 for West Germany. The rate of growth in car ownership in Great Britain is less than any other European Community country except Denmark and the Irish Republic, which have a similar rate.

The evidence from our neighbours and the USA is that there is still considerable growth to come in Britain. A simple extrapolation of current trends suggest Great Britain has 30 years of further growth to come at which time the number of vehicles will be about 650 per 1000 people. At this level there will be approximately one car for everybody holding a driving licence, so that any further increase in the number of cars is likely to be attributable to fashion and is unlikely to increase travel demand substantially. The growth will not be uniform across the whole country. Some counties, particularly in the south-east, already have over 470 cars per thousand people, while others have fewer than 300.

14.2 THE IMPACT OF OWNING A CAR

A family that has the use of a car makes more journeys, than a family that does not. Figure 14.2 demonstrates the point. The non-car-owning family makes just over three journeys per day by motorized transport. The majority of these journeys, over 85%, are made by public transport and the remainder as a private transport passenger. Upon acquiring a car, the same family averages over five journeys per day. The journeys previously made by public transport are reduced by almost 50%; the others transferring to the acquired car. More importantly, there are over 2 journeys a day that were either not made before or, in a few instances, were journeys on foot or bicycle. This behaviour is observed worldwide and becomes even more acute when the family owns more than one car.

The change in travel demand that results from owning a car has a dramatic effect on the total travel demand when it is coupled with the increase in the number of vehicles. Figure 14.3 shows the resulting passenger travel demand that has occurred in Great Britain in the past 40

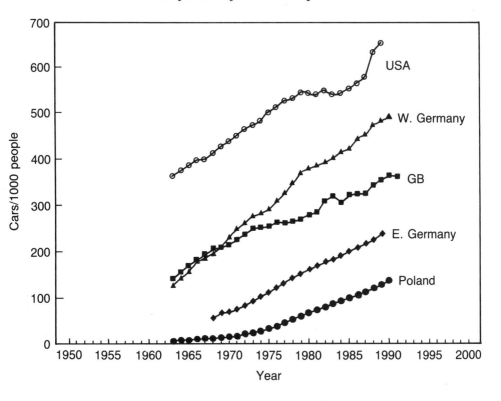

Figure 14.1 Growth in car ownership.

years. The increase in travel by private transport has been at the rate of about 3% per annum, compared to a 2.2% rate of growth in the number of vehicles, whilst the use of buses has declined steadily at about 2% per annum and the level of rail travel has remained remarkably constant.

The change in behaviour provides the opportunity to consider what might happen if the use of cars was restricted, perhaps through road pricing. The number of journeys by car would decrease and some would return to public transport. But, only those journeys that were made previously by public transport are likely to return. The new journeys made when the car was acquired cannot be expected to transfer to public transport as the public transport service did not offer the desired service prior to acquiring the car. New public transport services would have to be offered in order to capture any of the new car journeys.

There is further support for this view from the oil crisis of 1974. At that time the price of fuel increased by 31% in real terms with the result that there was a decrease of 12 000 million passenger kilometres (4%) travelled by car. This was not compensated by the increase of 2000 million passenger kilometres by bus and coach in the same period.

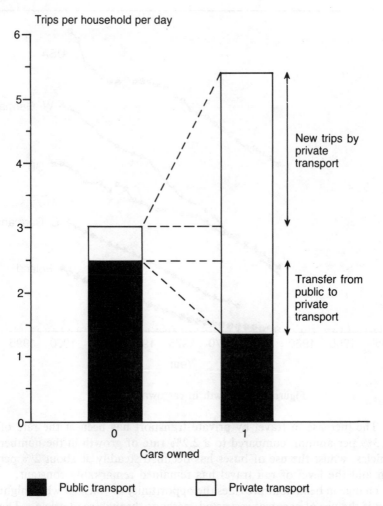

Number of trips per day for households in London with one working member and for an average income in a medium bus accessibility area

Figure 14.2 The impact of car ownership.

14.3 FREIGHT TRAFFIC

The growth in freight traffic shows similar characteristics to passenger travel and Figure 14.4 illustrates the strong trend in the increasing use of private goods vehicles and the decline in rail traffic in the UK. Rail is still an important carrier of freight, but it is used primarily for carrying bulk commodities whilst goods vehicles have proved their value in carrying most types of goods and offer flexibility and better travel times.

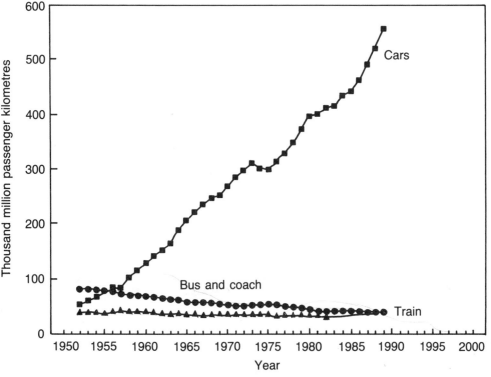

Figure 14.3 1000 million passenger kilometres by year.

The movement of freight by all types of transport has grown roughly in proportion to the growth in gross domestic product. In Britain, as in other northern European countries, the growth in freight tonne kilometres is not principally the result of more freight being moved. About three-quarters of the growth is the result of freight being moved further. Since 1952 there have been ups and downs in the amount of freight lifted, but the total has hardly grown, if at all. On the other hand, the average haul length has doubled, from under 40 km to about 75 km, and this is the main reason for the increase in road freight traffic since 1965.

The growth in the haul length for freight reflects trends in manufacturing, warehousing and logistics that lead to greater overall economic efficiency. For example, the trends to single, large, manufacturing centres to serve the whole country and single warehousing sites require more freight transport, but give economies of scale which lead to lower retail prices. Just-in-time logistics replaces warehouses with trucks. World sourcing gives customers a wider choice of goods and lower prices. There are many anecdotal accounts of materials being trucked to areas with low wages for goods to be manufactured and then trucked back to the country of origin (cloth

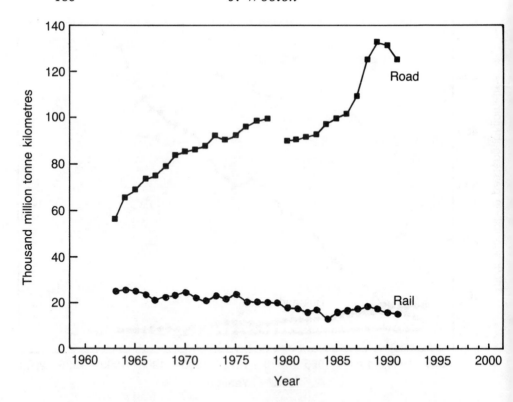

Figure 14.4 1000 million tonne kilometres by year.

and accessories from Germany to Turkey or Britain to Morocco, garments back to Germany or Britain).

While the British economy grows, the movement of freight will also grow. Attempts to restrict it would reduce consumer choice and increase prices. The growth of Europe as a trading area by the inclusion of the countries of eastern Europe, and the former Soviet Union, must also increase the movement of freight. With the longer hauls and the investments being made in high speed rail services it is likely that the longer freight journeys will be attracted to rail. This will be encouraged by the growing use of containers and swop-bodies (non-stackable containers). This type of traffic is the fastest growing form of inter-modal freight (road–rail or road–water) in Europe at present. Its use in Britain can only increase with the opening of the Channel Tunnel and the associated inland container ports that are being built. However, since in Britain road at present moves about eight times as much freight tonne kilometres as does rail, even doubling the freight moved by rail will only have a small effect on that moved by road.

For many years sites that generate or attract freight movements have been located to be served by road rather than by rail or water. Thus it is almost inevitable that most freight movements will include road stages at their origin and destination. Hidden freight movements should not be overlooked. One retailer estimates that for each truck serving a supermarket there are 500 car trips taking the goods from shop to home. This traffic is not insignificant.

14.4 TRAVEL PATTERNS AND THE SHAPE OF TOWNS

Towns and cities are places to transact business and their economies depend on this. They are also places where people live, work and spend their leisure time. History tells us that they are shaped by the transport facilities that are available. In seeking solutions to the problems associated with traffic growth, it is necessary to understand the interactions and the role that each form of transport can play.

Almost all transport movements are a consequence of activities at particular places, so the pattern of travel depends on the pattern of land use and the organization of activities within that pattern. In Britain, until about 1840, urbanization and its associated activities had located itself where it could be served by rivers and canals. Between 1840 and 1930 land use developments were located to be easy to serve by rail. By 1950 most land use developments were located to be served by road. This pattern of development, and the location of activities within urban areas, is largely responsible for the dominant role of road transport today. Similar changes have occurred in the other countries of Europe, but at different dates. For example, Britain urbanized between 1820 and 1880, while France did not do so until well into the twentieth century.

Mechanized transport made possible the geographic spread of cities with accompanying reductions in population density. Since 1951 the population growth in the south-east of England has been outside the area of Greater London, as has the growth of employment. The movement of over 2 million residing within London to living outside is one of the two most important factors – the other is the growth in the number of cars – to affect travel patterns and the viability of public transport within London.

The way in which cars are used to serve a diffuse pattern of travel, while buses serve high density radial routes into town centres, was illustrated by some of the urban land use/transportation studies carried out in the 1960s (Freeman *et al.* 1968; Traffic Research Corporation Ltd, 1969). Public transport tends to be used predominantly for radial trips into the centre of the conurbation, and sometimes to other town centres, and loads the main radial routes with traffic. Private transport tends to be both radial and cross-town trips, and loads all the main roads in the conurbation.

This pattern of bus and car travel is typical of large urban areas. As employment, shopping, health care and recreation relocate into the peripheral areas, it becomes increasingly difficult to serve them by public transport. Thus the switch to private transport from public is, to some extent, driven by the changing locations of activities. From a social perspective these changes reduce access to these activities by those who do not have cars – children, old people and poor people, for example.

The development of the private car and other forms of personal motorized transport have also had a major impact on the form of our cities. Much longer journeys can be made in the same time. Flexibility in choice increases both in terms of the direction of travel and the time at which journeys are made. Perhaps most importantly this flexibility encourages development in-filling and orbital movement.

The impact of increased personal mobility on the shape of our towns and cities is seen clearly in the building of ring roads, which in their most sophisticated form are orbital motorways. Most major cities of the world have an orbital motorway some 10–20 km from their centre. Paris has the Boulevard Périphérique, Washington its Beltway, Boston Route 128, Madrid the Almendra and London the M25. None of these cities have an orbital public transport route at this radius and no city can be found with one. One point of passing interest is that an orbital motorway could be used as a very high capacity public transport system, but none are used this way. A single three-lane carriageway of a motorway is quite capable of accommodating 3000 buses per hour with a carrying capacity of over 150 000 people. The collective demand is simply not present to justify such services.

While the main purpose of ring roads and orbital motorways is to provide a high quality bypass that relieves congestion and improves the environment and safety in the centre of towns and cities, they encourage people and business to relocate. The M25 provides many examples, such as junction 9, the Leatherhead intersection. Esso have moved most of their European Headquarters to within a mile of junction 9; a new industrial site accommodates the Puma division of Dunlop Slazenger; B&Q have constructed a superstore; 84 houses have been built on land severed by the motorway; and Tesco have built a large store on the site of a former garden centre. All of this new activity is within sight of junction 9 and there is much more new development in the adjacent towns of Epsom and Leatherhead. Leatherhead, for example, now has 9 business parks whereas it only had 3 before the M25 was opened.

The traffic impact of new development around the intersections on the M25 is significant, with somewhere between 10% and 25% of the traffic currently using the M25 associated with it. The sad fact is that no one has measured these impacts and our planning systems and assessment procedures do not take them properly into account when justifying new roads or new development.

Garreau (1991) argues that the provision of high quality roads and the desire for personal mobility has resulted in the growth of over 100 new post-industrial cities in the United States of America. This inextricable link between the location of buildings, the density and type of development and transport infrastructure and the impact the growth in private vehicles have had on shaping our towns and cities are only just being acknowledged in the planning, building and financing of our infrastructure.

One final example from the south-east of England. Although the population and employment in the south-east has been growing steadily for 40 years, the population and employment in Greater London has been declining. Since 1951 the population of Greater London has declined from 8.20 million to 6.38 million in 1991 and employment from 4.29 million to 3.25 million. Other conurbations show similar, though less dramatic, trends. This dispersal of population and employment was unforeseen and unplanned, yet it is one of the most important factors affecting travel demand and patterns of movement that could have occurred. The dispersal provides more space for garaging vehicles and again makes it increasingly difficult for public transport to serve the pattern of movement.

At a time when there is so much concern about transport provision, a deteriorating environment, the functioning of our cities and the sources of finance, can we afford to ignore the relationship between our transport facilities, the location of buildings and the density of development? Development may seem to take place slowly, but it is always present, the changes continually exerting their influence and shaping our urban form. Perhaps one of the most important things we have to do in seeking to improve urban transport is to understand the forces at work so that we can encourage them to provide the quality of life we desire.

14.5 THE EFFECTS OF FURTHER TRAFFIC GROWTH

The increased travel, that is implied by the current trends, will be important to our economy, but congestion, which manifests itself in the form of queues and long delays, seems likely to spread, both geographically and in duration. Stokes, Goodwin and Kenny (1992) have studied what the British forecasts (Department of Transport, 1989) mean for traffic on particular types of road, with particular reference to flows on non-motorway rural roads. They conclude that there is likely to be the road capacity for the extra traffic, but that parking difficulties are going to restrict the growth of ownership and use of cars in the larger towns. Some 60% of the total growth of traffic would occur on local roads. Congestion in urban and suburban areas would spread into off-peak hours and into currently uncongested areas. Congestion on rural roads would increase dramatically. Journeys would take longer and country lanes would become 'rat runs' to a much greater extent than at present. The pressures for new locational patterns for industry, retailing, health care, education and leisure facilities would create new 'business and shopping centres' at motorway junctions.

I see no reason to disagree with these views. The best we can hope to do is control the rate of growth and influence travel behaviour. Even so the amount of growth will be substantial. This implies that there must be more road space. Most of the new roads will not be built in urban areas as there is insufficient land available.

14.6 THE NEED FOR NEW ROAD CONSTRUCTION

The extent of the anticipated growth in traffic certainly means that there is a need for more road construction. The questions are where, when and why new roads should be constructed. Clearly a limitless supply of road space cannot be provided, since land is very precious and new rights of way are difficult to find. But there are some simple guidelines, the simplest of which is that they should be built to serve the needs of society.

Thus new roads may be built to aid the growth in the economy. For example, new roads in a hinterland allow goods to be brought to market; a new bridge across an estuary encourages new business activity by reducing travel times and making communication easier.

Where extensive road networks already exist, but there is also severe traffic congestion, cost benefit analyses can help to decide whether new road construction is worthwhile or not. But roads can also be built to simultaneously relieve congestion, improve the environment and safety. Bypasses are a good example of this as they allow the removal of through-traffic from urban areas thereby improving the mobility, safety and environment for local inhabitants.

The concept of separating and isolating the different uses to which roads are put is important. For example, traffic calming in a residential area enforces the nature of the area – the residents and pedestrians are more important than traffic – and yet access is maintained at an acceptable level. Jensen (1992) has given excellent examples of this concept applied in the Norwegian cities of Kongsvinger and Oslo.

14.7 CONTROLLING THE RATE OF GROWTH IN THE NUMBER OF VEHICLES

Conditions will not deteriorate as quickly if the rate of growth can be lowered. As we have seen, Britain has a level of car ownership that is below the average for the European Community, with only Portugal, Spain and Greece having levels that are much lower. Britain also has a rate of growth in car ownership, just over 8 cars per 1000 people per annum, that is less than any other EC country except Denmark and the Irish Republic, which have a similar rate. Denmark had a six-year period of an approximately constant level of car ownership, and in the Irish Republic growth stopped in 1981 after which car ownership remained almost constant at about 10% below its peak value for six years, and even by 1989 was still 5% below the level for 1981.

The low rate of growth in Britain, Denmark and the Irish Republic seem to reflect the relatively high purchase price of cars. All three countries have or, in the case of Britain, had special taxes to increase the price of cars. Denmark and Ireland both have high prices for petrol, but neither is as high as that for Italy, which has a high rate of growth of car ownership. Note also that the former West Germany, whose economy has grown strongly and whose cars are comparatively cheap, has had the highest growth rate in car ownership in Europe (Figure 14.1). Thus it seems we could use the purchase price of cars to reduce the future rate of growth in the number of vehicles.

14.8 A ROLE FOR PUBLIC TRANSPORT?

There is a popular belief that improved public transport services will satisfy people's travel demand and persuade them out of their cars. Sadly this is not the case. The dispersed travel demand in a city cannot be served economically and efficiently by current forms of public transport.

The majority of travel does not start or end in a high density activity area. Activities are now far too dispersed for that. So while public transport can, and should, continue to serve our town and city centres its role does not extend beyond this. For it to do so requires a change in lifestyles and a return to high density urban development with activities concentrated in the centre and along radial routes. It seems that existing forms of public transport have only a marginal, though important, role to play in changing traffic demand.

Technology can help support public transport. It can provide people with information on the status of the transport system, the services available and will also help with common ticketing and charging systems, but it does not change the fundamental hub and spoke nature of public transport systems. Bus and rail operate this way, airlines have developed along these lines and freight distribution shows the same characteristics.

Other forms of collective transport system must be considered. Success in persuading people to share transport facilities is helped by creating a focus. Elsenaar (1992) has suggested we should focus particularly on the management of the journey to work. He highlights the importance of motivating companies that are 'located near to each other to encourage their employees to use other means of transport than the private car for their journey to work and to offer them a so called transport plan'. For this to succeed he considers it is essential that the Government, businesses and transport companies co-operate in establishing the plan.

The importance of car and van pooling programmes have also been emphasized by Hoel (1992). He gives an example from Virginia 'where there are 17 ride sharing programmes in operation. These are run by individual localities with financial assistance from Virginia Department of Transportation ... In 1989, 89 new van pools were formed and 5421 applicants were placed in car pools. The computed savings were 1700 parking spaces, 700 000 gallons of fuel, and 11 000 000 vehicle miles of travel.' Professor Hoel argues that by manipulating the demand through these mechanisms greater person carrying capacity will result and the need for new infrastructure will be lessened.

These and similar ideas are ones we have yet to explore in Great Britain. By manipulating the demand through these mechanisms greater person carrying capacity will result and the need for new infrastructure will be lessened.

14.9 ENVIRONMENTAL IMPACTS

Transport activities produce a wide range of environmental and other unwanted side effects. Most commonly considered are the emission of chemicals to the atmosphere, water or land, the level of noise and the production of dust, smoke or soot. These are all physical effects whose magnitude can, in principle at least, be measured objectively. They may in turn have effects on people, animals or vegetation. But it is often very difficult to identify positive links between the emission of pollutants and their consequences.

Another class of unwanted side effects, which can be considered as part of the environmental consequences of transport, are social effects, which range from accidents to the effects on lifestyles of a mobile society. Yet another class is subjective effects. These include the nuisances caused by noise, exhaust smells and building vibration. It also includes the fear felt by pedestrians over the proximity of heavy traffic or by residents near airports.

Finally there are effects falling between the objective and subjective, and which are difficult or impossible to quantify. These include the effect on land use of transport provision (ribbon development in the 1930s, suburban sprawl in the 1960s, housing and industrial development around airports), the development of warehouse or industrial complexes at motorway intersections and the visual intrusion of highways.

The impacts may be global, regional or local. Most regional and global effects tend to be the result of the total emission of pollutants and are not remedied from local policies or design features. They do benefit from national or international policies that reduce emissions per vehicle km, but these benefits are eroded by continuing traffic growth. In the long term, regional and global effects can only be reduced either by dramatic technical change away from using fossil fuels, or by legislative or fiscal approaches to constrain further growth in traffic.

In general, the local effects of transport, such as noise and air pollution, can be much alleviated be technical improvements to vehicles and infrastructure, and by routing traffic away from where people live, work or shop. However, these technical improvements are not a long-term solution, because traffic growth erodes their benefits.

Local environmental effects of traffic can be reduced by diverting traffic away from people, usually by building bypasses, and by calming the remaining traffic to reduce its speed. Congestion can be reduced and safety improved by traffic management, junction improvements and very limited road improvements. Noise from traffic can be reduced by quietening vehicle powerplants and by using noise-absorbing road surfaces to reduce the tyre noise that is dominant at high speeds. There may be scope for designing tyres to be quieter without compromising the requirements for safety and durability. Emissions of air pollutants, particulates and smoke are being reduced by improvements to engines, to fuels and by exhaust after-treatment, using devices such as catalysts to convert harmful emissions to benign ones.

14.10 SAFETY

Many of the solutions that reduce local environmental impacts will also improve safety, though in general, safety should be built into our infrastructure and vehicles by design. For example, pedestrians, cars, buses and cyclists may all use a road, while houses shops, schools, etc. all front onto the same road. By deciding the most important function in an area and giving priority to the function, conflicts can be eliminated and a more pleasant environment created. Traffic will move more smoothly on roads that are not in conflict with pedestrians, shops or businesses. Pedestrian areas and traffic calming can create pleasant and safe areas where people can live work and play without the conflict of motor vehicles. The two can, and do, exist together without the economy suffering. Indeed it benefits.

14.11 AWARENESS

Many of the prescriptions that have been discussed would require people to change their present values and lifestyles. Before they will do this they must be aware of the pending problems, how they are affected, the benefits from changing their behaviour and what they can do personally to solve the problems. This implies the need for a continuous education and awareness programme which should be part of forward planning processes.

14.12 NEW TECHNOLOGY

Technology has played a fundamental role in creating motorized forms of transport and there is no reason why it will not play an equally important role in the future. The technology to construct canals, the steam engine and railways, the combustion engine and cars and the jet engine and aeroplanes are obvious examples from the past and electronics, computers and communications are the technologies of the present and future. These new technologies will change our behaviour and be used to provide travel information, change transport demand, modify the vehicles we drive and the way we control their use.

Telecommuting may be one of the ways in which people's travel behaviour is changed. In March 1990 President George Bush said in his Statement of National Transport Policy 'Sometimes the best transportation policy means not moving people, but moving their work . . . a trend known as telecommuting. . . . Think of it as commuting to work at the speed of light'. This thinking has been incorporated as part of the USA's National Transport Plan (Mokhtarian, 1990).

In the short term, technology is going to make travel safer and provide some additional capacity. It should help to keep traffic moving and minimize delays. My present view is that technology can increase the capacity of our roads at the rate of about 0.5% to 1% per annum, but this is an intelligent guess and should not be taken for granted. Clearly this is insufficient to keep pace with the increase in traffic growth and other measures are required.

The longer-term prospects suggest we could see radical changes in the form of our transport systems with it becoming more difficult to distinguish between collective and individual transport. The changes could increase the capacity of existing roads quite substantially. For the changes to happen it is necessary for us to protect the rights of way that currently exist as land is scarce and we cannot be sure what will be required. I expect to see any radical changes commencing around the year 2020.

14.13 THE TRENDS ARE NOT OUR DESTINY, WE SHAPE IT!

The message is that there will be substantial traffic growth in the next 30 years. There are many techniques and measures that can be used to improve the efficiency, safety and environmental quality of our transport systems and short, medium and long-term plans will help to ensure the measures are implemented.

The short-term measures are low cost improvements and will tend to be traffic management and minor road improvements. Regulations can be introduced to control traffic and to charge for parking. At the same time people can be made aware of the traffic problems we are likely to face.

In the medium term further transport management measures can be introduced and the separation of uses can take place so that there is an attempt to match land use with the growth of traffic. Travel patterns should be encouraged to change in an attempt to match the available supply of transport facilities and services to the demand.

In the much longer term a new balance between supply, in terms of new services and facilities, and the management of land use and travel behaviour can be undertaken. Also in the longer term we can expect new technology, as in the past, to influence the type of transport systems that we have available to us.

Finally, returning to the quotation (Wootton and Pick, 1967) at the beginning, there is no longer 'a rising number of accidents'. The Department of Transport set a target for the year 2000 of reducing accidents to two-thirds of the number in 1987. The serious and fatal injuries are already well on the way to meeting the target which seems as though it will be achieved. Secondly, the words 'a changing environment' no longer seem appropriate. 'A deteriorating environment' are more appropriate words today. If a target has been so successful in reducing the number of accidents perhaps we should have targets to improve the environment!

REFERENCES

Department of Transport (1989) *National road traffic forecasts (Great Britain) 1989*, Department of Transport, HMSO, London.

Elsenaar, P.M.W. (1992) Better Use of Road Space: Counter Measures; new measures to resolve traffic problems on main roads in the Netherlands. *17th International Study Week on Traffic Engineering and Safety, Warsaw Sept 1992*.

Freeman, Fox, Wilbur Smith & Associates (1968). *West Midlands Transport Study*, Freeman, Fox, Wilbur Smith & Associates, Birmingham.

Garreau, J. (1991) *Edge City – Life on the new frontier*, Doubleday.

Hoel, L.A. (1992) Better use of road space: US Solutions to relieving traffic congestion. *17th International Study Week on Traffic Engineering and Safety, Warsaw Sept 1992*.

Jessen, E. (1992) Better use of road space: Counter measures. *17th International Study Week on Traffic Engineering and Safety, Warsaw Sept 1992*.

Mokhtarian, P.L. (1990) The State of Telecommuting. *ITS Review*, University of California, **13**, August.

Stokes, G., Goodwin, P. and Kenny, F. (1992) *Trends in transport and the countryside*, Countryside Commission, Cheltenham.

Wootton, H.L. and Pick, G.W. (1967) A model for trips generated by households. *Journal of Transport Economics and Policy*, **1**, (2), London and Bath.

FURTHER READING

This paper has also used extracts from the following papers presented during the past two years to similar meetings and conferences in the past two years.

Wootton, H.J. (1991) *Road Transport Solutions with 2020 Vision*. A Lecture to the Fellowship of Engineering at The Institution of Mechanical Engineers on the 17 January 1991.

Wootton, H.J. (1992) Theme III – The Better use of Road Space. *17th International Study Week on Traffic Engineering and Safety, Warsaw Sept 1992.*

Wootton, H.J. Mitchell, C.G.B. and Poulton, M.L. (1992) *Transport in Europe – Demand, Environment and Energy.* Seminar on Energy, Transport and the Environment, Institute of Energy, 25 November 1992.

Wootton, H.J. (1993) Congestion, Traffic Management and Road Pricing. *Financial Times* conference, 'Transport in Europe', London, 2 March 1993.

Wootton, H.J. (1993) *Urban Transport, Planning and Construction – Planning.* Alan Brant Workshop, Institute of Highways and Transportation, Leamimgton Spa, 6 April 1993.

15

The intelligent highway: into the twenty-first century

P. Davies

15.1 INTRODUCTION

'Smart vehicles' and 'smart highways' form the key elements of intelligent vehicle-highway systems (IVHS), which promise to introduce dramatic changes to road transportation by the end of the current century. Automobile companies, electronics firms and highway agencies are coming together to set the standards for the highways of the twenty-first century. To address the current problems of congestion, accidents, energy and environmental concerns, advanced traffic control techniques and new information systems are being developed. Applications of advanced technologies are starting to make engineers and planners think in terms of truly intelligent twenty-first century roads.

Current generations of IVHS technologies, or Advanced Transport Telematics (ATT) to use the European term, have significant potential for helping relieve traffic congestion. This includes technologies such as motorist information and navigation systems, and demand-responsive, optimized traffic signal control. Longer-term development of intelligent driver support systems, electronic co-pilots and eventually, fully-automated vehicle control systems have the potential to revolutionize traffic safety and current concepts of highway capacity. Four main areas of IVHS have been recognized internationally, as outlined below.

- **Advanced traveller information systems** (ATS) provide drivers and passengers with current information on road conditions and route availability. They can assist travellers in making decisions before the trip begins, in selecting an appropriate route or travel mode, and through

Passenger Transport after 2000 AD. Edited by G.B.R. Feilden, A.H. Wickens and I.R. Yates. Published in 1994 by E & FN Spon, London. ISBN 0 419 19470 3.

reduced uncertainty as the travel situation changes. This field is examining the collection, processing and distribution of travel and traffic information to travellers at home, at work or during the course of the journey. Systems are currently being developed to provide information to drivers of vehicles, public transport passengers and fleet operators.

- **Advanced traffic management systems** (ATMS) build on established techniques for computer-optimized traffic control in urban traffic signal networks. In Europe in particular, ATMS is divided between urban and inter-urban applications. Technologies for tidal-flow systems, ramp metering, bus and light rail systems priorities at signalized intersections, all come under the ATMS umbrella.
- **Fleet management and control systems** (FMCS) represents the third area of IVHS developments. These are often subdivided into commercial vehicle operations (CVO) and advanced passenger transport systems (APTS). FMCS technologies include automatic vehicle identification, automatic vehicle location, two-way communications, and on-board computers.
- The final area is **advanced vehicle control systems** (AVCS). This offers the greatest potential benefits and the intelligent vehicle-highway environment. AVCS includes a group of technologies which can assist and support drivers in performing vehicle control functions. This group includes established systems such as vision enhancement, radar braking, and safety steering.

This paper examines the above areas of development primarily in Europe and within the DRIVE II framework, providing a background to the discussion of the potential benefits expected from the implementation of advanced transport technologies. Additional examples are provided from non-DRIVE initiatives including North American initiatives where appropriate. Major research initiatives are currently underway to realize the potential of advanced technologies in the transportation environment, and the paper sets these in the context of breakthroughs which will lead passenger transport into the twenty-first century.

15.2 ADVANCED TRAVELLER INFORMATION SYSTEMS

Advanced traveller information systems (ATIS) provide drivers and passengers with current information on road conditions and route availability. They can assist drivers in making decisions before the trip begins; in selecting an appropriate route or travel mode; in route following; and through reduced uncertainty as the travel situation changes.

ATIS technologies include travel information terminals, variable message signs, electronic maps and route guidance equipment in vehicles, bus stop displays, and traffic information broadcasting. These systems provide the user with directional or timetable information, location reference maps, and real-time updates on congestion, incidents, weather and highway maintenance activities.

ATIS benefits mostly accrue to individual system users. Providing drivers with accurate, real-time information may also help to remove a proportion of excess travel caused by less than optimal route choice. To the extent that this limits the overall demand for travel, wider social benefits are also anticipated. The greatest impact of ATIS, however, is likely to be reduced frustration and uncertainty for system users, who find these systems reassuring, and at least know what is happening when things go wrong.

Two broad groups of ATIS can be identified as follows:

- public transport information systems; and
- driver information systems.

The main DRIVE activities in these groups are outlined below. As ATIS has been widely recognized as being among the ATT technologies nearest to commercial availability this section represents a major focus of the report.

15.2.1 Public transport information systems

Research has shown the traveller's choice of the mode, time and route of travel is inefficient. The availability of more accurate information regarding routes, scheduling, route interchanges and fares encourages greater patronage and more efficient operation of the transport system.

A number of recent projects have aimed to establish standards and specifications for systems and to evaluate pilot schemes in public transport information systems. Between 1989 and 1991 seventy-one projects were undertaken in the DRIVE programme (Dedicated Road Infrastructure for Vehicle Safety in Europe). The programme was established by the Commission of the European Communities to investigate infrastructure requirements, operational aspects and ATT technologies of interest. The ATT (or DRIVE II) programme aims to take many of the systems developed under the DRIVE programme through to large-scale field trials. Five DRIVE II projects focus on public transport information systems. The main aims of these initiatives are introduced below.

The **SCOPE** project is a multi-faceted assessment of ATT applications. Three test sites are being used to investigate different technologies: Southampton (UK), Cologne (D) and Piraeus (GR). The work at the Southampton site (the ROMANSE project) is evaluating passenger transport information systems and the use of different forms of passenger information. The requirements and format of three types of traveller/passenger information are under investigation. These are:

- at home – pre-trip information;
- in-trip information; and
- in-vehicle/at stop information.

The SCOPE-ROMANSE project will provide real-time information to passengers at bus stops in the form of a countdown to the arrival of the next bus. A test of this is currently being developed, known as Stopwatch.

The **EUROBUS** project aims to define a European reference data model for public transport information systems and to design computed-aided tools for passenger information services. EUROBUS is a direct continuation of the DRIVE I programme CASSIOPE project.

Design of the man-machine interface (MMI) is a critical factor in the acceptance and utility of a passenger information system. A survey of the most frequent passenger enquiries and preferences was undertaken as part of EUROBUS. This survey, in conjunction with the level of complexity of the MMI, is being used in the development of prototype systems. Within EUROBUS, POPINS aims to develop advanced passenger information prototypes in three cities: Madrid (E), Marseille (F) and Thessaloniki (GR).

The **QUARTET** project (Quadrilateral Advanced Research on Telematics for Environment and Transport) is investigating a series of technologies associated with an integrated road transport environment (IRTE). Prototype systems are under evaluation in four cities: Stuttgart (D), Birmingham (UK), Athens (GR) and Torino (I).

The Birmingham test site is concerned with public transport management and information systems. The research is assessing the use of real-time schedule adherence information (countdowns at bus stops), and fixed schedule and service information. Such fixed schedule information includes information to drivers about other modes of travel such as train and bus schedules, and nearby park and ride facilities. A series of information systems are being evaluated in Birmingham including an enquiry office service, in-street terminal and in-home terminals. Additional links have been established with the PROMISE project to test portable terminals in this city.

The **PROMISE** project (Prometheus CED 10 Mobile and Portable Information Systems in Europe) is evaluating a multi-modal traveller information system. The prototype hand-held terminals it intends to trial can be used to provide traffic and travel information, public transportation information and parking services. PROMISE is continuing the work undertaken in the PROMETHEUS programme (Programme for European Traffic with Highest Efficiency and Unprecedented Safety).

PROMETHEUS is a research programme to define and develop advanced technologies for vehicles. It is a collaboration between European automotive manufacturers and other respective governments, organized under the EUREKA programme. Within PROMETHEUS the THETIS transportation information system was developed. THETIS enables the traveller to query travel databases for a large range of services. It also enables facilities such as reservations for flights, car hire and hotels.

Finally, the DRIVE II project (**ASTRA**) is undertaking a feasibility study of an integrated system incorporating various services for traffic and travel. This encompasses dynamic travel and traffic information, reservation and guidance services for traveflers. ASTRA's objectives are firstly to investigate traffic management and traveller requirement, and secondly to assess the technical and financial feasibility of the integrated system on two test sites. These are Bochum (D) and Helsingør (DK).

15.2.2 Driver information systems

Traffic congestion is at present one of the most serious problems affecting the highway network. With the continued projected growth in traffic levels, congestion is expected to be a worsening problem. The development of driver information systems in conjunction with traffic management measures aims to increase the safety, efficiency and control of the highway network.

Numerous schemes are under development by individual automotive manufacturers and component suppliers. The projects examined here aim to establish standards and evaluate prototype systems within the scope of the DRIVE II programme. They are only a subset of all the developments in this field, but should serve as an overview to the type of progress being made. The projects considered are:

- ATT-ALERT;
- PROMISE;
- PLEIADES;
- SOCRATES;
- LLAMD; and
- GEMINI.

The **ATT-ALERT** project (Advanced Transport Telematics – Advice and Problem Location for European Road Traffic) concerns the development and standardization of protocols for driver information across a number of communication bearers. The protocols enable co-ordinated information to be broadcast using existing communication channels such as pagers, RDS (Radio Data System) and cellular radio. ATT-ALERT will also monitor the TMC (Travel Message Channel) trials to finalize the existing ALERT C protocol which covers basic traffic events broadcast over RDS. The project is being conducted by broadcasters, national traffic authorities and manufacturers.

The **PROMISE** project, which has been described in the public transport information section, is developing a multi-modal traveller information system. In addition to public transport information, the prototype system will also access traffic information and parking services. The PROMISE system will collect data from a series of data sources, undertake processing and generate information in formats suitable for broadcasting. Operational systems may use a number of different bearers. Field trials will take place in Gothenburg and Birmingham.

A field trial of a wide range of ATT technologies is being undertaken in the **PLEIADES** project. This project aims to co-ordinate information from a number of sources and disseminate relevant information to drivers through a series of different media, including RDS-TMC, paging, cellular telephone and variable message signs (VMS). PLEIADES will investigate traffic information collection, weather monitoring, traffic monitoring and traffic control. The test site is the London to Paris corridor. A significant problem identified in the PLEIADES project is the generation of an accurate and extensive database of information. Existing databases are considered unsuitable due to the formats they exist in.

The **SOCRATES** project (System of Cellular Radio for Traffic Efficiency and Safety) has continued from DRIVE I into DRIVE II. It aims to develop a system for communicating driver information based on the proposed GSM digital cellular radio network. SOCRATES-based pilot projects are taking place in Hessen (D), Gothenburg (S), London (UK) and Amsterdam (NL). The proposed system aims to cover dynamic route guidance, driver information and parking information. As with other RTI systems, information is collected from diverse sources and then stored and processed in traffic control centres.

The **LLAMD** project (London, Lyon, Amsterdam, Munich, Dublin Euro-project) aims to demonstrate, test and evaluate a series of ATT technologies for a co-ordinated approach to an integrated road traffic environment. Each city will be a demonstration site for different ATT technologies including dynamic route guidance (both radio-based and road-side beacon-based), traffic management, traffic information, public transport management, and public transport information.

Finally, the **GEMINI** project (Generation of Event Messages in the New Integrated Road Transport Environment) aims to develop an integrated approach to the use of VMS and RDS-TMC. Two test sites are being used to evaluate the prototype system: the Trieste-Brescia corridor (I), the Birmingham motorway 'box' (UK). The trials will consider data collection, data processing and information processing, in particular to ensure that drivers do not receive contradictory information.

15.3 ADVANCED TRAFFIC MANAGEMENT SYSTEMS

Advanced traffic management systems (ATMS) build on established techniques for computer-optimized traffic control in urban traffic signal networks. Related technologies for tidal flow systems, ramp metering of commuters onto congested urban motorways, bus and light rail system priorities at signalized intersections, and electronic enforcement of traffic regulations, all come within the ATMS umbrella.

Existing systems for ramp control and signal co-ordination in urban networks have already been shown to provide very worthwhile payoffs in terms of reductions in delays and stops for vehicles. More specialized systems giving priority to travellers by mode or direction travelled can offer even greater benefits in appropriate situations. Finally, electronic enforcement can help sustain priority measures by deterring violators, in addition to benefitting road safety through systematic enforcement of speed limits and red lights.

15.4 FLEET MANAGEMENT AND CONTROL SYSTEMS

This third area of IVHS developments can be divided into two categories as follows:

- commercial vehicle operations; and
- advanced passenger transport systems.

Fleet management and control systems for commercial vehicle operations (CVO) of bus and truck fleets represents a third area of rapid IVHS developments. CVO technologies include automatic vehicle identification systems (AVI), automatic vehicle location systems (AVL), two-way communications using both satellite and terrestrial equipment, and on-board computers covering a whole range of fleet management and safety applications.

CVO benefits include real-time response to changing demand for services; non-stop compliance with safety and taxation checks on fleet vehicles; continuous tracking of hazardous or high-value cargoes; and easy monitoring/communication with large fleets in order to maximize management efficiency. Specific examples of CVO technology applications include interstate truck monitoring in North America; bus and light rail fleet management in Europe; and police vehicle location traking in several areas of the world.

Within the CVO division, the US HELP programme represents a major innovation. HELP (the Heavy Vehicle Electronic License Plate program) is a US$20 million programme to research and develop an integrated heavy vehicle management system, which utilizes automatic vehicle identification, weigh-in-motion and automatic vehicle classification technologies with a networked data communications system. The programme is directed by fifteen states, the New York/New Jersey Port Authorities, various motor carrier organizations and the US Federal Highway Authority. Operational tests are being undertaken at thirty-five sites along interstate highways through Washington, Oregon, California, Arizona, New Mexico and Texas.

15.4.1 Advanced passenger transport systems

There is a considerable degree of overlap between this development area and activities being undertaken within the ATIS field. Many public transport companies currently face a significant degree of competition from private vehicles for road space and communications facilities. Such competition usually produces disturbances to public transport services due to traffic congestion lack of passenger information and low public transport productivity. The development of ATPS aims to address such issues.

One major initiative in this field is the development, implementation and evaluation of the vehicle scheduling control system (VSCS) being undertaken by the PHOEBUS project. Such systems are being developed to improve the overall efficiency of public transport.

Functional requirements of public transport operators are largely dependent on the operational characteristics of the network. A basic function in the VSCS systems is getting information about the vehicle's location. This information will then be used by operators to ensure that timetable schedules are adhered to. The potential benefits arising from VSCS will be evaluated by the PHOEBUS project at test sites in Madrid and Gent.

15.5 ADVANCED VEHICLE CONTROL SYSTEMS

This final area of advanced vehicle control systems (AVCS) at once offers the greatest potential benefits and the most significant obstacles to the IVHS/ATT development programme. AVCS includes a group of technologies which can assist and support drivers in performing vehicle control functions. These systems may, in the longer term, relieve the driver of some or all of the driving tasks. Potential benefits of AVCS could include substantial safety enhancements and major increases in highway capacity.

AVCS technologies begin with established systems for antilock braking and traction control, including conventional cruise control systems. New intelligent cruise control systems are expected to be marketed during the early to mid-1990s, which will monitor the vehicle ahead and adjust the cruise speed and headway automatically to suit prevailing traffic conditions. Other AVCS technologies include vision enhancement systems, radar braking systems, and safety steering which defaults back to the centre of the traffic lane. The logical conclusion of current AVCS developments could include fully automated steering and headway control sometimes known as the automated highway, which would eventually revolutionize the way roads are operated and constructed.

This section introduces some of the more advanced technologies being developed in this field including:

- forward obstacle detection;
- blind spot detection; and
- intersection collision warning.

As AVCS offers significant potential benefits to all road users, this section forms another major focus to the paper.

Forward obstacle detection

These systems monitor the highway environment immediately ahead of a vehicle, reporting any obstacles in the travel lane. This form of detection system operate by one of the three following concepts:

- headway monitoring of the distance and closing rate between adjacent vehicles;
- monitoring the forward path of the vehicle for obstacles; and
- the use of vision enhancement systems to improve the driver's perception of the driving environment.

Headway monitoring systems monitor the separation distance and closing rate between the host vehicle and leading vehicle. A warning is issued when the separation falls below an acceptable level. The leading vehicle is identified as the target if it is detected over a certain period of time. Current headway detection systems have only single targeting capabilities which enables isolation of the leading vehicle. This permits a safe vehicle-to-vehicle distance to be determined.

Forward obstacle monitoring systems provide the driver with a warning if an object rests in the travel path of the vehicle. For this a multi-targeting capability is required.

Vision enhancement systems enable drivers to increase the level of visibility under poor visibility conditions. Such conditions are found during various forms of precipitation and fog. These systems fall into two categories of highway illumination techniques and enhanced vision camera based techniques, as described below.

Blind spot detection

Even with current vehicle design, it is almost impossible for the driver to be able to see all around a vehicle. Blindspot monitoring systems are designed to aid drivers' vision, thus helping to reduce the occurrence of lane changing and merging accidents. Blindspot monitoring systems alert the driver to the presence of vehicles or pedestrians in fixed zones around the vehicle.

Blindspot monitoring systems must have the ability to provide an accurate detection capability while travelling at high velocities and while the vehicle is travelling under a range of weather conditions. The technologies utilized for this application currently available on the market are:

- ultrasonic sensors;
- infrared sensors; and
- microwave sensors.

The sensors are located to monitor where the driver's vision is limited or obscured. These sensors are connected to a central microcomputer which analyses and processes the information and relays it to a display or warning system inside the vehicle. The majority of the systems described below only operate when the turn indicator is engaged. Alternative modes of operation are described where appropriate. This does, of course, have the disadvantage that the systems do not engage when the drivers move into another lane without signalling.

Intersection collision avoidance warning

This has been the focus of considerable research work during recent years. Such research aims to develop systems to alert drivers to hazardous situations at an intersection. Typically, a system performing this function will consist of the following fundamental features:

- the ability to gather information relating to the traffic situation at an intersection, e.g. vehicle positions, speeds and dimensions;
- the ability to process this information to build a complete picture of the current traffic situation at the intersection;
- communication facilities to enable the information to be relayed to drivers of suitably equipped vehicles; and
- an in-vehicle unit capable of receiving the information and translating it into a form suitable for communication to the driver.

Given that the functions listed above can be provided in a cost-effective manner, a range of warnings can be provided to the driver. At the simplest level, the two-way transfer of information from a roadside processing unit to a suitably equipped vehicle can be used to warn a driver if the vehicle's speed is excessive as it approaches an intersection. At the other extreme, it is technically possible to warn the driver of a vehicle approaching an intersection about the presence of oncoming or turning vehicles in the intersection itself.

15.6 SUMMARY

Traffic congestion, high accident and fatality rates, and increasing environmental impact are related to traffic growth. The relief of traffic-related problems by the expansion of the existing network is no longer a suitable option in many situations. The use of advanced technologies such as IVHS/ATT holds significant benefits in increased efficiency, convenience and safety in all modes of transportation. This paper has introduced the main development areas currently being researched within various IVHS/ATT programmes thus setting the context for detailed discussions of the anticipated benefits arising from such initatives. Examples of ATT systems mainly from the European DRIVE programme were reviewed focusing in particular on ATIS and AVCS. There is considerable interest in these areas as such systems offer immediate benefits to road users.

In addition to the European DRIVE framework, there are other major public and private sector initiatives underway in Japan, Europe and North America to realize the potential of advanced technologies in the transportation environment. International collaboration between these initiatives is vital if significant advances in global transportation are to be realized. The scene is therefore set for some exciting developments and major breakthroughs during the rest of the decade.

Part Five

Transport Systems 2

16

European air traffic control – applying the technology

P.C. Venton and C.R. White

16.1 INTRODUCTION

The aim of air traffic control (ATC), is to ensure the safe, orderly and expeditious flow of air traffic within the airspace. Air traffic ranges from the scheduled, public transportation flights of the airlines, to military aircraft on operational training sorties; from private pilots flying for pleasure, to agricutural crop spraying aircraft, gliders, balloons and parachutists.

Airspace is organized into Flight Information Regions (FIRs) worldwide. Responsibility for these FIRs and the associated Air Traffic Services (ATS), are assigned, by the International Civil Aviation Organisation (ICAO) to the nations over which the FIRs lie and for which the respective nations can provide effective air traffic services.

ATS provide the infrastructure of the ATC system, as well as the means by which the system can operate. In current ATC systems ground-based and on-board navigational aids assist the navigation of aircraft in accordance with a pre-determined flight plan. Primary and secondary radars provide positional and identity information about aircraft on air traffic control unit displays. This enables the air traffic controllers, through voice communications with pilots, to ensure safe and efficient flight in accordance with the flight plan. Extensive ground-to-ground telecommunications and data exchange networks link ATC units within and between FIRs.

Within FIRs there are two main categories of airspace – 'controlled' and 'uncontrolled'. In uncontrolled airspace, aicraft may fly when and where they like, subject to a simple set of rules.

Passenger Transport after 2000 AD. Edited by G.B.R. Feilden, A.H. Wickens and I.R. Yates.
Published in 1994 by E & FN Spon, London. ISBN 0 419 19470 3.

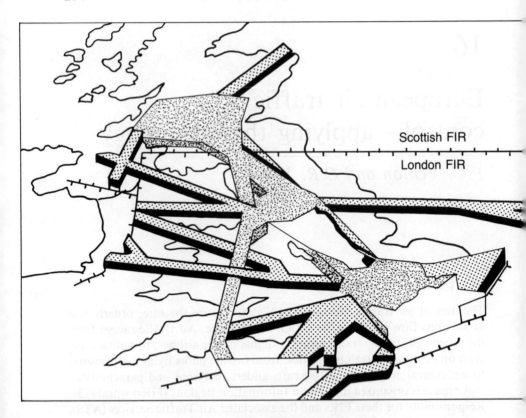

Figure 16.1 The UK airways system.

Controlled airspace is divided into three cateories: control zones – surrounding major airports; terminal control areas – normally established at the confluence of airways in the vicinity of one or more major airports; and airways – corridors of airspace connecting the terminal control areas and linking up with the airways of adjacent nations.

Airways are established to define the main traffic flow routes connecting centres of population within a particular geographical area. Invariably they link up with the major cities within national and adjacent states boundaries. Airways are normally 10 miles wide and they extend from between 5000 ft and 7000 ft up to a height of 24 500 ft (Figure 16.1).

To fly in controlled airspace, aircraft must carry special navigational equipment and pilots must hold the necessary qualifications. Pilots must obtain clearance from ATC to enter this airspace and, except in an emergency, they must follow ATC instructions implicitly. The prior notification to obtain clearance normally takes the form of filing a 'flight plan'.

In controlled airspace each aircraft must be kept separate from all others by internationally agreed standard distances. This is done by allocating different height or by arranging certain minimum horizontal distances between aircraft. These distances vary according to circumstances; for example, two aircraft operating under radar control may not come within five nautical miles of each other at the same height. If two aircraft are less than five nautical miles apart horizontally they must be vertically separated by a minimum of 1000 ft or 2000 ft if the aircraft are flying above 29 000 ft.

As was outlined above the ATC process is designed to achieve the safe, orderly and expeditious flow of air traffic in accordance with approved flight plans. The process starts with the acceptance and promulgation of an approved flight plan by a national, or international, Flight Management Unit.

16.2 A TYPICAL COMMERCIAL FLIGHT

Let us now look at the progress of a typical commercial flight. First a flight progress strip, generated from the flight plan, is issued to the aerodrome control function at the departure airport where the ground movement controller (GMC) instructs the pilot when to start the engines and move away from the stand. The GMC guides the aircraft across the apron and along the taxiways avoiding vehicles, obstructions and other aircraft and positions it in the correct sequence for take-off. During the daytime, when there is good visibility, aircraft and vehicles are controlled by direct observation. At night and during periods of poor visibility, aircraft are guided by red and green lights embedded in the taxiways and controlled from a visual control room at the top of the control tower. At large busy airports, the GMC makes use of a plan position display of aircraft movements from a short range, high resolution radar, known as an Airport Surface Detection Equipment (ASDE).

Whilst the aircraft is taxiing the GMC obtain, from the terminal control area departure controller a clearance for the aircraft to depart in accordance with the pilot's flight plan request. On arrival at the holding point for the runway used for departing traffic, control of the aircraft passes from the GMC to the air controller (AC). The AC's task is to instruct the aircraft when to enter the runway for take-off and, once it is airborne, control is transferred to the terminal control area departure controller in the air traffic control centre (ATCC). Flight strips are printed to warn of the impending arrival of the aircraft which have recently taken off from the departure airport, in the terminal area and the en-route sectors of the airways system. Co-ordinating clearance messages are passed from the departure controller in the ATCC to the AC, to accept the transfer of the aircraft from the terminal control zone into the terminal control area. The task of the departure controller is to start the aircraft on its climb to cruising level, applying, if necessary, radar separation standards to resolve any problem there may be with arriving, transiting or departing traffic.

Once the aircraft is airborne, the actual time of departure is entered into the computer system. This input message activates the computers to produce new flight progress strips for the sectors through which the aircraft will pass en-route to its final destination.

The ATCC is responsible for control both in the terminal area and the enroute airways. The centre's computers are programmed with the aircraft's flight profile from the flight plan i.e. climb/cruise/descent, speeds and the distances to be flown between reporting points; also the wind speed and direction at various levels. It is thus possible, following the activate message, to calculate and print flight progress strips giving the estimated time of arrival at various points in the flight. As the aircraft continues its flight and approaches the next sector, co-ordination is carried out and the aircraft is instructed to change its radio/telephony (R/T) frequency to that of the next sector. On receipt of the R/T call, the next sector controller continues the climb of the aircraft to its cruising level, once again using radar separation standards, if necessary, to resolve any conflicts. Prior to the arrival of the flight at the boundary of the destination terminal control area, co-ordination takes place on a direct telephone circuit between the en-route controller and the terminal area controller and the aircraft is instructed to transfer to the terminal area R/T frequency.

The terminal area controller has a radar display similar to that used by the en-route controller, showing the aircraft with its callsign and height. The controller also has the flight progress strip updated by any revised estimated times of arrival. It is the terminal area controller's responsibility to continue the descent of the aircraft until it is handed over to the approach controller.

Following the receipt of an R/T call from the aircraft, the approach controller gives the pilot an initial clearance. This may include instructions to enter a holding pattern, or 'stack', if an approach delay is expected. Aircraft in a stack circle at different heights around a reporting point until the way is clear for them to be guided into the sequence for landing.

Approach controllers work closely together to establish the correct landing intervals between aircraft on final approach, by instructing the pilots to adjust their aircraft's height, speed and route, so that they are correctly separated. The spacing between arriving aircraft depends on a number of factors such as the prevailing weather conditions, the size of aircraft involved and the number of aircraft waiting to depart. Because of their great size and weight wide-bodied aircraft, such as the Boeing 747, create more turbulence in the air through which they pass than smaller aircraft. This wake turbulence can upset the flying characteristics of lighter aircraft following behind, so greater separation distances have to be applied.

As outlined above, the flight plan registers information on a flight for two basic purposes; firstly prior information which is essential for the provision of air traffic services and secondly information which, in the event of an accident, is vital to the success of the search and rescue (SAR) services. It will be clear that air traffic control is dependent upon a knowledge of the aircraft's present position and the intentions of the pilot. Since the controllers cannot see the aircraft, it is necessary for them to build up a picture in their mind's eye of the relative positions and intentions of the aircraft under their control. The flight plan and the derived flight progress strip are, therefore, essential planning tools. The flight plan, which is an internationally agreed document, includes information on identification, type and callsign; aerodrome of departure, destination and alternates; estimated time of arrival at FIR boundaries, cruising speed, desired flight levels and the proposed route and is submitted at least 30 minutes before the planned departure time for the flight. For scheduled flights, which are of a repetitive nature, operating on a published timetable, a repetitive flight plan (RPL) is filed in the computer and automatically activated at the appropriate time.

The universal method of achieving the mental picture of the air traffic, is to transpose the received flight data onto the 'flight progress strip'. These are literally strips of paper which, when placed in holders on the controller's workstation, are used to display time, height, geographical and relative position information on aircraft.

16.3 THE INFRASTRUCTURE OF THE ATC SYSTEM

Apart from the various types of ATC units, concerned with air traffic management and control (ATM/ATC), the infrastructure of the ATC system consists of three elements: communications, navigation and surveillance (CNS). In current systems, communication from ground to air is by voice, utilizing very high frequency (VHF) and high frequency (HF) radio links. The communication of ATS data from one ground centre to another is by telephone or teleprinter utilizing the worldwide Aeronautical Fixed Telecommunications Network (AFTN). Navigation is achieved through the mandatory carriage of specific radio navigation equipment onboard the aircraft, and the provision and maintenance, by national ATSs of a large number of navigational aids which enable aircraft to fly the airways system with the necessary accuracy. These aids are VHF omnidirectional range (VOR) beacons, which are sometimes located with distance measuring equipment (DME) and non-directional beacons (NDB). Safe landings are assisted by the instrument landing system (ILS). Surveillance of aircraft along the airways and in terminal areas is provided by primary and secondary radars, strategically sited below the airways and at many airports. Outside radar coverage, over the oceans for instance, the positions of aircraft are tracked through regular voice position reports from the pilots.

Primary radar depends on the reflection from metal surfaces of some of the pulsed signal transmitted by the radar station on the ground. From this reflection, the range and bearing from the ground transmitter of a 'target' aircraft, can be determined. The reflected signal is, however, extremely weak and requires considerable amplification and processing to produce a clear 'plan position indication' of the relative position of the aircraft and the transmitter on the controller's display.

Unwanted reflections of the transmitted signal, from the ground or from precipitation in bad weather, can produce 'clutter' on the display. Further sophisticated processing to show only those targets moving at characteristic aircraft speeds, is required to remove this clutter.

Secondary surveillance radar (SSR) is a development of primary radar, in which the aircraft target co-operates with the ground-based radar system. This co-operation is achieved through the aircraft carrying a 'transponder' which transmits coded pulsed messages, in response to receiving coded pairs of pulses from the SSR ground transmitter or 'interrogator'.

Because the SSR system does not rely upon reflected energy from the aircraft to provide a radar echo, but utilizes the return signal generated by the transponder, the transmitter on the ground can be of lower power and employ simpler and cheaper technology whilst ensuring the certainty of a signal return unaffected by clutter.

The return pulse train can also be coded to provide specific information on each aircraft, such as identity and height at which it is flying. This capability enables the SSR ground receiver and processor to separate and identify targets in a manner which is not possible with primary radar.

Primary radar provides only basic information on the position of an aircraft in relation to the radar, but it does show all aircraft within the area of coverage. Secondary radar is selective and only displays information from aircraft equipped with transponders. All aircraft operating in controlled or special rules airspace must be equipped with a serviceable transponder.

Before an aircraft enters the airways system it is allocated an individual four-figure code so that, when it is interrogated by a SSR station, it replies through its transponder with the allocated code and the height at which it is flying. This information can then be displayed on the radar screen, in the form of a label next to the aircraft's position symbol. This makes it easier for the controller to associate the radar picture with the flight plan details for the aircraft. Combined with this displayed information on the radar screens, are computer-generated maps showing key geographical features, such as coastlines, and the airways structure. The controllers have the ability to select which information and maps they wish to have displayed.

Air Traffic control centres (ATCC), be they concerned with aerodrome, approach or area/enroute control, all depend upon modern computer and software techniques. The Vienna ATCC is one of the largest and most advanced air traffic control centres currently operational in Europe. The provision of data processing to assist the controllers in the safe conduct of air traffic requires the design of system functions which are extremely reliable, resilient to failures and capable of expansion to meet future needs. Within the Vienna system a distributed processor architecture, which provides a high degree of configuration flexibility with considerable scope for expansion, is adopted. The functions of the system fall into three major areas: flight data processing, radar data processing and display data processing. Each is assigned to a particular processor. The radar processor executes complex mathematical functions repetitively, on a large amount of data in a limited period of time, maintaining a record of all aircraft tracks recognized by the system. Every six seconds, corresponding to one rotation of the radar antennae, these track data are read out and broadcast to all the plan view display positions.

The central processor supports all the flight plan processing and other aeronautical information services, such as the provision of meteorological (MET) data. This processing is concerned with accessing and manipulating inter-dependent data held in a complex database structure. A processing transaction is stimulated on receipt of an external message or by a controller command or the occurrence of a timed event. This normally results in a change to the content of the database and the distribution of information to the display consoles.

The display processor maintains a local picture on the synthetic data display. Broadcast data from the radar processor are filtered according to the sector allocated to the controller's console and his or her local display selections. To achieve high system availability, both the central and radar processors are triplicated. Any pairing of central processor and radar processor may be set up to provide the processing power needed to support full system operation. In the event of either failing, an automatic change-over to a standby processor takes place.

The synthetic data display (SDD) is the main device for the presentation of aircraft movements derived from radar data, supplemented by flight plan and other information. The SDD is a cursive display with a 550 mm diameter cathode ray tube. The high definition of these displays permits a considerable amount of information to be presented using vectors, special symbols and alpha-numeric characters. The controllers can update flight plan data and change their picture whenever the need arises by using a light pen.

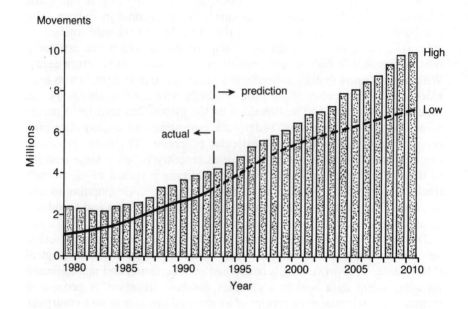

Figure 16.2 The projected growth of air traffic in Europe.

16.4 THE EXPANSION OF AIR TRAFFIC IN EUROPE

All regions of the world are expected to see significant increases in air traffic demand into the next century (Figure 16.2). Air traffic in Europe is increasing rapidly, the rate of growth is now higher than that forecast by the airlines and the authorities in the early 1980s. Traffic is currently increasing at 5% per annum and the trend is predicted to continue beyond the year 2000. The completion of the Single Market of the European Community and the development of Eastern Europe should increase both trade and tourism, and therefore traffic, throughout the continent. Whilst high speed rail services and the Channel Tunnel may absorb some of the growth on shorter routes, an increase in air transport can be expected on most routes linking the wider Europe now in prospect, as well as on the expanding inter-regional network.

The expansion of air traffic in Europe is a challenge to the entire aviation industry. The prime objective of the national air traffic services is to ensure that traffic is never allowed to rise to levels that cannot be accommodated safely by air traffic control at any given time or within any given flight

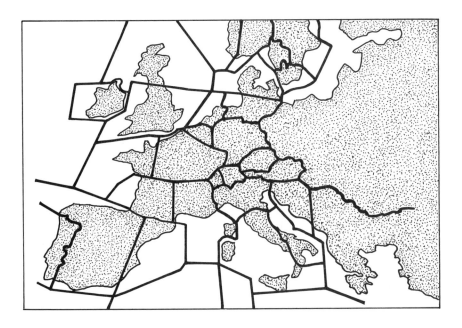

Figure 16.3 The Flight Information Regions (FIRs) of Western Europe.

information region or sector. This is achieved by 'flow control', a system in which the traffic loads on the various air routes are calculated and are 'held' on the ground until their passage through the airspace to their destination is cleared. In very heavy traffic situations, alternative routes are proposed to airline operators to keep the traffic load within safe bounds. A central flow management unit (CFMU) is currently in the process of being established in Brussels to manage the flow of air traffic throughout Europe. The penalty for this safety measure is delays on the ground. These are caused, primarily, by an overall lack of capacity in the European ATC system and secondarily through the difficulties of co-ordinating the ATC operations of the large number of states in Europe. There are, within the core of Europe, some 13 states with 22 FIRs. Difficulties within one FIR can have a 'domino' effect throughout the system. ATC industrial disputes can also add considerably to the problem (Figure 16.3).

In 1990, the Transport Ministers of the thirty-one European Civil Aviation Conference (ECAC) states, reacted to the delays and the forecast growth of air traffic in the European region. They agreed to adopt a strategy and action programme to harmonize and integrate their air traffic operations by the end of the 1990s. This programme is known as the European Harmonisation and Integration Programme (EATCHIP) and is managed, on behalf of the ECAC ministers, by Eurocontrol in Brussels. The programme is in four phases.

In Phase I all the significant technical characteristics of the air space and route structure, communications, navigation and surveillance, air traffic control system and human resources were appraised and evaluated. This work was completed in mid-1991 and has led to the short-term upgrading of the existing systems.

Phase II, in which the programme for harmonizing and integrating the European systems is developed, is currently in hand and should be completed by mid-1993. This involves the detailed planning for medium-term harmonization and integration of the systems, together with the development of recommendations and the production of specifications. Implementation programmes for specific areas are being developed and the initial implementation of new route and airspace structures, new facilities and common procedures, is in hand.

Phase III will cover the acquisition and installation of new advanced equipment and the continued implementation of new route and airspace structures and the development of common procedures. The harmonization and progressive integration of the air traffic control systems, throughout the ECAC area, will be implemented, and a start will be made on introducing new air/ground data link facilities. This phase is planned to be largely completed by mid-1995, with the new elements being completed by mid-1998.

Phase IV is planned for 1995 to the year 2000 and beyond, and covers the implementation of the future European Air Traffic Management System (EATMS). This integrated system is based upon the latest technology and new common operational requirements, which this supports. The studies, tests and applied research upon which the new system concept is based, are being undertaken in parallel with the other phases of the EATCHIP.

The new concepts for the EATCHIP are based upon ideas developed by the ICAO Future Air Navigation System (FANS) group, which have been endorsed by the worldwide aviation community, and the Future European Air Traffic System (FEATS) concept, developed by the ICAO European region sub-group.

Eurocontrol, in concert with the Civil Aviation Authorities (CAA) of the ECAC states, is progressing the new concepts in the EATCHIP through the Eurocontrol programme of Studies, Tests and Applied Research (STAR), the Programme of Harmonised ATM Research in Eurocontrol (PHARE), which co-ordinates the research programmes of the leading European CAAs, the Enhanced ATM and Mode S Implementation in Europe (EASIE) programme and the EATMS programme.

The European Community is keen to see a safe, capable and cost-effective air traffic control system, introduced throughout Europe, as part

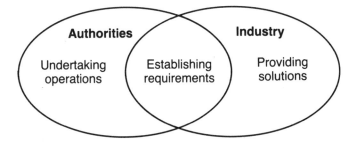

Figure 16.4 The key roles of the European ATC authorities and industry.

of an overall integrated transport system. Consequently, the European Commission (EC) is actively developing policies and procedures for the deregulation of European airlines, certification of aircraft, licensing of pilots, maintenance engineers and controllers and the establishing of specifications and standards.

Directorate General (DG) VII, the Transport Directorate, is leading these legislative initiatives and, in collaboration with DG XII, the Research Directorate, and DGXIII, the Information Technology and Innovation Directorate, is supporting the forward-looking Eurocontrol activities with the EURET, GAAS and ATLAS research programmes.

One of the major concerns in achieving the timescales planned for the EATCHIP, is the availability of adequate, appropriately skilled resources, to undertake the wide range of tasks required. It is generally appreciated that the appropriate skills within the European ATC community are contained within two major groups – the authorities, i.e. Eurocontrol with the national CAAs – and industry. These resources are finite and, to ensure the success of the EATCHIP, it will be necessary to use them effectively. The ECAC ministers have recognized this and called for industrial involvement and support to ensure the success of the programme.

Effective use of these resources is best achieved through the major groups concentrating on those tasks for which their skills are most appropriate and their experience is best suited (Figure 16.4). For the authorities the key skill is providing air traffic services, through managing and operating the air traffic management and control systems. From this operational experience, the authorities are in a unique position to specify the requirements for new systems. The primary role of industry is to design, develop and implement system solutions for these requirements, having worked with the authorities to establish the requirements.

The European authorities and industry have, over the last forty years or more, built up considerable experience of the specific requirements and the particular solutions relating to the European region, which has characteristics different from other regions. The concentration of states in central

Europe, results in the distances between major cities being relatively short. Unlike, for instance, the US, where the centres of population are widely separated, the centre of Europe is effectively a large terminal area, with a great deal of ascending and decending air traffic. Consequently European ATC operations and solutions are markedly different from those in the US, where much of the activity is en-route.

As indigenous organizations, the authorities and industry are best placed to meet the challenge of harmonizing and integrating the various national systems in the short to medium term, and developing and supporting the EATMS in the long term. There is no doubt that there is the capability, within the authorities and the indigenous European industry, to solve the European ATM/ATC problems and successfully complete the EATCHIP; however, this capability needs to be applied in a balanced manner. To date, there has been a tendency for the authorities to establish requirements and design solutions within their own ambit, with little industry involvement. This approach leaves the indigenous European industry at a disadvantage against other industry, particularly from the US where, in a closed market with very large development and implementation contracts placed by the influential Federal Aviation Authority (FAA), a desire to dominate the European ATC market has developed.

To ensure the success of the EATCHIP, the considerable experience and skills within the authorities and the indigenous industry in Europe, should be deployed in a balanced manner. The authorities should concentrate on establishing operational and functional concepts and managing the specification, procurement and operation of systems. In partnership with industry, the authorities should research these concepts and establish requirements and standards, so that the results of this work can flow through effectively and rapidly, to implemented solutions. Industry should concentrate on designing, building and supporting systems and software.

To ensure that indigenous European industrial resources, of proven capability, and significant size, are available to support the EATCHIP, Siemens in the UK and Germany and Thomson-CSF in France, have taken a lead by combining their ATM/ATC activities.

The ECAC strategy is pragmatic and is based on deriving the maximum benefit from the present air traffic control systems in the area and ensuring that future developments are co-ordinated. The strategy concentrates on the period up to the end of the century. Within that period a comparable level of system performance will be achieved throughout the ECAC area through the use of common operating procedures, system standardization and enhancement and the introduction of new equipment. At the end of the period, new advanced systems, currently under development, will begin to be introduced operational.

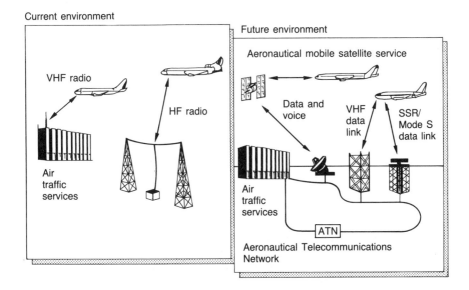

Figure 16.5 Communications: current and future environments.

16.5 THE FUTURE

In the ATC system of 2000 and beyond, the shortcomings of the present system will be overcome by introducing the new CNS/ATM concepts in an evolutionary manner. The flight plan will still define the intended flight path, and efficient use of airspace within Europe will be assured by advice from the central flow management unit (CFMU).

There will be increasing emphasis on the use of digital data communication over VHF, Mode S and satellite data links, provided by the Aeronautical Mobile Satellite Service (AMSS), to pass positional and control information between air and ground (Figure 16.5). These data links, which are sub-networks of the planned worldwide Aeronautical Telecommunications Network (ATN), will effectively connect together the airborne and ground computers of the air traffic management system. Digital data communications, through the ATN, will be increasingly used to pass handovers and clearances directly from one ATCC computer to another. A major development is the introduction of Mode S, to overcome the limitations of conventional SSR, with surveillance and data link capability. The format use and design of the data link are being studied under the Eurocontrol PHARE and EASIE programmes.

Under EASIE, a five-year study programme has started to address the design of the Mode S sub-network, including the Ground Data Link Processors, which control the interchange of data messages between ground and air, the VHF and satellite sub-networks, the Communications and Routers, for the new Aeronautical Telecommunications Network (ATN), the End Systems which interface aircraft and centre computers with the network and the key new ATM Functions in the centres, resulting from data link operations.

The use of area navigation (RNAV) techniques, in which aircraft with highly accurate navigation systems are allowed to fly unconstrained by the airway network, will allow the use of direct, fuel efficient routes. Airline use of ground based en-route navaids will gradually decrease, as the airspace structure is modified. There will be increasing use of on-board and satellite-based navigation systems to provide accurate positional information at all times. The major advance in navigation systems, as we enter the twenty-first century, is the increasing use of the Global Positioning System (GPS) to provide accurate, three-dimensional positional information, on board the majority of aircraft, for all phases of a flight. GPS is likely to form the basis for the Global Navigation Satellite System (GNSS (Figure 16.6)).

Precision guidance, for the crucial final approach phase of flight, will be provided by the Microwave Landing Systems (MLS). The introduction of MLS will overcome the siting, interference and frequency problems of the Instrument Landing System (ILS) and will facilitate segmented and curved approaches, helping to make automatic landing easier and to increase system capacity.

For surveillance primary and secondary radar (SSR) will continue to provide positional and identity information. The performance of primary radar, in terms of 'seeing' targets, leaves little to be desired these days. Clutter rejection is excellent and automatic extraction of target plots standard. These digital plot messages allow the networking of radar data to provide unproved coverage and redundancy. This is becoming standard within Europe. An important improvement in SSR is the introduction of monopulse, improving tracking accuracy and reducing interrogation rates. The major development is the introduction of Mode S, as an extension of monopulse SSR, with specific addressing of individual aircraft and data link capability (Figure 16.7).

Outside areas of radar coverage, over the oceans or uninhabited land masses, where currently aircraft position is obtained from pilot voice reports over HF or VHF radio, Automatic Dependent Surveillance (ADS) will be introduced. This involves the automatic report, at regular intervals, over the Aeronautical Mobile Satellite System (AMSS) data link, of the

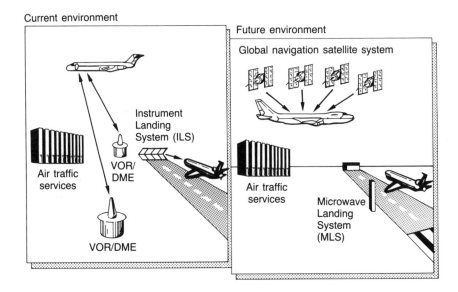

Figure 16.6 Navigation: current and future environments.

precise aircraft position as obtained from the Global Navigation Satellite System (GNSS).

The ability to transfer information from the aircraft to the ground by data link, will allow new ATM functions to be developed to support the controller. This information includes: meteorological conditions, aircraft dynamics and planned trajectories from the aircraft's Flight Management System (FMS). The new ATM functions include: planning across several sectors, trajectory prediction in four dimensions, three dimensions in space and time, probing for conflicts between predicted aircraft trajectories and monitoring for deviations from the predicted trajectories. It is expected that these functions, together with re-structuring of European airspace, will increase system capacity, whilst maintaining safety, without increasing the controller's work load and will eventually allow general use of area navigation.

The development of appropriate man–machine interfaces (MMIs) to support these functions is important. Considerable work is being undertaken in this area by Eurocontrol and the European authorities on activities such as the ODID (Operational Display and Input Development) programme. The best ways of presenting and handling control data are being researched.

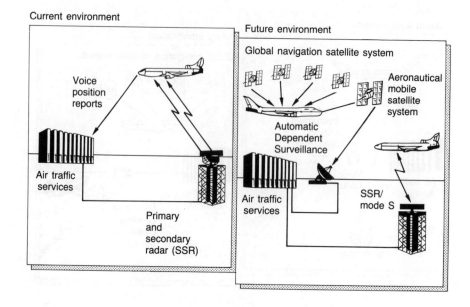

Figure 16.7 Surveillance: current and future environments.

An important aspect of this is the development of common operational procedures. Consideration is being given to the presentation of: electronic flight strip data, integrated situation displays, conflict displays, sector entry and exit displays, hand-over techniques and on-screen interaction with the data processing system and communications. The use of high definition, tv style, colour raster displays, is becoming established as the basis for the new MMI, incorporating Window, Icon, Menu and Pointer (WIMP) techniques.

The new concepts for the ATC systems of 2001 require systems of increased processing power which can evolve and expand as new requirements and functions are identified. The developing technology of distributed and 'open' processing systems provides these capabilities and is vital to achieving a harmonized and integrated system throughout Europe.

The basic technology is available to support these new operational and functional concepts which, together with harmonization and integration, will be able to provide the required improvements in capacity whilst the vital levels of safety are maintained. What is needed now is a combined approach by the authorities and the indigenous industry in Europe which, in partnership, will validate the concepts, quantify the capacity increases and cost benefits they provide, and establish, where appropriate, common operational requirements from which functional and technical specifications can be developed. Detailed programmes can then be developed for implementing solutions for harmonization, integration and enhancement of the existing systems and transition to the EATMS early in the next century.

17

Global systems: the challenge

P. Rochat

17.1 INTRODUCTION

It is, of course, a pleasure but also and first of all an honour – maybe a rather perilous one – to be the last presenter of these two days' meeting on 'Passenger Transport after 2000 AD'.

I have neither the authority nor the ambition to conclude this discussion in the name of my colleagues. I would like simply to share most of the views expressed so far that indeed passenger transport is more and more multimodal and must be considered, planned and operated globally, each mode of transport contributing in complementary, and at the same time, competitive terms to offer to our common customer – the passenger – the safest, most efficient and cost-effective transportation system, locally, regionally and world-wide.

It is a challenging task and credit should be given to the Royal Society to have assembled for two days most of those partners who have to work closer and closer together.

As far as civil aviation is concerned, Meredith (this volume) was absolutely right in promoting a co-ordinated policy on surface access to airports including road, rail and even water transport, in order to meet travel needs. Let me add that co-ordination is also essential at the airport itself among all service providers including customs, immigration and security officials, with a view to simplify and accelerate passenger treatment. That is what we call, in civil aviation terminology, facilitation – one of our major challenges, in particular since the coming out of high speed rail network. The French TGV in this regard, while becoming an ideal complement to long-haul flights, has also appeared as a tough competitor to short-haul air services, up to 500–800 km, in terms of travel duration, tariffs

Passenger Transport after 2000 AD. Edited by G.B.R. Feilden, A.H. Wickens and I.R. Yates. Published in 1994 by E & FN Spon, London. ISBN 0 419 19470 3.

and comfort (direct connection, without any change, from one city centre to another).

In the continuous development of a safe, orderly and efficient air transport, the aspects related to facilitation and multimodal integration constitute an important facet. Nevertheless, the flight itself, including take-off and landing, constitute the main operational elements of air transport, all of them showing specific characteristics and problems. Here, the key objective resides less in gaining speed – even if the supersonic flights deserve further attention into the next century – rather than in continuing to improve safety and punctuality.

17.2 CNS CONCEPT

As you know, the rapid growth of international air transport since the Second World War has created demands and operating requirements that can no longer be met using the existing ground facilities, techniques and procedures. It is a fact that the contemporary air communication, navigation and surveillance systems affected to air traffic control and management all over the world have not been able to prevent increased congestion and delays in expanding parts of the world.

The current systems are unfortunately characterized by a number of intrinsic shortcomings, for instance:

- the line-of-sight propagation of today's systems and the accuracy and reliability constraints resulting from the variability in the propagation characteristics of the available non-line-of-sight systems;
- the difficulty of implementing the present ground-based systems in large parts of the world (oceans and desert areas) and operating them in a consistent and reliable manner;
- the limitations of voice communications and the lack of digital air/ground data interchange systems to support modern automated systems in the air and on the ground.

More than ten years ago, the International Civil Aviation Organization (ICAO) recognized these shortcomings and the need for change to take civil aviation into the twenty-first century. A special committee on Future Air Navigation Systems (called FANS) was established with the view to developing a new concept, over a period of 25 years, capable of satisfying three basic operational requirements:

- global communication, navigation and surveillance coverage from very low to very high altitudes, embracing remote, offshore, oceanic areas and polar zones;
- digital data interchange between air–ground systems to exploit automatic control of the flying aircraft to a maximum extent; and

• navigation and approach guidance to runways and other landing sites within certain operational tolerances.

In its conclusions, the FANS Committee resolved that, complementary to certain redesigned terrestrial systems, satellite-based communications, navigation, and surveillance (CNS) systems would be the key to world-wide improvements and the only viable solution in the long term to overcome the shortcomings of the current system and to fulfil the global needs and requirements of the foreseeable future.

The new concept – called Communication, Navigation, Surveillance and Air Traffic Management (CNS/ATM) – is intended to gradually implement satellite technology without making existing CNS systems and technologies obsolete. It offers improvements that can be implemented through an evolutionary transition on a local scale, as requirements dictate, while at the same time meeting the need for global co-ordination. In general, the concept allows for a judicious mix of satellite technology and the best of line-of-sight systems to achieve an overall optimum result.

The concept has been endorsed not only by ICAO's 179 Contracting States but also by the whole civil aviation industry. Such a support is, of course, fundamental from the moment governments, airspace users and international organizations are required to co-operate on a global scale as never before to realize fully the benefits of the new systems.

17.3 COMMUNICATION

In the future, communications with aircraft will increasingly be accomplished by means of data transmission. Various communications media (e.g. aeronautical mobile-satellite systems (AMSS), very high frequency (VHF) data links, secondary surveillance radar (SSR) Mode S data link) will be integrated through the aeronautical telecommunications network (ATN). Communication with aircraft for both voice and data would be by direct satellite–aircraft link operating in the frequency band exclusively allocated to the aeronautical satellite service. In terminal areas and where line-of-sight limitations are not a problem, VHF and SSR Mode S would also be used.

17.4 NAVIGATION

As far as navigation is concerned, the central element will be the Global Navigation Satellite System (GNSS), comprising one or more satellite constellations and providing a high-integrity, high accuracy, world-wide navigation service for the en-route, terminal and non-precision phases of flight, and possibly for near Category I precision approach and landing operations as well. For precision approaches, the Microwave Landing

System (MLS) is still recognized as the future Standard System to replace ILS. However, this question will be re-examined by ICAO in early 1995.

17.5 SURVEILLANCE

Automatic dependent surveillance (ADS) is one important and early application of the air-ground data link technology. ADS is a function for use by air traffic services (ATS) whereby aircraft, via a data link, automatically provide data derived from on-board navigation and position-fixing systems. As a minimum, the data include aircraft identification and four-dimensional position. It will provide the capability of extending surveillance of air traffic operations beyond present radar coverage areas for en route traffic. SSR will continue to be used in terminal and high traffic density airspace.

In order to give you a more concrete idea of ADS potential advantages, I would like to refer you to a tragedy which took place 10 years ago. You will remember that on 31 August 1983, Korean Airline Flight 007 was shot down by a soviet fighter over Sakhalin Island in the North Pacific Area. According to the fact-finding investigation which ICAO completed recently, it is now established that the B-747, during its flight from Anchorage to Seoul, continuously deviated from its planned route due to an error in the selection of the proper navigation system. As there is no civilian radar coverage along the north Pacific routes, no Air Traffic Control Centre had been in a position to detect the deviation and inform the crew. With ADS in the future, the lack of radar coverage will be totally compensated by automatic reporting positions in real time.

17.6 AIR TRAFFIC MANAGEMENT

New CNS capabilities will make it possible to progressively improve the Air Traffic Management (ATM) which is the fourth component of the global concept. In general, the new ATM will enable aircraft operators to meet their planned times of departure and arrival and adhere to their preferred flight profiles with minimum constraints and no compromise to safety. ATM will improve the provision of information to users, including weather conditions and traffic situation. Oceanic ATM operations, in particular will become much more flexible, resulting in a greater capability to accommodate user-preferred trajectories. Improved flow management as part of the new ATM will help prevent excessive levels of congestion. These ATM improvements require a high degree of automation as well as a clear political support for:

• harmonizing national ATS globally;
• reducing the number of Air Traffic Control centres; and

• developing an increased flexibility between civilian and military use of airspace.

It is essential to understand that the system elements which constitute the ICAO global CNS/ATM concept have to be viewed as a menu of items which have to be implemented according to the specific need of each airspace environment.

17.7 TRIALS

Today, some components of the CNS/ATM systems are subject to trials and demonstrations, mainly within the Pacific Ocean region. Satellite communications are used every day, as well as Automatic Dependence Surveillance to send waypoint position reports. Pilots and air traffic controllers are enthused and see these trials as a giant leap forward, dramatically reducing in particular what is the biggest frustration in oceanic operations: voice communication over HF radio!

These trials are made possible by existing satellite constellations for communication and navigation. For mobile satellite communication, several services are available and have proven to be reliable and effective. For navigation, only one system is presently operational and will be fully operational before the end of 1993. It is the Global Positioning System (GPS) owned and operated by the US Air Force and composed of 24 Navstar satellites. This military system, as well as its Russian equivalent, which is called GLONASS and is not yet operational, have been offered free of charge to the international civil aviation community for a minimum of 10–15 years. As they have a military character and belong to individual states, some concerns have already been expressed within the international civil aviation community regarding the risk of a monopoly and the guarantee of continuous and uninterrupted GNSS service provision to all states without discrimination. Several options are presently under study in ICAO for the long term, including GPS, GLONASS, a combination of them, a combination of them with Satcom and, last but not least, an independent international GNSS system dedicated to civil aviation or shared with other users.

17.8 COST EFFECTIVENESS

The selection of the best option will of course depend on many factors of political, institutional, legal, economical and financial nature. In this regard, the costs of the CNS/ATM systems, including capital costs, maintenance and operating costs have been estimated globally at about 1 billion US dollars a year. Avoided costs resulting from the elimination of the existing CNS systems are also estimated at 1 billion US dollars a year.

On the other hand, the savings to aircraft operations are estimated to be around 5 billion US dollars a year and justified by more direct routes, lower fuel consumption, shorter flying time, better ATM in real times. This figure of US\$5 billion savings – which has to be considered as a very preliminary estimation – corresponds more or less to the financial losses of the airline industry in 1992. That is to say that the global CNS/ATM systems appear **spectacularly** cost effective. This impression is strengthened by the capacity of the same systems to improve safety, to reduce congestion and to contribute to a better environment. After all, without the significant capacity expansion which only the CNS/ATM systems can make possible, air traffic in crowded airspace, such as here in Europe, would become more congested. As a result, delays would increase to the extent of making air travel a largely ineffective mode of transport. And this would have serious repercussions for economic development all around the world.

But the system would also be of great benefit in those areas where the volume of air traffic is low and where adequate communication facilities are lacking because of the serious financial challenges faced by the states concerned. In such circumstances, these states could meet that commitment to serve international civil aviation by so to speak 'leap-frogging' technology and implementing the CNS/ATM systems, thereby avoiding having to invest in much costlier traditional technology facilities.

17.9 IMPLEMENTATION

As you will appreciate, the new systems represent a major revolution in technology and will have a profound global impact within the aviation community world-wide in financial as well as organizational terms never experienced before. This is because the capacity of the systems extends far beyond the traditional requirements of a single state and because of the huge investments involved, which similarly exceed the means of all but few states.

The successful implementation of the new CNS/ATM system will depend on a critical global planning and on the effective participation of all states, in order to achieve a global system and full benefits. The need for an evolutionary transition is critical indeed:

- to avoid degradation in system performance and maintain the required safety levels at all times;
- to ensure that aircraft are not unnecessarily burdened by the need to carry a multiplicity of old and new CNS equipment during a long transition cycle; and
- to ensure that differences in the pace of development around the world do not lead to incompatibility among elements of the overall system.

World-wide co-ordination is, thus, essential as well as regional coordination. The ICAO, as the world-wide intergovernmental body responsible for civil aviation, has of course a key role to play in this regard. We are in the process of producing a global transition plan based on the near term (1993–95), mid-term (1996–2000) and long term (2001–10). This plan, which will be completed next September, has to be a living document, providing guidelines for a transition which has to be as short as possible, consistent with all issues involved and immediate where the benefit of the new system is maximum (oceanic areas with low density traffic). This living document will be the frame for regional planning groups, created in most ICAO Air Navigation regions, to develop their own transition plans accordingly.

The global plan and the regional plans will have to be implemented by all ICAO states, without exception. This is essential. While the implementation of the GNSS may not, for practical purposes, offer many alternatives – this is why once more a truly international navsat system appears so important in order to avoid any state monopoly in that critical field – the other elements of the CNS/ATM systems offer states a number of implementation options. These options range from a state operating a system on its own, which is not often viable in light of the high costs, to contracting with certified satellite service providers, to various forms of international co-operation. International co-operation, in turn, may involve three such options as commissioning existing multilateral state organizations like EUROCONTROL to act on their behalf in dealing with service providers; forming an *ad hoc* group of states or a new international organization; and/or using a mechanism within ICAO to act on behalf of states in dealing with service providers.

17.10 ICAO MECHANISM

Different options may be selected by different states or groups of states, but much attention has been focused on international co-operation, one reason being that states collectively would be able to exercise more system control than where states would individually contract with service providers. I should add that, at the international level, particular note has been taken of the possible use of an ICAO mechanism. This is based on the successful management by ICAO for over 40 years of agreements covering the provision of air traffic control, communication and meteorological facilities and services on the North Atlantic, and the organization's reputation as an independent and neutral body with expertise in the various disciplines pertaining to international civil aviation. Also, in so far as aircraft operators are concerned, and where costs have been recovered through charges, ICAO's involvement has offered the protection of the costs being recovered having been determined in a sound and equitable manner.

Consequently, one solution now being actively considered within ICAO is establishing a new structure, such as an agency, under the strict control of ICAO, which would provide various CNS/ATM implementation assistance to individual states or groups of states. This includes assistance with regard to, for example, cost/benefit and cost-effectiveness assessments, selection of implementation options, multinational co-operative arrangements, system financing and management, how to proceed with cost recovery, etc. The agency could be financed by user charges.

17.11 CONCLUSION

As aviation continues its move towards globalization into the twenty-first century, states and the civil aviation industry face unprecedented challenges imposed by: traffic growth; emerging new technology; a rapidly changing commercial and regulatory framework; a growing awareness of the need for protection of the human environment and a requirement for substantial investment in infrastructure, equipment and staff at a time of increasingly competitive pressures for financial resources.

I am well aware of the magnitude of the challenges and mindful of the tasks before us. However, I am confident of the commitment of the aviation community to a future of continued growth and achievement. With that commitment, ICAO will be able to continue planning and developing a civil aviation system which meets the needs of the peoples of the world for safe, regular, efficient and economical air transport.

Part Six

Conclusions

18
Summary and conclusions

T.M. Ridley FEng

I am sure that you will agree that I have a very challenging task to sum up the wealth of information and ideas we have been presented with over the past two days, but I have accepted the challenge from the Royal Society and the Royal Academy of Engineering.

In the United Kingdom we have a picture of the 'mad scientist' (much resented by the scientific community) – wild of hair, wild of eye and scruffy of dress. An ordinary member of the public might be forgiven for thinking that a joint meeting of the Royal Society and the Royal Academy of Engineering was nothing less than the uniting of the 'mad scientist' and the 'mad technologist' – except that, at least with transport, science and technology could not possibly ignore everyday life.

There are 7 million experts on the subject of London Underground in our capital city – 20 000 on the payroll and 6 980 000 in the rest of the population. We are all experts on the subject of transport.

We have been here to discuss 'Passenger Transport after 2000 AD' and we ranged widely, from the gentleman who wanted to challenge British Rail's policy on the carriage of bicycles to Professor Thring. He wanted us to reflect on the second half of the twentieth century when, with ever greater population and democratization of the consumption of resources, there will not be nearly enough resource for all our needs. Extrapolation, he said, is not good enough.

We have, of course, heard a great deal about science, about engineering and about technology. But we have heard about much more:

- the Single Market, image, land use planning, regulatory framework, speed, policy, co-ordination, markets, interchange, safety, survivability,

Passenger Transport after 2000 AD. Edited by G.B.R. Feilden, A.H. Wickens and I.R. Yates. Published in 1994 by E & FN Spon, London. ISBN 0 419 19470 3.

affordability, standardization, frequency, reliability, cost reduction, training, values, lifestyles.

Thus we see that transport has characteristics and a context wider than that which is traditionally considered to be science or technology or, as I frequently tell my students – there is more to engineering than engineering.

We started with an overview from my old friend Phillipe Essig. We first met when I was developing the Tyne and Wear Metro and he was running the Paris Metro. We were in no doubt that our jobs were not fundamentally about technology, but about passengers (or customers), about people – both the users and the providers of the system.

Essig spoke about the relationship between people and transport but expressed a fear that ecological concerns might imply, if taken to the limit, that we should all stay at home.

Transport is about the movement of people and goods and only coincidentally about the turning of wheels, as spokesmen for water transport and the pedestrian certainly understand. But the concept of staying at home reminds us to draw a distinction between mobility and accessibility, the latter emphasizing that satisfying travel needs by bringing origins and potential destinations closer together is a land use based policy which we must examine.

For as each year passes we are not only making more journeys, our journeys are getting longer. It is the length of journeys as much as the number which is contributing to ever greater congestion and the only issue about congestion, it has been said, is how quickly it will get worse – over the day or over geographic areas.

Finkbohner told us about the splendid transport system in Zurich in Switzerland. Zurich is remarkable for having both high car ownership and high use of public transport. Zurich, a friend of mine has said, is the place where even the 'gnomes' ride on trams, leading another friend to dub them the 'metronomes'. Braagaard described the transport system covering a large region in northern Europe. He demonstrated how new infrastructure is expected to increase speed and, therefore, significantly to reduce travel times.

Meredith stressed the need for good access to airports. He called for policy co-ordination, though that sometimes implies the arrangement of matters in the rest of society to suit 'my own purpose'. But we would all surely agree that, at very least, Government should encourage individual operators to come together to produce co-ordination. The Heathrow Rail Link, being jointly developed by the British Airports Authority and British Rail, is a case in point.

There are no easy answers to co-ordination problems. Clearly, we must have more lanes on the M25 west of London or we must do without new capacity at Heathrow airport. Meredith reminded us that airport access from non-city-centre locations is as important as from centres themselves.

Kemp described plans for the European High Speed Train Network – competitive, he believes, over the distance range of 150–500 km at speeds up to 300 km h^{-1}. He was concerned about national railways' failure to make their infrastructure compatible and thus handing the market to more effective competitors. He did question the benefits of very high speed and wondered whether problems of energy consumption and environmental impact would make it worthwhile pursuing. He believes it is basically frequency and reliability which the customer wants.

A speaker from the floor, from London Business School, asked who was going to pay for all of the new infrastructure and will it pay? It is clear that governments can no longer pay, with our tax money, for all the infrastructure which seems to be needed. The private sector will have to be joined with the public through partnership. Equally clearly, however, Government must take a lead.

Miller told us about high speed Maglev systems, but most of us probably believe that it will be a long time before they are financially viable.

Ambrose spoke for regional airlines and made a fairly bitter attack on railways. He called for equal treatment, though I suspect that Sir Alistair Morton, if he had been with us rather than facing his shareholders in Paris, would have drawn attention to the duty-free privileges of the air transport industry.

Schaffler described regional and commuter aircraft while McKinlay gave us an excellent picture of the development of Airbus. He spoke about pressures which will bring about change including both political and industrial issues.

The mood changed in the last session this morning. Road transport presents some of the most difficult transport problems but, at the the same time, is newest in terms of looking at systems as a whole from the technological point of view. To date, a large part of the highway system has been in the hands of private individuals – the drivers.

Wootton showed us the link between traffic growth and economic growth and emphasized that neglected subject, the relationship between transport and land use. He said that growth trends are not our destiny – it would be terribly sad if they were – but neither he nor I, nor you, know exactly how we can grasp our destiny to ensure that we are not overcome by trends. He and Davis both gave an excellent coverage of the potential contribution of new electronic and communications knowledge in the field of highway transport. There were calls for better recognition of the role of environmental problems in transport. I would just comment here that I recently served with a group of academics on behalf of the RAC – the Royal Automobile Club – looking at the automobile and the environment into the next century. We concluded that there is a strong likelihood that industry in the next

10–15 years will overcome the technical problems of emissions from automobiles, with the exception of the important and unresolved CO_2 problem. But there is no clear indication how we are going to overcome the problem of the sheer numbers of cars that are forecast.

Venton made clear the challenge for technology in European air traffic control and Rochat described the challenge of global systems. He made the point too that there may be a priority for safety and punctuality over speed.

Bradshaw spoke about the young, the elderly and women. What I thought was particularly interesting at what I would call this high-tech conference was that he, representing the old and somewhat tired but not glamorous bus mode, was able to indicate the way in which new technology can perhaps encourage a revival of the use of buses. In virtually every city in the world the bus carries more passengers every day than does urban rail. I say that as one who has been committed to urban rail for most of my life. Bradshaw also said that buses cannot carry out their task on their own. Unless society provides right-of-way, then buses cannot fulfil their essential role.

Just a small story. When I was in Newcastle and we were building the Tyne and Wear Metro, my colleagues who had served in Newcastle for the previous 20 years told me they had repeatedly asked the authorities to provide bus lanes for buses through the centre of the city. They had never been able to obtain them. The irony was that when we came to build the Metro, because of the need to do some traffic management to provide for its construction, bus lanes were provided and, happily, have not been taken away. This says something about the ludicrous way in which we make decisions – and not only in this country.

Bradshaw and his colleague also talked about the introduction of alternative fuels, noise reduction and the development of batteries, and also about 'smart' cards, suggesting that – and this point was made when we met the Press yesterday – we might be beginning to see the development of common transport technologies, technologies which are common to all modes of transport.

I particularly enjoyed Green's presentation as an example of what an enthusiastic manager can do when he brings together customer needs and technical possibilities, and also, technical realities, together with a clear statement of business objectives. He also presented some interesting facts that were new to me – the number of passengers travelling every day between Tokyo and Osaka as compared with those between London and Manchester, for example. When we say 'why can't we do what they do in Japan?', and we have done so in the last two days, we frequently look only at the supply side of the equation and not sufficiently at the same time at the demand side.

The Royal Society and the Royal Academy of Engineering bring together people involved in the development of science, engineering, technology and innovation, a subject I know which is close to the heart of the Chairman. I thought Davis' presentation from Boeing was an interesting example of this, bringing together and building bridges between those areas, talking as he did about sound engineering development based on physical principles. He talked about maintenance, frequently overlooked in engineering development – the cost of ownership.

Recently at Imperial College, in our Railway Technology Strategy Centre which is supported by British Railways, we have been looking at the position of research and development in the supply chain of the railway industry. As an aid to that examination we have given some consideration to that position of research and development in the automotive, telecoms and power generation industries. I thought that Davis' presentation gave an interesting insight into that so far as the aerospace industry is concerned. Boeing, he said, is reinventing itself. I believe we also heard today that highway systems are reinventing themselves. As one who has spent a lot of my life in railways I ask – is the railway industry really and truly reinventing itself, and is water transport reinventing itself? Now, of course, we did have a commercial from Boeing, which I personally enjoyed, having lived in Seattle for one year of my life.

Nordstrom talked about the nature of automobile transport. I was sad that Professor Kurti got in first with my joke about Greta Garbo wanting 'to be alone', but I think the point was well made about the special privilege that using a car brings to individuals. The difficulty and the question of course is – do I or you as a driver pay the full cost to ourselves and others of operating that car in grossly congested situations? I believe we must move in the direction of demand management, of charging people at the point of delivery the true cost of operating their transport systems.

So, Chairman, I would like to congratulate yourself and the other organizers for the very rich mix of presenters that you have brought to us in the last two days. As the meeting has gone on you may have decided, and I certainly have reflected, that some reorganization might perhaps have been in order. Perhaps the first morning might have benefited from a discussion of the issues and the problems, discussion of demand before discussion of supply, before turning to see what science and technology can offer. In that way we would perhaps have avoided what I would call modal obsession, in certain cases even modal sneering between one group and another.

We have to some extent, in common with everybody who ever meets to talk about transport, talked past each other. Too often in transport we all compete in putting forward solutions before we have sat down and agreed what the questions are. I make no apology to those of my friends who have heard me say this from rostrums in other places at other times. The first question should always be – what are we trying to achieve? I suspect that different speakers in the past two days have had different agendas, but of course we, the public, will all face the same problems with passenger transport after AD 2000. Now, I cannot tell you precisely what passenger transport will be like after AD 2000, nor even what all the problems are likely to be, but I will close by highlighting what I believe are some of the issues.

Unless disaster strikes the world, there will continue to be economic growth, and if there is economic growth there will be traffic growth, and if there is traffic growth there will be increasing congestion. Customers will demand at the same time higher standards and lower costs, and there will be a powerful imbalance between the wish for mobility and the wish to protect the environment. There will be a desire for many more facilities and much more infrastructure at the same time that there is an increasing shortage of money. My personal opinion is that for all modes we will want and need some new possibility of a substantial underground road network in London. Whether it ever comes about or not remains to be seen, but there will be new infrastructure, whether underground roads, bypasses or whatever, and the same can be repeated for all of the modes.

There will be increasing use of electronic means of providing information and of guidance control. However, while I believe that is very important and I urge all of us to get behind it scientifically and technologically to push the frontiers forward, there is a limit to the amount of additional capacity that such means can actually provide. Thus I am sure that, by pricing or other means, there will be increasing use demand management.

But it may also just be that, because of what I earlier called the sheer number of cars and of movement by air, transport people, scientists and technologists, may have to look afresh at the way we run business and plan transport. We may then come up with policies and strategies which, contrary to the past where transport was seen to be in conflict with environmental protection and energy conservation – incidentally a subject not greatly considered during the course of the last two days – turn out to be those which are consistent with environmental protection and energy conservation. I hope that all of us scientists, engineers and technologists can change the perception of the public, which has existed for some time, that we are consumers of wealth and destroyers of the environment, and organize ourselves so that we are seen to be, and in fact are, creators of wealth and protectors of the environment. I would urge this upon the Royal Society and the Royal Academy of Engineering in all of their work in their area. But I finish by returning to the beginning of the meeting yesterday morning, and join with Philip Essig in asking us all to keep an open mind and not to confine ourselves to a single mode.

Index